# THE HORNETS NEST

## A History of 100 Squadron

# ORIGINAL SQUADRON FLAG

The Original "Squadron Standard". A treasured relic of the Squadron's early years which finally disintegrated in a Japanese POW camp after the fall of Singapore.

# THE HORNETS NEST

## A History of 100 Squadron

## Arthur White

A SQUARE ONE PUBLICATION

First published in 1994 by
Square One Publications, Saga House
Sansome Place, Worcester WR1 1UA


© 100 Squadron Association

British Library Cataloguing in Publication Data

White, Arthur
  Hornets' Nest: History of 100 Squadron
  Royal Air Force, 1917–94
  I. Title
  358.41310941

  ISBN 1-872017-82-7

Typeset by Avon Dataset Ltd, Waterloo Road, Bidford-on-Avon, B50 4JH
Printed by Biddles Ltd, Guildford, Surrey

# CONTENTS

# Acknowledgment

100 Squadron would like to acknowledge the financial help given to the Association by Allied Lyons (J. Tetley Ltd); British Aerospace; Rolls Royce and the Canadian Group of 100 Squadron Association.

# LIST OF ILLUSTRATIONS

# FOREWORD BY AIR VICE-MARSHAL
# W.J. HERRINGTON CB, RAF (Retd.)

100 Squadron celebrated its 75th Anniversary in 1992. This auspicious landmark was the spur to revising and up-dating the Squadron's history, a task undertaken enthusiastically and with great dedication by Arthur White who was a navigator on the Squadron during the Bomber Offensive in World War II.

This new volume draws extensively on "The Annals of 100 Squadron" (the late Major Gordon Burge OBE) and on the Official History (Wing Commander A.J. Brookes) for operations in World War I and during the post war period to 1977 respectively, and has been admirably brought up to date by contributions from members who have served on the Squadron in more recent years. It has been enhanced and enlivened by the many personal accounts of members' experiences and reflections on the Squadron's activities throughout its history, including hitherto unknown details of the Far East operations in the dark days of early 1942.

The Squadron was one of many formed during the expansion of the Royal Flying Corps to meet the demands of the Western Front in 1917 but it was immediately selected for a role prophetic for its future and for air power-strategic bombing. It became a founder member of Trenchard's 41st Wing,* which had been established to respond to German bombing raids on Britain, by attacks on German targets. Then, in May 1918, it became part of the 83rd Brigade of the new Independent Air Force, formed at the direction of the British Government for "an extended and sustained bombing offensive against German industries", in which role it continued until the end of the war. It survived the severe post-war cuts to play its part in the independent Royal Air Force.

Throughout its history, as this record shows, the Squadron's contribution to Royal Air Force operations, in a variety of roles, in peace and war, has been outstanding: it performed with great heroism, valour and distinction most notably in Malaya and the Bomber Offensive during the war, but

---

*[It is noteworthy that of the squadrons originally assigned to the Independent Air Force, only 100 is still operational after Options for Change.]

later, in smaller but no less important actions in Malaya again and in Kenya. The years of the Canberra and, later, the Victor at Wittering were crucial in the development of weapons and the maintenance of Britain's nuclear deterrent. Finally, the part the Squadron has played, and continues to play in testing and improving the Air Defence components of the United Kingdom and NATO is of immense value.

A great deal of work has been devoted to researching and marshalling a mass of historical records and data to ensure completeness and accuracy; the many illustrations, photos and appendices embellish the narrative and serve to remind readers, now and in the future, of the devotion, courage and fortitude as well as the humour, cameraderie and esprit of those who have served on the Squadron. The book will arouse many a nostalgic memory among former members from all eras and, I believe, inspire those who serve on 100 in the future.

All of us who have been privileged to serve on 100 Squadron share pride in its history and achievements. I express on everyone's behalf our congratulations to Arthur White for bringing that story together with such success.

W.J. Herrington CB.
Air Vice-Marshal RAF (Retd.)

# AUTHOR'S FOREWORD

My first thought, on embarking on this History of 100 Squadron, was to seek a unifying theme which would weld together the thoughts, the spirits, attitudes, humour and dedication to duty of three generations of men, spanning 75 years, who flew with 100 Squadron.

The answer was comparatively easy to find and lay in the Squadron motto: 'Sarang Tebuan Jangan Dijolok' surmounted by the skull and cross-bones. The Squadron, however, did not receive its first [official] badge until March, 1938, twenty one years after its birth as the first night bomber squadron. Some rudimentary research, however, traced its origins back to 1917 which led to some, to say the least, eyebrow raising revelations!

The original emblem was a red, hand painted flag bearing the skull and cross-bones. According to the late Group Captain R. McKendrick the flag was purloined from a French 'house of ill repute' soon after the first young Fe 2b flyers arrived in France. With the addition of the words, 'Blood and Brains', this became the first, unofficial 100 Squadron badge. This emblem survived the First World War and the inter-war years until it was carried into a Japanese prisoner of war camp by Flight Lieutenant Trillwood in 1942. Despite his care the flag decayed during his captivity although he retained the iron flag pole until he was freed in 1945. How frustrating it must have been for him to be forced to abandon this sole, remaining symbol of a squadron's spirit at a transit camp in San Francisco.

In 1930 'A' Flight Horsleys carried a bulldog badge on their fins and an emblem was designed showing a bulldog mounted over the motto of the Order of the Thistle: *nemo me impune lacessit* — no one provokes me with impunity.' Wing Commander A. J. Brookes, in his Official History of 100 Squadron, recalls an amusing anecdote about its origins.

'A previous Flight Commander had owned a bulldog which he treated very badly and, one day, the beast rebelled and turned on its master. The unfortunate officer was then seen fleeing from a hangar with an irate bulldog firmly attached to his nether regions and when the animal returned, triumphant, with a large piece of barathea between its teeth, it became much revered.' However, Wing Commander Brookes goes on to state that the bulldog was always regarded as subordinate to the skull and cross-bones which eventually became the squadron's official badge.

'*Sarang Tebuan Jangan Dijolok*'. These words of a Malayan proverb appeared on the first official Squadron badge in November, 1937, when it was approved by H.M. King George VI, twenty one years after its formation and after five years in Malaya. The proverb has been, variously, translated as:

'Do not attack the hornets' nest.'
'Do not disturb the hornets' nest.'
'Don't let anyone attack the hornets' nest.'
'Let no-one dare disturb the hornets' nest.'
'Don't put your finger in a hornet's nest.'
'Do not stir up a hornet's nest.'

The last version is the officially accepted interpretation quoting the Department of Education of the Straits Settlement as the authority for the translation from the Malayan text. Each version carries a warning to the would-be aggressor but they all carry more than a strong hint of retribution most adequately describing the spirit of 100 Squadron from its birth in 1917 to the present day.

In their own way each of these mottos summarises the spirit, the determination, the valour and the comradeship of men from all walks of life who have flown with 100 Squadron over the past 75 years. Perhaps this empathy was most evident at the first reunion of the 100 Squadron Association in September, 1985. Gathered together were men from all eras of the Squadron's history. From Roy Shillinglaw, an Observer on Fe 2b's to serving officers flying Canberras. Men in their 70s and 80s mingled with 'youngsters' in their 20s but they all spoke the same language: they had experienced the same risks and dangers; the same sense of adventure; the same joie de vivre, songs and pranks and had felt the same sense of loss when their comrades failed to return.

Although this story is primarily concerned with the flyers of 100 Squadron tribute must be paid to those unsung heroes who kept the 'planes flying — the ground-crews.

Time and time again one reads of their devotion to their aircraft and the Squadron. They worked in impossible conditions of rain, cold and mud on the Western Front; in the insect infested jungles of Malaya and the winter-time snow and ice-bound airfields of Lincolnshire. Wherever they were, shelter was at a premium and most of their work was done in the open. They were sustained by their own, dry sense of humour; only they understood the idiosyncrasies of their own particular aircraft and only they could identify a problem that wasn't mentioned in the manual.

The common bond, through three generations, between air and ground crews was 100 Squadron whose story I hope to unfold in the pages which follow.

Arthur White
March, 1992

# CHAPTER ONE

## The Background

At the outbreak of the First World War the Royal Flying Corps (R.F.C) component of the British Expeditionary Force (B.E.F.) consisted of a mixed force of 63 aircraft. On Armistice Day, 1918, the new Royal Air Force had a first line strength of 3,000 with thousands more in reserve. For the first two years of the war the principal role of aircraft on the Western Front was that of reconnaissance, artillery spotting and aerial photography. It was a natural progression for other, "fighter" aircraft, to defend these aerial observers and from thence it was not a big step for these "fighters" to carry bombs to attack enemy airfields. Nevertheless, when Major General Hugh Trenchard (later Lord Trenchard) took command of the infant R.F.C. in France in 1915, any attempts to extend the role of aircraft beyond that of reconnaissance were greeted with suspicion and, even, downright opposition by the General Staff. It is to Lord Trenchard's credit that he resisted the objectors and transformed his air force into a major offensive weapon.

During the first two years of the war Germany used Zeppelins as heavy bombers for attacks on England. Early in 1917 these Zeppelins were transferred to the German Naval Air Service and their place taken by the twin engined A.E.G.s and Gothas. These aircraft, with their greater speed and ceiling, stepped up their daylight attacks which necessitated the withdrawal of R.F.C. and Royal Naval Air Service (R.N.A.S.) fighters from the Western Front to combat them. In this they were successful as the German attacks turned to night raids and, eventually, ended in May, 1918.

Endless trench warfare and a succession of unsuccessful offensives were taking a dreadful toll of the armies:by the end of 1916 Britain and France had suffered half a million casualties on the Somme alone whilst France had lost hundreds of thousands more at Verdun. In November, at the Conference of Chantilly, plans were drawn up for an all out offensive in February, 1917. Lloyd George, Minister of War, strongly objected to the plans which were, eventually, postponed to April. In December his hand was strengthened when he succeeded Asquith as Prime Minister. Without attempting to go into the minutiae of conferences between allies, army commanders, service chiefs and politicians in general one clear objective became apparent: the war would be concentrated in France with the sole object of ousting the Germans using all the means at the disposal of the Allies.

It was in that context that Major General Trenchard came into his own. Whilst maintaining its reconnaissance role, his expanding Flying Corps would take the war directly into the enemy camp and homeland. His strategy of, first, attacking enemy air bases and then his lines of communication and industries was similar to that followed by both the R.A.F. and Lufwaffe in World War 2.

Part of that strategy, which entailed making the best use of his available resources, led to the formation of squadrons which would bomb their targets at night. The first of these squadrons, which would pave the way for a host of others in the years to come, was designated 100 Squadron. In his book, "Royal Air Force Squadron Badges", Peter C. Smith suggests that, historically, 100 Squadron was the predecessor of the 1,000 bomber raids of World War 2. It is a nice thought even though, by the time of the first 1,000 bomber raid on Cologne in May, 1942, the Squadron had been wiped out by the Japanese. Yet, it is significant that, in less than a year, 100 Squadron rose from the ashes and took its place again as a bomber squadron in that conflict.

From our standpoint in 1992 it is difficult to appreciate the significance of night bombing in 1917. The experience of those of us who lived through World War 2 was that night bombing was par for the course. In 1917 to fly "in the dark" as Air Vice Marshal John Herrington, so simply and admirably put it, in an address at the Squadron's 75th birthday party, was almost unheard of. How did these flyers find their way? There was no radar, no W/T, just a weird system of "lighthouses" strung along the allied lines on the Western Front. The only concession to night flying was a luminous instrument panel. More often than not this would only comprise inaccurate compasses, air speed indicators and altimeters. Which brings us to the Fe 2bs.

World War 1 saw a tremendous development in aircraft design from the frail, single-engined, single-seaters of 1914 to the multi-engined bombers of 1918. Amongst the dozens of different aircraft types that flew in World War 1 was the rather elderly Fe 2b. In the early years of the war this was flown by Home Defence Wing but the higher speeds and ceilings of new enemy machines made it more and more unsuitable for this role.

To those of us looking back on those days the Fe 2b appears to have been a very strange aircraft indeed. Basically, it had an engine and cockpit up at the front, a pair of wings and, then, an open latticefuselage joining the tail plane to the enginelcockpit assembly. Ridiculed by Baron von Richtofen as "an old lattice tail" it was described by 2ndlLieutenant Reg Kingsford, when he first saw one, as "a weird looking contraption." He goes on to say, "The whole thing had an appearance of insecurity. Painted black, many were decorated with crests of various designs, the favourite being the skull and cross-bones. Those old night bombers certainly

Lieut. Col. M G Christie, C.M.G., D.S.O., M.C.
*Annals of 100 Squadron*

presented a terrifying sight. It made me shudder every time I looked at mine."

Such remarks put one in mind of the Duke of Wellington on the eve of Waterloo. Discussing his army he is reputed to have said: "I don't know if they will frighten the French but, By God, they frighten me!"Despite these uncomplimentary remarks we learn, from the "Annals of 100 Squadron" and Roy Shillinglaw, our oldest, known, surviving member of the era, that the Fe 2 bs were held in the highest regard and affection by those who flew them. Asked, at the 1987 reunion of 100 Squadron Association, what he thought of the new Handley Page 0-400, introduced in 1918, which was conceived as "a bloody paralyser of an aeroplane" (Commodore Murray F. Sueter) Roy replied:

"Yes, it was alright, but I liked the Fe 2b best."

It would be too facile to say that these 1917 airmen flew by the seat of their pants or "by guess and by God" as one contemporary put it. They must have developed some strange affinity with their machines: their discerning of minute fluctuations in engine noise; the changing sound of the wind whistling through the struts. They learnt the importance of delicacy of touch on throttle, stick and rudder. Added to all this was the occupational hazard of forced landings, common enough in those days, when, perhaps through engine failure, the pilot would put down in a convenient field, remedy the fault and take off again! And they did that at night as well!

Against all these odds the men of 100 Squadron performed brilliantly and laid down the criteria which their successors have taken as the norm ever since.

# CHAPTER TWO

## The Western Front 1917

In February, 1917, Home Defence Wing (H.D.W.)was given the responsibility for organising a completely new unit which was to specialise in night bombing. This was a logical assignment to H.D.W. with its expertise in night patrols against Zeppelins. The new unit was designated 300 Squadron but on 8th February the War Office altered this to 100 Squadron with successive night bomber squadrons following in numerical sequence. On 11th February authority was given to the Officer Commanding Administrative Wing to mobilise the new squadron at South Farnborough where it was to be equipped with Fe 2bs. However, the only squadron in H.D.W. operating this type of aircraft was 51 Squadron which was based at Hingham, Norfolk. Hence, 51 Squadron was to undertake the training of the new unit at its own base. Just over two weeks later, on 23rd February, 100 Squadron officially came into existence when its personnel began to mobilise at South Farnborough under the command of Major M.G. Christie and his three Flight Commanders. On 21st March they set sail for France.

As already described the Fe 2b was a strange and 'elderly aircraft'. 100 Squadron's Fe 2bs had a top speed of 81 mph at 6,500 ft. and a ceiling of 11,000 ft. Their aircraft came from 23 Squadron after being modified at No. 2 Aircraft Depot with 120 hp Beardmore engines taken from 27 Squadron's Martynsyde G 100s. Twelve of the modified aircraft were flown out to St. Andre-aux-Bois where they were fitted with luminous compasses, rev-counters, altimeters, air speed indicators and watches. Their bomb dropping gear was designed for 25 lb. and 112 lb. bombs. The top-planes were painted brown, with red, white and blue roundels and, to prevent detection from the ground, the rest of the 'plane was painted black with dark grey nacelles whilst the underwing roundels were replaced by white circles.

On 1st April the Squadron moved to Izel le Hameau as part of III Brigade. The original twelve Fe 2bs were augmented by four BE 2cs and one Fe 2c taken from day fighting units and modified in the same way as the Fe 2bs. Before going on to describe the new squadron's first operation, on 5th April, it is rather sobering for World War 2 crews and their successors to reflect on the time-scale outlined above. In the space of six weeks the pilots of 100

F. E. 2 B. Ready for a Raid
*The Annals of 100 Squadron*

Squadron had learnt to adapt to a new type of aircraft and fly it at night in a strange country with little or no navigational aids. And part of those six weeks were spent waitng for delivery of aircraft.Compare that with months at O.T.Us and conversion units!

On the night of 5|6 April the new squadron was ordered to attack Douai aerodrome, the home of von Richtofen's 'Flying Circus', which was the scourge of both the army and R.F.C. on the Western Front. The operation was carried out in two waves with the aircraft gliding in low, throttles closed, dropping 132 bombs on and around the hangars and then roaring away. Writing in 'The Annals of 100 Squadron' Major Gordon Burge gives the following description of the Squadron's initiation as a night bomber force:'The results of the raid, together with those obtained during a second offensive, the night following, were deemed excellent and portended well for the future success of the Squadron. The introduction to the Hun was well executed and came to him with sudden unexpectedness as it was the first night bombing raid undertaken on a large scale in France.'

Baron von Richtofen, writing in 'Der Rote Kampfflieger' disagreed:'One night when we were sitting in the Casino the telephone bell rang and we were informed that the British were on the way. Great excitement prevailed, of course . . . The Englishman was flying very high. First he circled round the aerodrome and we began to think that he was looking for some other objective. All at once, however, he shut off his engine and came down. We fetched our rifles and began to fire at the Englishman. At last he was caught in the beam and the whole aerodrome shouted with surprise for it was quite an old machine. He was not more than a kilometre away and was flying straight for our aerodrome and coming still lower. It wasn't long before the first dropped and then there came a rain of small bombs. It was a fine display of fireworks and might have impressed a rabbit. So this old lattice-tail dropped his bombs, and that from a height of 50 metres. It was a regular bit of impertinence . . .'

The facts were, however, that four hangars were destroyed and a number of smaller fires were burning around the airfield. On its first operation of the war 100 Squadron had its first casualties when 2nd Lieut. Richards and 2nd Air Mechanic Barnes were interned as P.O.W.s. The following night 2nd Lieut. Butler and 2nd Air Mechanic Robb were lost on a raid on Douai railway station.

100 Squadron's initiation into battle coincided with the Battle of Arras – a memorable part of which was the Canadian attack and capture of Vimy Ridge. For the next eight weeks or so the Squadron was engaged almost exclusively in attacks on the railway system behind the German lines. The principal targets ranged from Menin and Courtrai on the Belgian border through Lens, Lille, Wervik, Orchies,to Douai and Valenciennes facing the centre of the Allied front. The method of attack on trains at night makes fascinating reading:

"Their method of attacking trains at night was to glide down with the

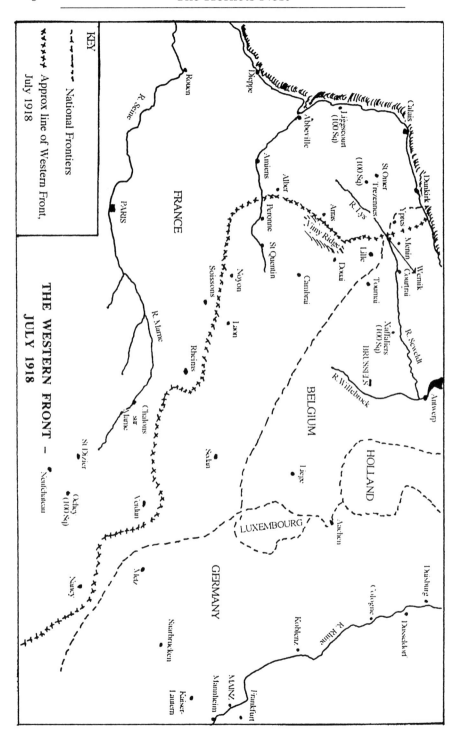

engine cut and then open up for a slow run along the track. Bombs were then dropped in sticks along the trucks or carriages and a flare released afterwards to observe the results. Such sorties were, mainly, carried out in moonlight and, sometimes, the aircraft were rapidly turned round and sent on another mission the same night." After just one month's operations the Squadron had bombed and derailed 17 trains, damaged stations, track and sidings, destroyed some German vehicles in an M.T. park and bombed a German convoy on the Arras – Cambrai road. In an attack on Dorignies aerodrome on 7th May the Squadron lost 2nd Lieut. Holmes and 2nd Air Mechanic Ekin and 2nd Lieut. Eccles was wounded.

Despite the crews' affection for the Fe 2b all felt that its bomb load of 200lbs.was inadequate as all aircrew "wanted a good strafe". In the early days a crew of pilot and observer would carry six or eight 20lb bombs but by the end of April 112 lb bombs were in use and a month later the largest was 230lbs. From the Operations Reports in "The Annals" one is bound to assume that pilots dispensed with their observers on many occasions in order to carry a heavier bomb load. Weight is given to this theory in a conversation between the late 2nd Lieut.Angus McCreath and his brother, Norman. He said he often flew alone in order to increase his bomb load and also flew quite low – well below the operational height of the 'plane. On such occasions his 'plane was often tossed up in the air by the force of his exploding bombs.

The British and Canadian successes at Arras and Vimy had cost 84,000 casualties including 316 airmen. To the south, at the ill-fated Chemin des Dames, France had suffered 118,000 casualties and serious mutinies were breaking out in the French Army. That was the background to the British summer campaign in Flanders – more generally known as Passchendaele – with the Battle of Messines and the Third Battle of Ypres. For this part of the campaign the Squadron was moved to Trexennes, near Aire, on 16th May, where, records the "Annals", the Squadron reached concert pitch.

In 1917 the German Air Force concentrated a large number of aerodromes well behind the German lines. These were bases for attacks on the Allied communications, fuel and ammunition dumps. One branch of the German Air Force, however, was known as the "Storm Squadrons" whose main purpose was trench strafing – the murderous machine gunning of troops in trenches and open ground – and aiding the German Army in its attempts to repulse Allied forces. Hence, from the beginning of July until the end of September, the "Annals" record German airfields as primary objectives. At the same time the Squadron's penchant for "train bashing" is still evident for, time and time again, one reads of attacks on trains, sidings and stations.

From "The Annals" we have the following description of the organisation at Trezennes to illustrate the daily life of the Squadron:

"Within easy reach of St. Omer, outings for the troops could easily be arranged and a well stocked canteen could be kept up. The billets were fairly comfortable and a recreation room, fitted up with a stage, enabled the concert party, organised by Sgt. Major May to entertain the troops on wet evenings. The officers' quarters were situated well away from the aerodrome and consisted of bell tents, a comfortable mess and an ante room in which 'many a merry night was held.'

Another institution, which had its origins in the Squadron, the operations room, was a place of interest, especially before a raid, when all pilots and observers went to get the last details before going to their machines. In this were all the maps, charts, photographs of targets and details of the numbers of raids carried out by individual pilots and observers as well as congratulatory telegrams received by the Squadron from Headquarters.

Just before dark the machines would be got out of their hangars and loaded up with bombs in accordance with the armament laid down in the daily operation orders. Then they would be got into line of flights and readied to be taxied out to the flare path. Flares were out and ready for lighting at the appointed time. Pilots and observers would arrive, climb into their machines and await the order to start. Presently, an orderly is seen doubling down to the flight ordered to start first. Directly afterwards the roar of an engine was heard and machine number one was on its way to the flare path. A hurried shout to the Flares Officer, conveying to him the names of the pilot and observer together with the number of the machine and time away. In less than a minute machine number one was on the flare path, engine all out and fast disappearing in the failing light until its navigation lights, fast fading into twin stars, were all that could be seen.

Hardly had this machine left the ground when the second was after it, soaring into the night, its twin lights following the first, and so on until all the machines were in the air which seemed full of the drone of engines, getting fainter and fainter until the silence of a summer's evening once more reigned supreme. The mechanics, who had been engaged in the despatch of the machines, are seen strolling back to pass the time in what manner they cared until the return of the machines. The average time taken on a raid was about two hours according to the distance away of the targets. Quickly, the time slips by and all are beginning to cast their eyes around the sky to try and pick up the lights of a returning machine.

Soon, the drone of an engine could be heard; the pilot could be seen blinking his lights, intimating that he was going to land, and required the flares on to give him his position. These were put on and, sometimes, a searchlight beam was displayed on the ground. One last turn to get into the wind and the machine is gliding towards the flare path. The roar of the engine gradually lessens and dies away and, in a few moments, the slight shock of the machine landing is heard. Immediately, the engine roars out again and the pilot taxies the machine towards the hangars. He shouts his name to the Flares Officer, who notes the time of arrival of the machine, and then hands his machine over to the mechanics who either overhaul it and load it up for another raid, or put it away in its hangar. The pilot then makes his way to the C.O.s office to hand in his report and then returns to the mess for a little well earned refreshment."

Shortly after its arrival at Trexennes the Squadron had its first contact with enemy night bombers. The aerodrome was situated about 1½ miles from the important French steelworks at Iseberges which was a regular target for the German Air Force. Despite being well defended by anti-aircraft guns and searchlights the steelworks received a number of hits although the aerodrome itself was undamaged. By July, 1917, the enemy was well aware of 100 Squadron's role in its attacks on their own bases and, on the 17th, Trexennes came under attack from a long range gun.

Only half a mile away from the aerodrome was a large ammunition dump which, as the "Annals" state, made the position 'precarious'. The first shell exploded outside an empty hangar but the next hit a hangar containing two Fe 2 Bs which were being serviced by Air Mechanics Evans and Sowerby who were killed instantly. As it happened, this was the sole attack on Trexennes and damage was reported as slight. Nevertheless, rumours abounded that the Germans were determined to destroy the aerodrome so steps were taken to 'outwit the Hun' by building a dummy airfield on waste land about two miles away. Two airmen, Air Mechanics Templeton and Fisher, were based on the dummy aerodrome operating a lighting set to illuminate dummy flares. "Judging from the number of bombs dropped on this field Air Mechanics Templeton and Field must have spent some exciting nights together!"

From July to September, in particularly favourable weather, there were nightly raids behind the German lines, principally against German aerodromes in a bid to gain allied mastery of the air as a pre-requisite for success on the ground. After one, particularly successful operation the Officer Commanding 100 Squadron received a letter from the G.O.C. Royal Flying Corps stating:"Please congratulate all pilots and observers on their splendid work last night when the night was particularly dark. This bombing, by 100 Squadron, is, according to the prisoners' statements, of the greatest use to our operations."In a letter to a relative on the 5th July a member of the 6th German Army Aircraft Park, near Tournai, wrote:" The night before last the English again bombed us; they set fire to a large hangar which was completely burnt out including the twenty machines which were inside. Let us hope this nightmare will soon cease."

On the following pages there are extracts from the Operational Records giving some idea of the Squadron's operations in this period.

By the autumn of 1917 Germany had increased its scale of raids on England and had replaced its Zeppelins, which were particularly vulnerable to tracer bullets, with the Gotha and A.E.G. bombers. The resultant outcry in England led to demands for retaliation on German cities. At the beginning of October, 1917, Major General Hugh Trenchard, then commanding the R.F.C. in France, was instructed to commence attacks on whatever German targets of

## 100 SQUADRON

Date: 11|12 July, 1917.
Objective: Ramegnies Chin Aerodrome and Ingelmunster Aerodrome.

*Taking Part*

| Pilots | Observers. |
|---|---|
| Capt. Collison. | Lieut. McNaughton. |
| 2|Lt. Kemp. | "     Price. |
| "     Carpenter. | Corpl. Hunter. |
| "     Boret. | ———————— |
| "     Blaney. | Lieut. Goddard. |
| "     Turnbull. | "     Steadman. |
| "     Kent. Sergt. | Doyle. |
| "     Duncan. | ———————— |
| Capt. Schweitzer. | 1st Air Mech. |
| | Crickmore. |

Bombs Dropped: 7 230 lb. 4 112 lb. and 10 20 lb.

Results:     2 230 lb. on Ramegnies Aerodrome from 1200ft.
            3 230 lb 2 112 lb and 6 20 lb. on Ingelmunster Aerodrome.
            2 230 lb. seen to have exploded close to hangars at Western end
                of aerodrome and 1 230 lb, near hangars at Eastern end.
            1 230 lb. and 2 20lb. from 2000ft. on Menin.

Remarks:   Intelligence later state that one shed containing 12 machines
                completely destroyed at Ramegnies Chin.

importance could be reached from the area around Nancy in Eastern Lorraine. Once again 100 Squadron was at the forefront and on 2nd October received orders to move to Ochey, near Nancy, which would put the Fe 2Bs in range of the Rhineland region around Saarbrucken and, later, when equipped with the H.P.0-400, within range of major German cities along the Rhine.

The ground party left Trexennes on the 3rd October entraining at St.Omer for a two day journey to Barisey-la-Cote north east of Neufchateau. After two nights on the train it was not a happy party that made its way to Ochey in pouring rain and the uncertainty of not knowing what sort of a place they were heading for. Spirits soon revived, however, with the arrival of a Staff Oficer who, quickly, made arrangements for the supply of rations on the French scale. Ochey itself, a former training ground for French Aviation, was a large aerodrome with permanent hangars and good hutted accommodation. An added bonus was its proximity to the well stocked shops and restaurants of Nancy and Toul.The Fe 2Bs, held up by bad weather at

100 SQUADRON

Date: 13|14 July 1917.
Objective:Heule and Chateau du Sart Aerodrome.

*Taking Part.*

| Pilots | | Observers. |
|---|---|---|
| 2|Lt. | Blaney | Lieut. Goddard. |
| " | Nock | ———— |
| " | Kent | Sergt. Doyle. |
| " | Carpenter | Corpl.Hunter. |
| " | Bean | 2nd Air Mech. Lem |
| " | Boret | ———— |
| " | Lewis | Lieut. Thompson. |
| Capt. | Schweitzer | Lieut. McNaughton. |
| 2|Lt. | Duncan | 2nd Air Mech. Cuss. |

Bombs dropped: 9 230lbs. and 18 20lbs.

Results:  3 230 lb and 6 20 lb. on Wervicq Station.
1 230 lb on sheds alongside.
3 230 lb and 6 20 lb on station N. of Lille and just S. of St.Honore.
1 230 lb and 4 20 lb from 1000 ft. on goods sorting station at La Madeleine triangle N.E. of Lille. Small fire started.
230 lb from 1500 ft. on sheds alongside Railway at Halluin.
1 230 lb and 2 20 lb from 1500 ft. into large rest camp just N. of Gheluvelt on Menin-Ypres road.

Fismes, finally arrived led by Major Christie who had the distinction of being the first pilot to land in the new Independent Air Force Area.

The first operation from Ochey was directed against trains, junctions, stations and sidings between Falkenberg and Saarbrucken. Twelve Fe 2Bs, each with a bomb load of 1 230 lb and 2 25lb. bombs, took off and bombed junctions at Merlenbach and Saarbrucken. Two trains and Falkenberg and Homberg stations were hit as were buildings near Saarbrucken station. Two 'planes were lost and their crews taken prisoner.

German reaction was instant. Aircraft and transport were destroyed or damaged by repeated German night attacks despite the addition of more French anti-aircraft batteries. 216 R.N.A.S. Squadron and a French night bomber squadron shared Ochey and also suffered from the attacks. It was obvious that the base risked being wiped out and drastic steps were taken to minimise the disruption of operations.Each evening MT transport was moved to a wooded area a mile away whilst hangars were emptied of all equipment

Fe 2 B (I.W.M.)

Be 2 E (I.W.M.)

Major W. J. Tempest, D.S.O., M.C.
Commanded the Squadron from 11th December 1917 to 12th June 1918
*Photo – The Annals of 100 Squadron*

and taken to the other side of the aerodrome. The following day it was returned to prepare aircraft for the next night's operations. The strain on all concerned was tremendous but it was particularly hard on the ground crews who had to have their aircraft ready by late afternoon. The Squadron carried out further raids on railway targets at Falkenberg and Saarbrucken and the steel works at Volkingen in the last days of October after which, it seems, operations were curtailed by the onset of winter.

One amusing incident, which could have turned out otherwise, occurred about this time and is recalled by Mr. Norman R.J. McCreath, brother of the late Lieut. Angus McCreath, an Fe 2B pilot with the Squadron:

"I recall my brother telling me about returning from a raid in very bad visibility and being unable find base. With fuel running low he realised that he might have to crash land. Just then, he saw a light ahead which he took to be the airfield. He put the 'plane down only to find that he had landed on a railway track and the light had been a signal!

Completely lost and not knowing whether he was behind the Allied or German lines he set off to find help. Eventually he came to a farm house and knocked at the door. Despite repeated knocking and banging he could get no response. In desperation he took out his Verey pistol and fired it in the air. There was a great commotion and the farm house door flew open. Running straight at him came a cow followed by the French farmer and his family. 'Are you the Boche?' asked the farmer in terror. In a mixture of English and pigdin French Angus assured the Frenchman that he was not, in fact, a German and was thankfully put on the road for his base."

Today, amongst 100 Squadron's memorabilia, can be found Lieut. McCreath's log book and personal items together with a little black toy dog which flew with him on all his operations.

Mr. Norman McCreath presented the collection to the Squadron and it is believed that the toy dog was taken on a refresher flight in a Canberra by former Squadron Commander Wing Commander Keith Douglas.

# CHAPTER THREE

## The Western Front 1918

More than three years after the outbreak of war the opposing forces were still deadlocked on the Western Front. The futile offensives and counter offensives of 1914, 1915, 1916 and 1917 had moved the battle lines barely a few miles one way or the other. With the collapse of Russia on the Eastern Front Germany was now able to reinforce its armies in France ready for its hoped for coup-de-grace in a Spring offensive. The Allied strategy, under Marshal Foch, was to absorb the German attack until it had spent itself and then counter attack to, finally, rout the German army.

In its own sector of the Western Front 100 Squadron's task was threefold: to continue its attacks on the railway system; to build up attacks on German industry and to safeguard itself by destroying German air bases responsible for the repeated raids on Ochey.

On the night of 3|4 January five aircraft bombed the steel works at Mazieres, where a large explosion was caused, and a railway station and junction near Metz was attacked. The following night nine crews dropped seven 230lb bombs on the blast furnaces at Mazieres and one 230 lb and a number of smaller bombs on Courcelles junction. Again, on the night of the 5th, Conflans station was hit by five 230lb and some smaller bombs causing a large explosion. Between the 14th and 21st January 17 sorties were flown against the steel works at Diedenhofen in the Saar. On the last of these raids one machine was lost and its crew, 2nd|Lt. Piele and Lt. Reid taken prisoner.

Towards the end of January 2nd|Lieut. Kingsford was posted to the Squadron and it is from him that we have a description of the "lighthouse system" and his first operational flight.

"But for the excellent system of lighthouses used on our side of the line it was quite an easy matter to get lost. These lighthouses were placed at intervals of, roughly, fifteen miles, some running towards the line and some parallel. They each flashed a letter in Morse so that any pilot, once he picked up a lighthouse, knew his position. Unfortunately, the enemy was not so considerate . . . and, once over the line, it was a matter of 'by guess' plus a very erratic compass which often acted in such a way as to make us doubt its acuracy."

After a few hours familiarisation by day and night on the Fe 2B 2nd|Lieut.

Kingsford appeared on orders for a raid on Courcelles railway junction through which enemy troops and supplies passed on their way to the Verdun sector of the Front. Also making his first trip was 2nd/Lieut Swart, a young South African. Discussing tactics prior to take off Swart mentioned that he would go in at 500ft whilst Kingsford, on the advice of old hands, decided on 2000ft. After shaking hands and wishing each other 'Good luck' they took off.

"We climbed into the darkness and headed for the lines. Ahead, I could see the tail lights of three machines while "D" lighthouse flashed below. Looking back, the wing tip lights of four machines could be seen and the flares of our aerodrome away in the distance. As we neared "C" lighthouse, three miles from the lines, I switched off our lights and set a course NNW."

"Our target was about 40 minutes flying time from the line which we crossed at 3000ft. There was not a light to be seen – just blank, inpenetrable darkness everywhere and broken only by the red glare of the exhaust and the glow from the instruments on the dashboard. Suddenly a searchlight pierced the darkness and caught us lighting the whole machine. My observer,Edwardes-Evans, was immediately on his feet and, grasping the gun, signalled me to swing round. Throttling back we dived right down the beam, Evans firing a good burst, but they held us . . . We could not frighten them so, kicking over the rudder, we side slipped out of the beam. Evans was keen to have another go so, while they scanned to and fro we dived down to 1000 ft. and, when directly overhead, Evans let go a whole drum. The light switched off immediately and we went on our way undisturbed."

"Ten minutes passed and I consulted the map; we could not be more than five miles from the target. On very dark nights our instructions were to watch for the leader's phospherous bomb and then drop ours as near to that as possible. I was just wondering whether, perhaps, we had flown past the objective when, away to the right, the leader's bomb exploded lighting up the surroundings for miles. We immediately swung round and made for it . . . I waited while the leader dropped the remainder of his bombs and then, as I guided the 'plane over the burning buildings, Evans let go two of our nine bombs. At this moment a searchlight lit up, its long thin beam pointed in our direction. We managed to dodge it and, coming down to 2000 ft., let go two more bombs. Looking over the side I could see the railway track. Another searchlight now frantically scanned the sky – shells were bursting everywhere – things were livening up."

"We decided to drop the rest of the bombs so, coming in again, Evans let go four more keeping the huge 230 pounder to the last. We wanted to get a good shot with this so we flew round to the north and came in from that direction. It was a good shot, slightly to the side of the track, but sufficiently near to have caused considerable damage."

"At this moment we were caught by one of the searchlights. I tried to dodge and, instinctively, looking over the side, saw a whole string of phospherous bullets coming towards us. Things were getting too hot and, as we had dropped all our bombs, I headed south west at 800 ft. for "C" lighthouse. Looking back we could see the searchlights still busy. Bombs were dropping everywhere and shells were bursting. A good strafe was on – we pitied the last machine to arrive for we had stirred up a hornets' nest and and someone was going to get it hot and strong. In the excitement of the raid we had forgotten the cold but, before ten minutes of the return flight had passed, we froze. We gazed intently ahead trying to pierce the darkness with the hope of picking up the welcome flash of "C" lighthouse. As time went on we realised we must be drifting off course. I swung the 'plane a little to the south and on we flew but, still, no light. We were lost. For a moment a feeling of panic came over me – the intense darkness adding terror to the thought of a forced landing."

"Just when things seemed hopeless a tiny speck of light, away to the left, caught my eye. I pointed it out to Evans and then made in the direction. We both glued our eyes to the tiny speck and, as we approached, I fancied it flashed. Evans leaned over and shouted: 'That's it!' and we shook hands away up at 3000 ft. In twenty minutes we were back safely and my first raid over the German lines was over."

The British official report of the raid was as follows:

'On Saturday night our night bombing machines carried out a successful raid into Germany although the weather was by no means good. Nearly a ton of bombs was dropped with very good results on the important railway junction and siding at Courcelles les Metz. One of our machines is missing.'

The missing machine was that of 2nd|Lieut Swart who, with his observer, Fielding-Clarke was taken prisoner.

On the nights of the 16th to 19th February the Squadron was out at full strength on railway targets at Conflans, Trier and Thionville. Trier, in particular, was subjected to 'round the clock' bombing on the 19th by VIII Brigade. 100 Squadron's share of the action consisted of dropping 2856 lbs of bombs. The official German report stated that there were five hits on the station destroying the station-master's house; one bomb on the market and another which destroyed the local Chancery Court. One aircraft flew so low that it just missed the tops of houses causing German civilians and mayors to demand that German air raids should stop so as to prevent retaliatory strikes. The crew involved were Lieutenants A. Wald and S.M. Duncan.

During the following month the Squadron launched three attacks on an important German aerodrome at Frescaty. On the 26th February three crews dropped 1048 lbs. of bombs on the base. On the 6th March one crew, Lieuts. Bright and Rose completely destroyed one hangar with all its machines inside. On the 23rd eleven crews dropped 2800 lbs. causing considerable damage. One pilot saw 16 'planes waiting to take off and dropped his bombs on them.

Writing in 'The German Air Force in the Great War' G.P. Neumann describes 'the unfair method' of night attacks on Aincourt aerodrome, home of German No. 2 Bomber Squadron. Although 100 Squadron was not involved here his description gives an insight into the tactics used by some of the night bomber forces.'We heard the sound of the machines and ran outside. One of them flashed the squadron's Morse landing signal so the landing lights were lit up but we then found we ourselves were being bombed. I do not think this was very honourable of the enemy.'

The "Annals" describe another example of a forced landing during the winter of 1917l18:

Returning from a sortie behind the German lines one crew flew into heavy rain. Blinded by the driving rain with 'water cataracting off their goggles' it was impossible to see the instruments and they lost all sense of direction. Instinct told the pilot that he was flying nose down and he heaved back on the stick 'until he could feel her rear and swoop upwards.' Clear of the rain he found them flying north instead of west. The pilot brought the 'plane down to 200 ft. but could see absolutely nothing to indicate their position.

They climbed again to 1000 ft. on a westerly heading believing they should be somewhere near the Allied lines when they flew into a snow storm. Blinded now by the snow, the cockpit clock out of action and running low on fuel the pilot flew along on instinct. After a few more minutes they fired Verey lights in an attempt to get a glimpse of the ground but to no avail. Gingerly the pilot brought the 'plane down to 200 ft. and, in the glow of another Verey, saw a field. The pilot fired a landing light which gave him just enough vision to put the 'plane down in quite a good landing when he promptly shut off the engine.

Neither pilot nor observer had any idea where they were and the observer was about to set off to seek a farmhouse when they saw vague lights and gun flashes in the distance. They called out repeatedly but received no reply until lights appeared moving towards them. It was then that they heard voices. They were German! They had landed behind the German lines!

Pilot and observer ran to the 'plane and as the pilot climbed into the cockpit the observer wound the prop back to suck fuel into the cylinders."When she starts," called out the pilot, "jump to the wing tip and pull her round. You'll have to jump for it and climb in as we go!"

The voices were now louder and, after two swings, the cold engine refused to fire. Lights and shouts were directed at the 'plane and, in a last desperate effort, the observer swung the prop again and the engine roared into life. As the 'plane taxied forward, to the accompaniment of rifle shots from the Germans, the observer swung the 'plane round and, as it lumbered down the field, climbed in. Relying solely on the feel of the force of wind on his face the pilot judged the moment right to pull back on the stick and head for the lights of the trenches. Half an hour later they landed on their own 'drome.

As the 'plane came to a stop the Duty Officer walked over to them.

"Hello you two. Where the blazes have you been till this time? We'd just about to put you down as missing." The pilot and observer were standing in their cockpits and, without a word, were solemnly shaking hands. The pilot looked overboard at the officer on the ground: "You may believe it, Johnny,

or you may not," he said, "but we've been down in Hunland."
    "Down into hell?" said Johnny. "Quit joking. What kept you so late?"
    "You've said it Johnny. Down into hell – and out again."
    They shook hands again, solemnly.

...............................................................

In the early years of this century the German rail network was developed as part of military strategy to provide rapid movement of large armies in an area where mobility was limited. As Professor A.J. Taylor stressed in his history, "The First World War", it was a crucial factor in the 'Schlieffen Plan' where timetables were worked out in minute detail. They became equally important in the Spring of 1918 as the High Command launched its huge push for victory. For the next three months rail targets were 100 Squadron's primary objectives.

    From the end of March to the end of June there were nineteen major attacks on the German rail system – 174 individual sorties. The first of these, on the 24th March, was directed on the Metz – Sablons Triangle in two raids with thirteen crews in the first and five in the second. A total of 3353 lbs of bombs were dropped. The German report of the attack states:

DH 9 (I.W.M.)

'Last night, from 8.55 p.m. onwards, hostile aircraft appeared over Metz. The fall of bombs was as follows: Several bombs fell on the main No. 6 track in the station. 15 trucks caught fire and 7 munition wagons amongst them exploded. Tracks No. 6 and 16 were very extensively damaged and others also suffered (20 in all).The whole train exploded, blew up and burnt itself out. Seven houses were very seriously damaged. The northerly gasometer in the triangle was struck and damaged. The force of the explosion was so great that the building south of the gasometer had its roof blown off and exploding shells damaged the machinery. Traffic was held up for hours. Only six men were killed and two wounded.'

On the 28th March the Squadron was moved to Villesneux aerodrome, west of Chalon sur Marne, to strike at more rail targets vital for the German advance. Throughout April and early May repeated attacks were made on railways at Juniville, Mohon, Chaulnes, Ham and many other centres until the German advance was halted.On the 12th May the Squadron returned to Ochey and, for the rest of the month, resumed its attacks on Metz, Thionville and Saarbrucken railway targets. On the 22nd and 27th May there were two full Squadron attacks on the power station at Kreuzwald where large explosions were caused and fires started. Photographs showed two direct hits on what was believed to be the power house.

# CHAPTER FOUR

## The Independent Air Force

The new Indedependent Air Force was born on the 5th June 1918 under the command of Major General Hugh Trenchard and 100 Squadron marked the occasion by another attack on the Metz – Sablon railway triangle. On the following night it was the turn of the Mazieres blast furnaces and the Metz and Thionville railway system. Metz received another visit from the Squadron on the 23rd when German reports stated that one track was completely destroyed and several lines rendered unserviceable.

By the end of June the German offensive was running out of steam and the Allies were marshalling their forces for the counter-attack which was to end the war. There began a round-the-clock onslaught on the German airfields during which 100 Squadron repeatedly put up every available machine for its night raids. On the 25th 15 aircraft attacked Boulay aerodrome completely destroying four hangars containing stores. Six crews attacked Boulay again on the following night damaging three 'Gothas' on the ground. Five crews attacked again on the 27th setting fire to two hangars and hitting the railway at Metz and Contilon. On the 29th twelve machines attacked Frescaty aerodrome and trains near Metz. Throughout July the Squadron operated at maximum effort with up to 16 crews. The targets were, almost entirely, aerodromes behind the German lines – Boulay, Friesdorf, Morhange – interspersed with individual attacks on trains, stations, sidings, searchlight and anti aircraft batteries.

On the 10th August the Squadron moved to Xaffevilliers airfield and, three days later, it bade farewell to its faithful old FE 2bs. "It can be truthfully stated here," said 'The Annals of 100 Squadron', "that there was no machine that served its country so well as did this type. It was, undoubtedly, a most excellent machine for night bombing and the whole personnel of the Squadron made the best of the machine and did it more than credit." The main disadvantage of the FE 2b though, which even the 'Annals' admitted, was its limited bomb load which was "a decided drawback to pilots and observers out for a really good strafe." So in order to strike deeper into Germany with more telling loads the Squadron re-equipped with Handley Page 0-400s instead. The H.P. 0l400 was the main heavy bomber of World War 1 being an improved version of the 0l100 with a top speed of 97½ mph, a bomb load of 2,000lbs and a range of 700 miles. The whole of the industrial Ruhr and Rhineland cities were now in bombing range.

Throughout the month the Squadron, now under the command of Major W.J. Tempest, D.S.O., D.F.C., who had taken over from Major Burge in June, gradually converted to the new machine. A study of the "Annals" shows that the attacks on enemy airfields went on unabated. On one attack on Friesdorf Lieut. Johnson, Pilot, and Capt. Wilson, Observer, attacked an enemy machine below them and watched it crash on the flare path.

On the 25th a tragic accident occurred when one of new 0-400s crashed on take off. It was piloted by Lieut. Box with Lieuts. Inches and Boyd as observer and gunner. Seventy years later, on the occasion of the Squadron's 70th birthday, former Observer, Roy Shillinglaw, recalled the crash:

"We were sitting in our machine, waiting to take off, when we saw this Handley over to our right on its take off run towards a row of poplars. It failed to make height, perhaps twenty feet or so, when it struck one of the trees with its starboard wing. The machine slewed round and crashed – I knew the bombs would go off – they did. The blast blew back the trees. One engine was found 250 yards away and the other 100 yards away. I think eight men were killed and fifteen injured.

The next day Lord Trenchard came to visit us to express his sympathy. He sat back on his stick and spoke to us:'Yes, this is a bad accident but I have my targets to attack. We have plenty more machines and plenty of pilots and observers so go to it!'

So we went to it!"

Throughout September and early October the Squadron made repeated attacks on enemy airfields and railways. A typical bomb load was now 13 or 14 112 pounders but they were soon to be delivering 550 and the latest 1600 lb bomb. On the night of the 21st October one of the first of these bombs was dropped on Kaiserlautern. The Gernan report stated:'About 9.25 p.m. a machine dropped a very large bomb in the N.E. corner of the town. The result was terrific. Several houses were very badly hit by pieces from this bomb which burst in a field 50 – 100 yards away. Several families are left homeless. The whole quarter is extensively damaged.'The following night another 1600 pounder was dropped on Saarbrucken with other attacks on Metz and the Burbach works.

100 Squadron's war drew to an end with attacks on Mannheim, Frankfurt and Karlsruhe at the end of October. The last Squadron attack of the war was flown by Lieuts. Crocker and White, pilots, with their crews, 2ndlLieuts. Greaves,Best, Loftus and Gwyther. Wing Commander Brookes records:'It was a fitting end for the Squadron, that was the first to bomb Germany, that the last R.A.F. aircraft to return from a raid, the night the cease fire came into force, also belonged to 100 Squadron.'

On the Western Front the Squadron carried out 213 raids; dropped 185 tons of bombs; fired 450,000 rounds of ammunition and brought down five enemy aircraft.

Twenty nine officers and men were killed in action; eleven were wounded and three others died from illness or injuries received. A further 29 were taken prisoner.

There were 34 awards and citations for bravery including eight Military Crosses, eight D.F.C.s, three Meritorious Service Medals, four Croixs de Guerre, one Albert Medal,one Medaille Militaire, one Belgian Legion d' Honneur, one Medaiile d' Honneur en Argent and one Medaille Militaire en Bronze. Four officers and men were Mentioned in Despatches and Sgt. P.J. Adkins was awarded the D.S.M., D.F.M. and Medaille Militaire.

In a letter to Major Burge, the last wartime CO, Sir Hugh Trenchard wrote:

'I would like you to know what I think of 100 Squadron. It arrived, as you know, in March 1917 and was under my command for practically its whole time in France. It started with a splendid name and within a few weeks I was counting on it as one of my best weapons for hitting the enemy . . .

The pilots and observers were always cheery and ready to carry out any work asked of them and, in the worst weather, they showed the utmost determination to get to the targets they had been ordered to bomb, very often in thunderstorms or thick fog and mist; many times they attempted the work when it was impossible to see the ground from above 100 feet owing to mist.

The rank and file were noted amongst squadrons for being exceptionally good at keeping their engines and machines in serviceable order; this was not easy and the men, very often, worked all day and all night . . .

I can only say that it was 'one of the great squadrons' of the war. I was very proud to have had the honour to command such an efficient squadron.'

Perhaps the spirit of 100 Squadron in The Great War is best summed up in this condensed extract from an article by Irvin S. Cobb, an official American Correspondent on the Western Front, published in "The Saturday Evening Post" on 15th June, 1918.

### "HAPPY LANDINGS"

'The affair dated from a certain spring noontime when two of us were temporarily marooned at the press headquarters of the American Expeditionary Force. Suddenly a big biplane came into sight glittering like a silver flying fish and landed in a meadow behind the town. Two persons, muffled in great-coats, decanted themselves out of it and tramped towards us. They were two very young, very ruddy gentlemen and unmistakably English. My companion knew one of them and we were introduced.

"What brings you over this way?" enquired my friend."Well, you see, we were a bit thirsty – Bert and I – and we heard you had very good beer at the French Oficers' Club here so we ran over for half an hour or so to get a drink and toddle back again. Not a bad idea, eh, what?"

The speaker, aged about twenty one, had the complexion of a very new, healthy cherub and wore the twin crowns of a captain on his overcoat. On the way towards beer and lunch my friend asked:

"Anything new happening at the Squadron since I was there?" Quiet enough to be a bore – weather hasn't suited for our sort lately." stated the taller one. "We got fed up of doing nothing so, night before last, a squad started across the border to give Fritzie a taste of life. But just after we started the Squadron Commander decided the weather was too thickish so he signed us back – all but the 'Young – un', who claims he didn't see the flare and kept on going all by his little self." He favoured us with a tremendous wink.

"It seemed a rotten shame, really it did, to waste the whole evening," said the 'Young un', he of the pink cheeks, " so I just jogged across the jolly old Rhine until I came to a town and I dropped my pills and came back. Nice quiet trip – lonely and not a bit exciting."

It was then that a light dawned on me. I had heard of these bombing squadrons of the British outfits – of young and seasoned flyers now retaliating for the German attacks on unprotected cities. For each pair of flyers this meant a flight by darkness at 60 or 70 miles per hour above and beyond the enemy lines; it meant the peril of attack from anti-aircraft gun or speedier German scouts; it meant finding the objective and loosing off the explosive shells and winging back again – if they got back – in time for a late dinner at the home hangars.

Personally, I craved to see more of these men; men who could talk of dropping pills when they meant spilling destruction on German supply depots and railroad terminals or men who could refer to their machine as 'The Red Hen' and their task as 'laying an egg or two'. Out of this luncheon was born a trip – a trip to see more of these young men at their base. (Ochey)

The Mess was decorated with newspaper illustrations and sporting prints; there was a wheezy phonograph and a piano which, by authority, was mute until after dinner; there were guitars and mandolins; there were glasses and bottles upon the tables and cushions, plainly the handiwork of some fellow's best girl, upon the settees.

For guests of honour there were we four and, for hosts, there were sixty or seventy members of Night Bombing Squadron Number 100. This group of young daredevils represented every main division of the Empire's domain: Englishmen, Cornishmen, Welshmen, Scots, Irishmen, Canadians, Australians, New Zealanders, an Afrikander or two, a dark youngster from India as well as recruits gathered in from lesser lands and colonies where the Union Jack floats in the seven seas that circle this globe.

Their average age was twenty two and a half years. Veteran airmen will tell you that when a fellow reaches twenty five he's getting too old for the game. " 'Tis a man's game, if ever there was a man's game in this world; and it's boys with the soft fleece of adolescence on their cheeks that play it best."

Major C. G. Burge. O.B.E.
Commanded the Squadron from 13th June 1918 to the end of hostilities
*The Annals of 100 Squadron*

Well, we had dinner but before it an event befell which was as dramatic as anything could possibly be. Glasses had been charged to drink the toast of the British aviator when two things happened. The electric lights flickered, leaving us in shadows, and a servant entered, saluted and handed the Squadron Commander a slip of paper bearing a bulletin received by telephone from a sister squadron. The young Major read it aloud: "Eight machines of Squadron — made a daylight raid this afternoon. The operation was successfully carried out." There was a pause. "Three machines failed to return."

That was all. Six men, mates and friends to these youngsters assembled here had gone down – to death? To captivity in a German prison camp? No-one spoke nor did anyone refer to the matter afterwards but the glasses came up with a jerk, the lights flipped on and then together we drank the airmen's toast:

"Happy landings!"

The rest of the evening passed in a sing song and story telling round the piano and we, very reluctantly, left them in the small hours when, as they said, the fun was just starting.

When next I passed that road the hangars were empty. The great offensive had started and, on the third day of it, we learned from other sources that Night Bombing Squadron Number 100 had climbed by pairs into their big 'planes and had gone winging away to do their share in the air fighting where the fighting lines were locked fast. I doubt whether many of those blithesome lads came out of that hell alive or whether I shall ever see any of them again. So I shall think of them as I saw them last – sixty or so – average age twenty two and a half – grouped in the doorway with the candle light and fire light shining behind them and their glasses raised, wishing to us:

"Happy landings!"

# CHAPTER FIVE

## Between the Wars
## November 1918 to January 1934

Almost immediately after the Armistice the Independent Air Force was ordered to move North. On the 16th November the Squadron proceeded to Ligescourt, north west of Abbeville. The aircraft arrived there the same day whilst the M.T., stores, ammunition and other equipment arrived on the 22nd and from there they awaited orders to return home.

Writing on the 14th February, 1919, in his conclusion to "The Annals of 100 Squadron", Major C. G. Burge, O.B.E., paid tribute to the Squadron:

"My task as C.O. was considerably lightened by the energetic and whole hearted support which I, at all times, received from one and all serving under me. Pilots and Observers, always full of determination and keenness, unselfish and cheerful at all times, won for themselves and the Squadron the greatest admiration. Like gentlemen and sportsmen they played the game throughout. The every day order of our much respected chief, General Trenchard, to 'keep it going,' was carried out to the letter.

No less can be written concerning the Ground Personnel. Their task was no light one and their devotion to duty greatly contributed to the success of the pilots and observers. Although their work was less romantic their task entailed great hardships and hard work . . . They experienced frequent and, at times, severe aerial bombardment but their courage was not undermined in the least. They too 'kept it going.' Lastly, I cannot speak too highly of the "Esprit de Corps" which so strongly existed."

At the time of writing Major Burge thought that the Squadron was on the verge of being disbanded and went on to quote General Trenchard's words to him:

"It's traditions which count and which make people keep straight and, although the Squadron has been disbanded, those who belonged to No. 100 Squadron should remember, in the future, what a *Squadron they belonged to!*"

By June, 1919, Major Burge had learnt that the Squadron would, after all, have a peacetime role and sent his best wishes to all who serve in the Squadron concluding with his exhortation:

*"Keep up the good name of '100', carry through its traditions, 'KEEP IT GOING,' and play the game!"* Although under the threat of disbandment

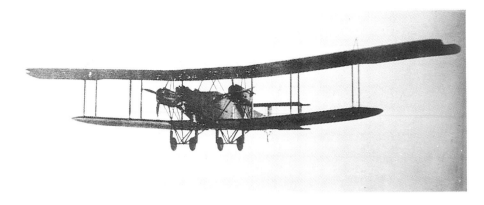

Vickers Vimy
*(I.W.M.)*

Handley Page 0–400
*(I.W.M.)*

from June, 1919, the Squadron's proud record in France must have caused delays in executing the order.In June, 1919, the Squadron, consisting of an HQ and two Flights moved to St. Inglevert, south west of Calais, where it took over 207 Squadron's aircraft. In September it returned to England where it was severely reduced in size to cadre strength after which it was posted to Baldonnel, Co. Dublin, as part of No.11 (Irish) Group.

From September, 1919, to February, 1920, there seems to have been some intense lobbying by Major Burge and other ex Squadron members to keep their old squadron alive. It also seems likely that Lord Trenchard himself would want to keep 100 Squadron as part of the new Royal Air Force. The outcome was that 100 Squadron returned to full strength by absorbing the cadres of 117 and 141 Squadrons at Baldonnel on 1st February, 1920.

It was based there for almost a year flying Bristol Fighters on duties against the Sinn Fein which consisted, mainly, of dropping propaganda leaflets and delivering mail. When Eire gained its independence all British forces were withdrawn and, on the 4th February, 1922, the Squadron moved to Spitalgate, near Grantham. There was one occasion when the Squadron was almost called into action when the new Irish Government was faced with rebellion and the seizure of the Four Courts in Dublin. The Irish Government requested a bombing attack on the rebels so a "D" Flight Vimy was fitted with bomb racks, sights and guns which, according to Flight Commander Flying Officer Alan Perry Keene, was an almost forgotten art. In the event the rebellion petered out and the operation was cancelled.

1922|1923 was a period of contraction for the R.A.F. and the Squadron, adapting to the new circumstances, became a training unit in March, 1922, flying Avro 504s and DH 9As which had been erected from storage. In September 6 FTS was disbanded and the Squadron received four of its Vimys to form "D" Flight, referred to above. These were identical to that flown by Alcock and Brown in their trans-Atlantic flight of 1919 with the exception of extra fuel tanks. Pupils converted to the Vimy, from the Avro 504, by flying five hours solo. One exceptional pupil, Pilot Officer Basil Embry, completed the course in one day.

1923|1924 saw another switch in political thinking and began to expand the R.A.F. again. In May, 1924, the Squadron moved to Eastchurch to equip with Fairey Fawns, a light day-bomber which replaced the DH9. Now, officially designated No. 100 (Bomber) Squadron, it formed part of the new, U.K. based, day bomber force. In June, the following year, the Squadron had the distinction of leading four squadrons at the Hendon Air Display. Back at Spitalgate it returned to routine training and bombing exercises until May, 1926. Between the 4th and 19th May the Squadron was engaged in carrying mail by air and lorry during the General Strike. Four Fawns were sent to Catterick to deliver 'The British Gazette' to Newcastle and to drop copies on isolated farms and villages in the north east.

Between August and December the Squadron was, again, re-equipped with a new aircraft; the Fawns were replaced with the Hawker Horsley day bombers powered by a Rolls Royce Condor engine which had an endurance of ten hours and could carry a 600 lbs. bomb load. For three months every year the Squadron was detached to Western Zoyland in Somerset to practise bombing and fire the aircrafts' guns. "C" Flight operated as a target towing facility for anti-aircraft gunners at Watchet. Wing Commander Brookes, in his Official History, describes this period as the hey-day of unrestricted flying for the home based R.A.F. He describes one occasion, in 1927, when a motorist, ignoring all danger signals and confused by the fact that the airfield was unfenced and level with the road, parked his car under the approach path of a Horsley. The irate pilot swung round and chased the petrified motorist down the road in his aeroplane!

In January, 1928 the Squadron moved to Bicester in Oxfordshire, where, in addition to its normal work, it took on a similar role to that of the '70s and '80s. Formations of Horsleys would act as targets for fighter squadrons and provide the bomber force for 'Redland' against 'Blueland' in mock attacks against such fighter bases as Tangmere, Andover and Upavon. In October, 1928 the Squadron came 7th in the Lawrence Minot Bombing Trophy Competition with a score of 68 yards. Other work at this time included testing experimental WIT and RIT aircraft fixes and DIF trials. Warrant Officer Gledhill spoke of their jubilation when they obtained a

100 Squadron    Donibristle 1933/1934
*W. J. Herrington CB RAF(retd)*

Vickers 'Vildebeest' Torpedo Bomber
Pegasus Engine
*D. G. Bell*

direct fix of one of the aircraft over the Forth Bridge. In May, 1929, "A" Flight also tested the new Hawker Hart and Avro Antelope, two high performance day bombers.

A log book, found in the roof space of a house in Cleethorpes almost 50 years later, gives a deeper insight into, what might be thought, the dull routine of the Squadron's work in those days. Pilot Officer E. H. Irving recorded hours and hours of practice and test flying with the Horsley in all kinds of weather. The success of the W/T fix came after hours of frustrating tests and further refinements led to its importance as a valuable navigational aid in World War 2. More hours flying decided the selection of the Hawker Hart in preference to the Antelope which was prone to cracks in the engine bearings.

Apart from regular bombing practices and mock Redland|Blueland battles, Pilot Officer Irving recorded aerial photography exercises, dummy parachute drops, three drift wind finding exercises, gunnery exercises and an altitude test when the Horsley's engine froze up at 18,000 ft.

It was on the 3rd November, 1930, when the Squadron adopted yet another role which was to lead to the most glorious, yet tragic, period in its history. The Squadron moved to Donibristle, Fife, where its Horsleys were converted to carry 2,150 lb. torpedoes. For the next two years 100 Squadron Horsleys were regularly engaged in making attacks, with dummy torpedoes, on any

Royal Navy warship entering or leaving the Firth of Forth with many 'kills' being claimed by both sides. The Horsley's conversion from a day bomber to a torpedo bomber, however, was never considered satisfactory and the R.A.F. issued a specification for an aircraft designed for the special role of coastal defence.The outcome was the Vickers Vildebeest, a 49ft. span biplane, deliveries of which commenced in November, 1932.

The new 'plane, designed by Rex Pierson, was powered by a 622 Pegasus engine and had a specially divided undercarriage to accommodate the torpedo. The pilot had an excellent view and controlled a Vickers gun whilst the Wireless Operator|Air Gunner defended the rear with a Lewis gun. 100 Squadron was the first squadron to be equipped with the Vildebeest and,in 1933, was officially designated 100 (Torpedo Bomber) Squadron. On the 8th December, 1933, 100 Squadron, with its Vildebeests packed in crates, set sail in the S.S. Rampura from London docks to Singapore. Travelling incognito on the ship was General Allenby for whom a boxing tournament was arranged by the Station Warrant Officer, Warrant Officer Rutley. Christmas was spent aboard ship in Aden and, on the 5th January, 1934, 100 (Torpedo Bomber) Squadron began to settle in at Seletar.

Yet, the new aircraft were hardly out of their crates when Air Marshal Chilton, then a navigation instructor at the Central Flying School, warned of the vulnerability of the torpedo bomber. He all too accurately forecast that, at the moment of release, a torpedo aircraft would be an easy target for ship's guns.

# CHAPTER SIX

## MALAYA
### January 1934 to September 1939

Before recounting the Squadron's role in Malaya it is useful to examine Britain's policy for the defence of Singapore and, in fact, Malaya as a whole. In the 1920s Japan was regarded as a "friendly power" particularly after the signing of the Naval Limitation Treaty, or "552" Treaty of London in 1922 which limited Japanese naval strength in the Far East to the third most powerful navy in the world after Britain and the United States. In the early '30s, however, Japan ceased to be an upholder of the League of Nations and took on an aggressive and expansionary role.

As an industrialised, island nation, practically devoid of raw materials and energy, with limited agricultural resources and with a rapidly growing population, Japan began to expand westwards annexing Manchuria in 1931and attacking Shanghai a year later.The ultimate aim was to establish hegemony over Malaya, Dutch East Indies and French Indo China or "The Greater East Asia Co-Prosperity Sphere" as Japan called it in July 1940. Standing in the way of achieving this aim was the U.S. Pacific Fleet based at Pearl Harbour and the Royal Navy at Singapore. Japan's overall strategy was to take out the two fleets, capture air bases in Malaya and take Singapore from the north. The Dutch East Indies would then be quickly overrun to obtain the much needed Sumatran oil and the whole operation consolidated by the capture of the Phillipines. In mid 1941 Japan had about a year's reserves of oil and she gambled that her aims could be achieved before America could recover and retaliate. Japan realised the long term potential of U.S. industrial might but gambled on America accepting the fait-accompli rather than face a long war.

In 1934, however, the West was largely ignorant of these, perhaps, over-simplified Japanese aims but Japan's encroachments in China caused rising concern in Britain. The Chiefs of Staff reacted to the ominous developments by asking their Government to reverse its policy of limited defence expenditure, stressing, in particular, "that it would be the height of folly to perpetuate our defenceless state in the Far East."

British policy for the defence of Singapore was based on the assumption that, in the event of trouble, the British main fleet could reach the island within seventy days. It was argued that Singapore need, therefore, have only enough arms to defend herself until the main fleet arrived and all measures taken were designed to deal wholly with enemy attacks from the sea. The Air Ministry was not happy with this assumption and was probably alone in believing that "Singapore might be assaulted from other directions than from the sea," but, in spite of their protestations, the role of the R.A.F. was seen as only of secondary importance in the defence of Singapore. As a result the total air strength of Singapore was to be built up in a leisurely fashion from two to three squadrons by the addition of No. 100 Squadron which began to move from Donibristle in December, 1933. It spent Christmas in Aden aboard the good ship 'SS Ranpura' and finally settled at Seletar on the 5th January, 1934 joining the Horsleys of 36 and the Albacores of 205 Squadrons.

"The British Command in Malaya had almost come to regard the jungle as a natural Maginot Line. As a British soldier explained:

'It's like this. Our colonel would say: 'Now this is thick jungle here and this is mangrove swamp . . . We can rule this out . . . all we have to concern ourselves with is the road.'

'Why, I went through a mangrove swamp the other day and nowhere did I go down in the mud over my ankles. Anyway, you can walk on the roots in almost any swamp.' And the Japanese did!" ('The War.' Ed. Flower and Reeves. Michael Joseph Ltd.)

As the late Flight Sergeant Sedgley, a fitter at Seletar, remarked,"As the Japs came in from one end we cleared out from the other."

In January 1934, however, all this was a long way ahead but it may serve to explain the tragedy seven years later.


In his memoirs of life with 100 Squadron in the 1930s former Warrant Officer G. Bell describes Singapore as one of the best overseas postings. Most routine work was done in the mornings beginning with Reveille at 06.30 and ending with tiffin at 13.15. There was a two hour "quiet" period until 1600 hrs.unless there was some emergency work to be done. Football and hockey were two favourite pastimes. There were frequent games and competitions with 36 and 205 Squadrons but, on many occasions, visiting Royal Navy crews were invited to join in. The Army, at Changi barracks, also took part and Seletar's hospitality was reciprocated whenever possible. On one particular naval exercise H.M.S. Eagle and a number of submarines paid a visit and a number of airmen were entertained by the ship's company and also took part in some of the exercises. As WIO Bell states, "All this liaison fostered a great spirit of comradeship between the various forces."

One young aircraftman, a former Halton Apprentice, who was posted to the Squadron in 1934, was Arthur Ernest Lowe. more popularly known as 'Lapper' Lowe. Arthur had trained as a Wireless Operator Mechanic and, on gaining his L.A.C.,became an air gunner with the Squadron. Following

100 Squadron   Seletar. Singapore c1934/35
*D. G. Bell*

a spell with 208 Squadron at Heliopolis he was posted back to England from where he flew a number of sorties on Whitleys. He was commissioned in 1941 and, in a distinguished career, was promoted to Wing Commander and became the first air gunner to command a squadron (77 Squadron at Elvington.) He was awarded the M.B.E. for his work as No. 4 Group Gunnery Officer and went on to be awarded the D.F.C. for operational work with 77 Squadron. Subsequently, as Group Captain Operations at H.Q. Fighter Command, he was created a C.B.E. in 1961.

There appears to have been plenty of time for leisure activities apart from football. A popular diversion was to hire a sampan and paddle up the straits to Frank Buck's Zoo, of 'bring 'em back alive' fame', which was situated near Changi Barracks. Water polo was popular as, of course, were weekly visits to the Union Jack Club and a cinema. 'Raffles', naturally, was the centre of social life for officers of all services who met and mingled with Singapore society.

One of the 'perks' of serving at Seletar at this time was the opportunity to take an 'indulgence passage' to Hong Kong in the Trooping Season which

Squadron Leader L. G. Le B. Croke (O/C 100 Squadron 1931 – 1935)
W/O2 Bow (Armaments), Corporal Emery (Torpedo Fitter)
L. A. C. Layton (Torpedo Fitter)
Photographed with some of the Squadron silver. c1935
*D. G. Bell*

lasted from April to October. The only charge was ration money for the return voyage to Hong Kong where one could stay for about ten days.

A highlight of 1934 was the MacRobertson Air Race from Mildenhall to Melborne in which Seletar was a recognised re-fuelling stop. All participants were refuelled by maintenance personnel from the three squadrons. The race was won by C.W.A. Scott and Campbell-Black in their DH 8 with a time of 70 hours 54 minutes. In second place was a KLM D.C.2 piloted by Parmentier and Moll. Two years later Miss Jean Batten landed at Seletar for refuelling on her record breaking solo flight to Australia and Flight Sergeant Beer, N.C.O. ilc "A" Flight had the task of guarding her Percival Gull from enthusiastic onlookers.

At the business end of life in Singapore the Squadron was kept busy although it got off to a tragic start when Pilot Officer Parrish and crew member L.A.C. Ginello were killed in a flying accident. Their loss was keenly felt on the Squadron as they had been two of the original members at Donibristle.

The Squadron's role in Singapore was to attack enemy shipping in order to 'hold the fort' for those vital 70 days in the event of war. To that end there were daily and, sometimes, nightly 'strikes' against any vessel entering territorial waters. Mock attacks were made with 'runner', unarmed, torpedoes which sometimes got lost. A regular target for mock torpedo attacks was H.M.S. Terror, a former World War 1 vessel, which was anchored close to the dry dock. The torpedoes were picked up by an R.A.F. launch. Former Corporal Roy Mager describes a typical 'attack' on a naval co-operation exercise.

"Returning from Kuala Lumpur where we had been taking part in Naval co-operation duties we immediately got six aircraft ready for a dawn attack the following day on a couple of Royal Navy cruisers – H.M.S. Norfolk and H.M.S. Birmingham. Take off was 05.15 hrs., about an hour before dawn. Tuesday and Wednesday were quite normal days and on Thursday we carried out a midday attack on two cruisers and five destroyers. Unfortunately the Navy couldn't find some of the torpedoes so the afternoon was spent flying round the area of the attack searching for – and finding – those missing tin fish and then directing destroyers to their positions in order to retrieve them."

To be effective the torpedoes had to be dropped from a height of 15 ft. which was just possible in daylight but almost impossible at night. Just how dangerous this was can be judged from the photographs of a 36 Squadron Horsley which didn't get it quite right and ditched in the Straits of Johore. The method was for a Flight or the whole Squadron to fly out with only blue, backward shining 'streaming lights' for guidance. One aircraft would illuminate the target from 5,000ft. with parachute flares when the rest of the aircraft would go in individually. Eventually, improved torpedo racks were designed so that the torpedoes could be launched from 100 ft. Former Sergeant Claude Thmpson, R.N.Z.A.F., wrote soberly and prophetically

Straits scene off Kampong

Visit of minister of State for Air
Left: Sir Philip Sassoon
Centre: GP. Capt. Sydney Smith (Base Commander)
Right: Flg. Off. Hobler (Adjutant, 100 Squadron)

about one such exercise:"The Navy told us the torpedoes would score hits but we would lose all our aircraft."

On two mornings a week the Squadron would also practise high level bombing from 8,000ft. to 10,000ft. using 8 lb. practice bombs. There were regular air-to-air and air-to-sea gunnery exercises, photo and visual-reconnaissance and target towing. On one of these latter exercises a pilot crash landed in the jungle. The following condensed extract from "The Straitsman" (January, 1935) describes the salvage operation. In charge of the ground party was the late Flight Sergeant J.W. Sedgeley whose widow, Yvonne, sent the original report.

## THE SALVING OF K 2931

A group of Malays had found the wreckage of the Vildebeest which had crashed in Northern Johore. On the 28th October two officers and five airmen with rations for nine days left Singapore by train for Bekok, 80 miles to the North.After changing into marching kit and making up 40lb. packs of food, tools and personal gear the party was met at Bekok by the Inspector of Police.

The party was transported in an ancient Ford and an equally ancient Fiat to a Chinese village four miles away where they met up with 40 Malay and Saki baggage carriers, guides and a police escort. An hour later, at 13.30, the march began. Initially, it was comparatively easy going but soon deteriorated when the party encountered heavy mud and a rough cut jungle path. Hourly breaks were made for a smoke and change over of arms which consisted of a rifle, pistol and shot gun carried by the police. The jungle path took the party up hill and down dale gradually rising to 1,000 ft. above sea level where the aircraft had force landed on the south side of Bukit Tankop.

Tea was made, nets rigged and bedding unpacked and all made snug – the wireless operator lighting the hut from bulbs and accumulators from the wrecked aircraft. (It seems that, earlier, two huts had been erected by Malays. They were built of small trees, fern and bark and set two feet above the ground.)

Salvage commenced on Monday, 29th October, at 07.30 hrs. By 11.00 hrs. a party of Malay and Saki had left for Bekok with 30 loads of parts. A cookhouse was built and some pieces of cowling were used to make a top over the fireplace – the piece over the Vickers gun being extremely useful for holding the kettle and saucepan whilst the hole, through which the stoppages are cleared, made an excellent range top. A parachute container, which was being carried to Alor Star, was used as a bread store whilst the aircraft rudder made a table. Each night, every member of the party had a 10 grain quinnine tablet and a tot of whisky "to keep away fever and other cold." Operations were hindered by heavy rain but salvage was resumed in the clear spells and, on Tuesday, more bearers returned to Bekok with engine cylinders, Vickers gun and wheels. The WIT gear was dismantled and the

The end of a 36 Squadron Horsley on a torpedo dropping practive in the
Johore Straits just prior to the arrival of 100 Squadron in Singapore
*G. Bell*

100 Squadron Vildebeest on torpedo practice Johore Straits 1934/35

Crashed 100 Squadron Vildebeest in jungle c1935/36
*G. Bell*

tail section removed and lowered to the bottom of the hill side.

Salvage continued in this manner for the rest of the week – often halted by torrential downpours. Returning bearers brought supplies of fresh water and took new loads of engine parts back to Bekok. On Wednesday evening the natives were treated to a fireworks display by the firing of distress signals. By Thursday, all that remained was the airframe – mainplanes, fuselage and the shattered undercarriage. This was the first fine day and the party was able to dry their clothes and wash in a dammed – up stream.

Camp was broken on Friday at 07.20 hrs. Earlier, a party of bearers had left with the crank case and had taken six hours to clear a mile of track. This eased the task of the main party as they began the march back. At last, the Chinese shop at the end of the road to Bekok was reached. Two motors were requisitioned and the R.A.F. party covered the last stage in comfort.

All members of the party were unrecognisable by the state of the beards and clothing but, at the police station, they had a much needed bath, shave and a change of clothes. "The services of two Chinese barbers were requisitioned who took off the week's growth with their 'patients' sitting outside the police station."

"The expedition closed on November 5th by the arrival of the engine by goods train at Singapore."


A vital part of the Squadron's work in the late 'thirties was familiarisation with the terrain and airstrips of Northern Malaya which were to become prime targets for the Japanese in 1941. In co-operation with the Signals Section at Singapore the crews on cross country flights would often carry pigeons to be released at various stages on the flights. It can only be assumed that the purpose was an experiment in communications and there is no record of pigeons being used operationally. The most famous pioneering flight was led by Squadron Leader L.G. Le B. Croke, Commanding Officer at the time, when he led three Vildebeests from Seletar to Risalpur to prove that the Indian N.W. frontier could be reinforced in an emergency. The expedition took nine days out and ten days back covering 7,000 miles in a flying time of 70 hours. Wing Commander Brookes describes the organisation of the Squadron and aircrews who made such feats possible.

'The standard crew consisted of a pilot and Wireless Operator|Air Gunner – about half the pilots were officers and the rest N.C.O.s with tradesmen's qualifications. The W|Op|Ags were also tradesmen – generally of lower rank – who also had responsibility for navigation, bomb aiming, signalling, firing the aft Lewis gun and photography! It was the tradesmen's talents which kept the 'planes flying on detachments away from Seletar. It is worth noting that crew members did not simply service their own aircraft but also co-operated in the servicing of all the machines in the flight. Roy Mager

Four "B" & "C" flight Vildebeests, 100 Squadron over Malaya
*(Photographed from an "A" flight Vildebeest, c 1935)*

gives us some idea of what was involved on an exercise from Seletar to Akyab in Burma.

There were two daily inspections – before and after flights; twenty, forty and hundred and twenty hour inspections and refuelling duties. On one occasion they had to prepare another aircraft for handing over to No. 4 Anti-Aircraft Co-operation Unit. "The handover entailed much hard work as everything connected with the aircraft had to be, not only there, but in full working order."

Another example, quoted by Wing Commander Brookes, occurred on the flight to Risalpur when the port lower wing tip was damaged at Rangoon. "This caused major damage to some two feet of alloy tubing so Flight Sergeant Beer, i/c aircraft fitters, went into the jungle, selected a suitably curved branch, trimmed it and cut it to size and used it to replace the damaged wing tip section. The fabric was then replaced and doped and so the wing remained until we returned to Singapore. Similarly, on the return trip, an engine change was required at Allahabad so a replacement was sent up by rail and the aircrew replaced the engine by means of sheer legs, made from railway lines, and a rope block and tackle normally used for lifting bullocks."

When the Squadron was flying long distances over the South China Seas it was usually escorted by a Singapore flying boat to maintain long range radio contact and provide navigational assistance. In all this 'peace time' work the Squadron paid dearly. Violent storms and unpredictable weather together with the dangerous nature of some of the exercises took a heavy toll. In 1938 eleven aircrew were killed in three consecutive months, six of them in a mid air collision. On another occasion the Commanding Officer led an expedition through twelve miles of Malayan swamp to recover every bit of it.

And so it was that the 1930s ticked by until the outbreak of war on 3rd September, 1939. On 15th March, 1938, Air Vice Marshal Tedder presented the Squadron with its first official badge, though it did not receive the original painting, which was kept in safe keeping in England until May, 1943. In the meantime the Squadron still retained its original skull and crossbones with the motto, "Blood and Brains."

# CHAPTER SEVEN

## The Malayan Campaign
## September 1939 to January 1942

Twenty four hours after Britain had declared war on Germany on 3rd September, 1939, a message appeared upon the screen of the station cinema at Seletar ordering certain personnel of 36 and 100 Squadrons to report to their hangars immediately. Nine airmen of "B" Flight, 100 Squadron, were told that three aircraft were to be prepared for take off the following morning for an undisclosed destination up country. They were not to carry bombs or torpedoes but all guns were to be loaded and they would carry extra spares and up country equipment for a stay of unknown duration.

The crews were:

K6384 Flight Lieutenant Smith (Flight Commander); Sergeant Leslie (Air Obs.|W|Op)

L.A.C. Hampson (W|Op|A.G.)

K6385 Pilot Officer Richardson, L.A.C. Miller (Fitter II|A,G.)

L.A.C. Mager (W|Op|A.G.).K6379 Pilot Officer Davis.

L.A.C.Hunt (Fitter II), Corporal Perritt (Armourer).

All these men were familiar with the airstrips and aerodromes in both Malaya and Burma and had hundreds of flying hours experience on the Vildebeest. The versatility of the Vildebeest crews is well illustrated. Between the the three aircraft there only two gunners but both Cpl. Perritt and L.A.C. Mager were capable of handling a Lewis gun in the air. Five of the six crew members could use a Lewis gun; four could use the camera and were bomb aimers and three could navigate. The three pilots could navigate, drop torpedoes and dive bomb and, with the four bomb aimers, do high and low level bombing.

At 09.00 hrs. on the 5th the crews were briefed by their Squadron Commander, S|Ldr. R.N.McKern. They were now on a full war footing; all flying, other than testing, would be regarded as operational flying. Each pilot was given sealed orders, with details of destination, which were not to be opened until airborne. There was to be radio silence although a listening watch would be kept. At their destination they were to be on continuous stand by for take off with ammunition and bombs ready to be loaded.

It was with mixed feelings and, no doubt, some trepidation, that the crews

No. 100 (Torpedo Bomber) Squadron goes to War. The First Operation. 5th September 1939 *From the painting by John Mitchell Webster. Presented to the Squadron and 100 Squadron Association by Bob Hampson "On behalf of former members of the Squadron who served in Malaya". 30th September 1989.*

listened to their orders. This was the real thing; they were carrying live ammunition and, sometime, somewhere, they would be loading up with live bombs or live torpedos.

The Vildebeests took off at 09.45 hrs. and the crews were greatly heartened to see the whole Squadron lined up to wave them off on 100 Squadron's 'First Op of the War'. On opening their orders they found their destination was Alor Star which they reached after an uneventful flight of four and a half hours. After tiffin they unpacked their personal gear and began the task of moving 112 lb. and 250lb. bombs, each packed in its own wooden crate, held together by screws, to rows well away from the aircraft. There were no bomb trolleys and each bomb had to be manhandled to its position.

Roy Mager took over the wireless station at the airstrip and established contact with R.A.F.H.Q. Far East in Singapore. Whatever the reason for this move to Alor Star – the presence of armed German merchantmen had been suggested – it came to nothing and two weeks later the three Vildebeests returned to Seletar. And so, as Wing Commander Brookes writes, "the first two years of war passed almost unnoticed – apart from the occasional submarine scare in the Straits of Johore." To conserve fuel Squadron flying time was halved but every effort was made to keep the maximum number of aircraft available at short notice.

Meanwhile, back in the U.K., plans for the defence of Malaya can be described as nothing short of chaotic with inter-service bickering about an overall strategy. In 1941 Churchill, himself, was at loggerheads with the Admiralty regarding a naval force in the Far East and eventually got his own way by the despatch of the ill-fated "Force Z" to Singapore. The Admiralty preferred the steady-build up of a much larger force based on Ceylon. The role of the Army was designated for defence of the air bases and an extra division was sent from India for that purpose. Churchill maintained that the strength of the R.A.F. did not warrant such a move but the General Staff got their own way.

As far back as 1937 the G.O.C. Malaya, Major General W.G.S. Dobbie actually forecast the precise Japanese strategy for the invasion of Malaya and Thailand – even to the approximate time, the N.E. Monsoon period from October to March – and stressed the importance of defences for Northern Malaya and the Thai border. The only concession to his assessment was to allocate £60,000 for machine gun emplacements in Johore commencing in 1939.

Air Marshal Sir Robert Brooke-Popham, as C.in C. confirmed this in December 1939. He and Lieutenant General A.E. Percival, who succeeded him as G.O.C., were concerned about a possible Japanese landing at Singora and devised "Matador", a plan to occupy Southern Thailand and thus forestall a Japanese attack on Malaya. The plan was thrown out by the Chiefs of Staff because they didn't want to present Japan with a casus belli. In all these deliberations the designated strength of the R.A.F. was to be 31 squadrons or 566 aircraft, reduced by the Chiefs of Staff to 336 which, in any case, could not be achieved until 1941. In August, 1940, the R.A.F. in Singapore consisted of 88 obsolete aircraft which, by the time of the Japanese invasion, had risen to 158 but with no modern fighters. At this point 100 Squadron possessed 18 Vildebeest MkIII, ten officers and 82 airmen, including six airmen pilots,under the command of Squadron Leader R.N McKern. These aircraft, plus 16 Vildebeests of 36 Squadron and five Albacores of the Naval Flight were the torpedo bomber force available to defend Singapore. Lieutenant General Percival wrote: "There were no transport aircraft, no long range bombers, no army co-operation aircraft, and no special photographic reconnaissance aircraft. There was, in fact, no really effective striking force in Malaya. Nevertheless there was, throughout the fighting services, a firm resolve to do our best with the limited means at our disposal."

"In other words," wrote Wing Commander Brookes, "No. 100 Squadron was ready to pay the price for ten years of gross negligence and apathy."

Despite the above there was, in Singapore and Malaya, from September, 1939 to December, 1941, an air of "it won't happen here." Social life progressed as before and Eric Hallam, a 100 Squadron fitter, described the easy going life in much the same terms as Warrant Officer Bell in 1934. Even Malayan planters resented the interference with their normal routine by armed forces sent to defend them.

Roy Mager writes of an unusual weekend in February, 1941, when he and thirty or forty 'other ranks,' from all the armed services, were invited to a reception held by the Governor, Straits Settlements and High Commissioner for the Malay States, His Excellency Sir Shenton Thomas Whitelegge Thomas G.C.M.G., O.B.E. Despite the preponderance of all the 'top brass' it appears the soldiers, sailors and airmen had an excellent evening being plied with excellent food, all the drinks one could imagine and entertainment by an orchestra playing light music. Amongst the guests were a number of ladies – wives, daughters of officers and civilians and so there were also partners for dancing. After a very pleasant evening they all returned to their units in taxis specially laid on for them after receiving a personal "Good night" from the Governor himself.

The following morning, Saturday, started as normal with three Vildebeests of "B" Flight, which was on stand-by, to be prepared. Both air and ground crews co-operated to have all ready – bomb sights fitted, guns loaded and checked, cameras fitted etc.and Forms 700 signed. All was normal until 10.55 when the Klaxon sounded and it was made clear to all that this was not a practice but the real thing. Roy had not been on the 'battle order' but the Flight Commander substituted him for duty. At briefing they were told that a Japanese submarine had been sighted near the Johore Shoal Buoy – the entrance to the Royal Navy Base at Singapore. Ten minutes later they were airborne.

Immediately after take off six aircraft of "A" Flight were armed and loaded with four 250 lb. bombs to await a sighting report from the two reconnaissance aircraft of "B" Flight. After an hour's search they were recalled. Up to this point the whole affair could be dismissed as a false alarm but the subsequent official report raises a few questions. First, it refers to "the suspected presence of an unknown submarine" and then goes on to state that *TWO* more aircraft were bombed up with *TWO* 250 lb. bombs when, in fact, six aircraft were bombed up with four bombs each. One is bound to ask if this was another example of Britain's determination not to strike the first blow against Japan or was it a genuine error?

Nevertheless 'Hope springs eternal . . .' as the saying goes and the hopes of 100 Squadron rose appreciably in late 1940 when they heard that their lumbering Vildebeests were to be replaced with Australian built Beauforts – then regarded as the fastest medium bomber in the world. On the 15th August the Squadron received two Blenheims to begin the process of converting the pilots to twin engined aircraft.

Flying Officer Michael Britten described how he and five others made up an advance party to fly out to Fisherman's Bend, Melbourne, in July, 1941 to acquaint themselves with the new aircraft. There followed crew training under the command of Wing Commander McKern, OIC 100 Squadron, after which they flew back in six Beauforts via Alice Springs, Darwin and Sourabaia to Seletar. This, "Q" Flight, arrived just a few days before the Japanese invasion of Malaya and the first air raid on Singapore.

The arrival of the Beauforts must have been an occasion of joy, pride, relief and hope for the airmen at Seletar. Eric Hallam, Eric Redshaw and Flying Officer Basil Gotto all describe the feeling of excitement and anticipation as the whole station, led by Air Chief Marshal Sir R. Brooke-Popham assembled to greet the Flight as it arrived on E.T.A. at 15.00 hrs. on the 6th December. Four days earlier the population of Singapore had been heartened by the arrival of "Force Z" consisting of the battleships 'Prince of Wales' and 'Repulse' with a destroyer escort. Amazingly there was no aircraft carrier with the force. H.M.S. Indomitable should have been there but was beset with 'working up trials' in the West Indies.

Such elation, however, was to be short lived. According to the official history only one Beaufort sortie was carried out although Michael Britten refers to several. The first recorded sortie took place the next day when a Japanese convoy had been sighted heading south west from Saigon which proved to be the Japanese spearhead of three divisions which established beachheads at Singara and Patani in Thailand and Khota Baru in Malaya. Flight Lieutennant Mitchell was detailed to photograph the convoy and, on his return, was attacked by Japanese Navy Zeros and badly shot up. However, he managed to land safely at Khota Baru where he destroyed the 'plane and eventually reached Seletar with the photographs with the help of a 'Buffalo' based at Khota Baru. The only other Buffalo was damaged when it taxied into a Hudson.

Spirits on the Squadron were further dampened by the general unserviceability of the new aircraft. Eric Hallam describes faults which

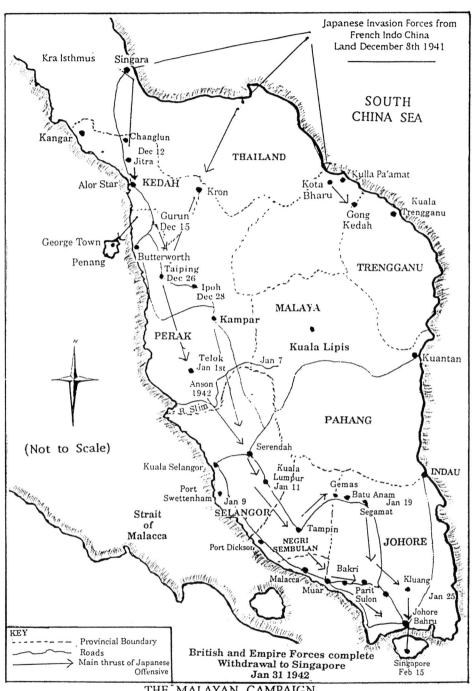

THE MALAYAN CAMPAIGN

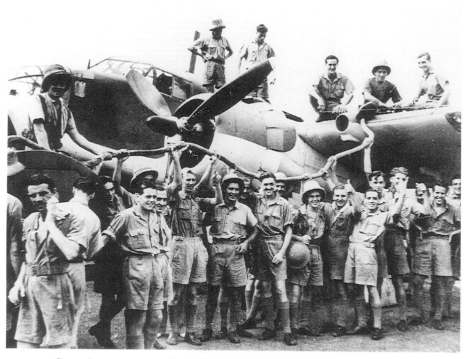

Ground crews greet arrival of Beauforts in Singapore, December 1941
Most unidentified but, left to right on 'plane: Ted Geldard, ?, Bill Simkin, ?,
Joe Castledine, Ted Drake.
Bottom: 7th from left; Eric Hallam, 7th from right; 'Wimpie' Wringer, 4th
from right; ? Moulscombe.
*Eric Hallam*

included 'popping perspex panels' and the unpreparedness of the 'planes for combat being unarmed and without bomb or torpedo racks. The first Japanese air raid on Singapore came on the 8th with reports of landings in Thailand and Northern Malaya. It was decided to return the Beauforts to Australia for modification and, later, await more reinforcements. The Squadron History states that a prime reason was to prevent the 'planes falling into enemy hands. The outcome was that the R.A.F. was back in Square 1 with only its Vildebeests, Albacores and Hudsons to defend Singapore.

It had been decided that the Vildebeests were too vulnerable to be used in daylight attacks and they were to be held in reserve to deal with any sudden emergency or sea-borne attack on Singapore. The Japanese attack on Seletar caused little damage and the Squadron was sent to Kuantan to join 36, the Hudsons of Australian 1 and 8 Squadrons and 62 Blenheim Squadron although 35 and 62 Squadrons returned to Singapore the following day. **Basil** Gotto describes how, just after lunch, Kuantan was attacked by three separate waves of Japanese bombers including nine aircraft in a low flying formation strafing the base from 100 feet. There was no fighter defence. Apart from one Vildebeest destroyed the raids caused only minor damage and there were no casualties yet Basil writes of the sheer panic, lack of leadership and sheer incompetence of the powers that be. In the first two days of the war the R.A.F. had lost three bases although Kuantan was not occupied by the Japanese for another two weeks. In fact, the Squadron, assisted by 36 Squadron, made return trips to collect torpedoes!

Disaster struck again the following day when 'Repulse' and 'Prince of Wales', which had sailed to attack the Japanese landing fleet, but without air cover,were lost. Initially damaged by torpedoes from Japanese submarines the battleships were finished off by high level bombers. As the 'Prince of Wales' followed 'Repulse' beneath the waves a squadron of Buffalos arrived but they were too late. Sergeant Thompson, then on detachment at Kluang converting to Blenheims,writes:"Suddenly we saw a Buffalo coming in to land. It made no circuit and taxied at great speed to the watch office. As the pilot ran to the stairs he shouted,'Get me Kalang on the 'phone!' He then told Kalang to get all the 'planes they could as the 'Prince of Wales' and the 'Repulse' were both sunk and that the sea was full of bodies and that the Japanese were shooting them in the water."

The tragedy of "Force Z" is a story in itself but only serves to illustrate, further, the muddle, indecision and lack of forethought and coordination which pervaded the whole of the Malayan chapter of World War 2. It was, in fact, the beginning of the end.

In late December, 1941, the remaining five Beauforts returned to Australia. En route, one of them crashed at Sourabaia.

Michael Britten arrived with Wing Commander McKern on the last one out from Singapore who handed his 'plane to the stranded crew. In due course, with the help of the Dutch Naval Air Service, Michael repaired the Beaufort and arrived in Australia in late January. A number of ground crew had been flown out separately by QANTAS to Sydney and they eventually arrived at R.A.A.F. Richmond to make up a total of 38 R.A.F. personnel servicing Beauforts for R.A.F. and R.A.A.F. operational training.

Throughout December Allied ground forces were obliged to make one withdrawal after another in Malaya with the Japanese capture of Singora, Khota Baru, Alor Star, Georgetown, Butterworth, Penang, Taiping and Ipoh. By the 9th January the Vildebeests were called on to make bombing missions in an attempt to halt the Japanese advance to the south. One Army officer who met Basil Gotto sometime later expressed the Army's appreciation of the Squadron's efforts: "Your Vildebeests are the only R.A.F. machines we ever see near the front line."

Despite the bombing missions the Japanese advance continued. Kampar fell on 2nd January; the Slim River was crossed on the 7th and Kuala Lumpur fell on the 11th. On the 20th eleven Squadron Vildebeests attacked the enemy held airfield at Kuantan destroying six enemy aircraft. On the 24th, accompanied by three Albacores, they destroyed a vital railway bridge at Labis after illuminating the area with parachute flares. The following night the Squadron took part in an action covering the evacuation of an Australian battalion trapped near Batu Bahat for which they were commended by A.H.Q. Singapore. The Squadron had, barely, returned to base when news came in of a large Japanese invasion force sighted twenty miles north east of Endau. The force consisted of two cruisers, eleven or twelve destroyers and two 10,000 ton merchantmen. A successful landing at Endau would mean that the Japanese could link up with their forces on the west coast of Malaya, cut off our armies to the north and isolate Singapore. It was vital that the invasion force be stopped but also meant that the Vildebeests would have to go into action in daylight despite earlier promises to the contrary. For 100 and 36 Squadrons this action was to be the beginning of the end.

"I saw the Squadron setting out on that last raid on Endau. Their actions were more than the ordinary fulfilment of duty; for, flying Vildebeest aircraft on a daylight raid, they knew they had little chance of coming through unscathed. As I spoke to many of them before they set off, I knew a good deal of their own feelings: their gallantry, therefore, to me, is a very real thing." (Padre A.S. Giles.)

The first force took off in the early afternoon of the 26th January. It consisted of ten 100 Squadron Vildebeests and two from 36 Squadron, nine Hudsons and a mixed fighter escort of eight Hurricanes and fifteen Buffaloes. The low speed of the Vildebeests, however, and the distance to the target made adequate fighter protection almost impossible. Although encountering heavy fighter and anti-aircraft fire they made the best possible use of cloud cover in their first attack. They scored direct hits on a 10,000 ton and 8,000 ton merchant ship with further hits on a cruiser and landing barges and troops on the coast. Despite this initial success it was already too late as the enemy landings had been in progress for four and a half hours and they were now well entrenched. British fighters shot down nine enemy aircraft but 100 Squadron had paid dearly losing their C.O., Squadron Leader J.T.B. Rowlands and five Vildebeests and their crews.

"It was not until I had been posted from the Squadron in the Spring of 1941, after a period of more than two years, that I realised how much I owed 100 (T.B.) Squadron, its traditions, principles and its personnel. I was never to meet their like again during the rest of my service career. I well recall one afternoon after return to base from a Catalina reconnaissance trip on January 26, 1942, standing to watch J.T.B. Rowlands leading his Vildebeests on the Endau Mission. They made a brave sight as the Vildebeests circled the airfield and then headed outwards towards their target on the east coast of the peninsula. Bravery itself, however, was not enough. The Endau airmen remain unsung heroes." (R.H.B. Hampson.)

A last, desperate effort to halt the advance was made in the late afternoon.

Nine Vildebeests from 100 and 36 Squadrons, led by three Albacores and escorted by four Buffaloes and eight Hurricanes, took off from Singapore. They were met by a large number of Japanese Zero and Army fighters but, although hits were made on a transport, the whole operation was futile. Five Vildebeests, all the Albacores and one Hurricane were lost. Both Commanding Officers were killed and many of the surviving crews were wounded. For the decimation of three squadrons the survivors were, "congratulated by the A.O.C. who told them they would never again be sent on a similar mission."

The reader may form his own opinion of the the situation and air of complacency in Singapore before the invasion from the following quote from the Official History:"The Station Commander at Tengah was summoned to A.H.Q. to explain why his handful of Hurricanes, most of which had only recently arrived without groundcrews and their guns still packed in grease, had not prevented the debacle. For a man who, like many others, had argued in vain against complacency, and who had been forced to watch his squadrons destroyed and his Station's morale deteriorate, it was the last straw. He had a final drink with his remaining crews, bade everyone 'Goodnight', and retired quietly to his room where he shot himself."

# CHAPTER EIGHT

## The Dutch East Indies and Australia
## January to May 1942

At the end of January the remnants of 36 and 100 Squadrons loaded up with torpedoes and took off for Kemajoram in Java. According to two sources, Bill Rafter and David Vincent, the remaining Vildebeests of 100 Squadron were handed over to 36 Squadron and operated under the command of Squadron Leader J.T. Wilkins as 36 Squadron at Tijikampok on the 8th February. There was certainly some resentment on the part of 100 Squadron crews at the loss of the Squadron identity but, unknown to them at the time, the Beaufort "Q" Flight was operating as 100 Squadron at Richmond in Australia. Basil Gotto reports that, even today, there is still friendly rivalry, in Australia, between the survivors of the two squadrons. Another bond was forged between the two squadrons when Flight Lieutenant Hutcheson, a 100 Squadron Flight Commander, became the last Commander of 36 Squadron. Now Wing Commander, he survived three and a half years as a prisoner of war and died in 1992.

Les Hughes and Doug Scott, former Corporal electricians with 36 Squadron, give their account of their last days at Seletar and evacuation to Sumatra.

"During the last week of 36 and 100 Squadrons' we were under constant fire from Japanese positions at Johore Baru and it was decided that all personnel would be taken by coach,each night, to a Chinese cinema theatre at Paya Lebar near the centre of Singapore. They would return to camp the following morning for breakfast and duties. One morning the coach failed to arrive so I took a taxi back to camp to see what had happened.

The camp was completely deserted and, on my return, no-one would believe my story. Doug and I, however, decided to find out more in Singapore itself. Singapore was in a state of chaos – the docks had been bombed and fires were burning everywhere – but nobody knew anything about the two Squadrons. Thanks to an Australian officer we were able to get a meal at Raffles Hotel although other residents didn't take too kindly to us and were carrying on as though it was peace-time. We were told by a Sergeant MP that the Japs had crossed the Straits and were fighting on the island and advised us to try to get away by boat.

That evening, about 9 pm, we saw the lights of a small ship making its way to the coal wharf and when we reached her she had tied up and the Malay crew were leaving in a hurry. The Captain, a Scot, told us the crew had deserted but if we found more helpers to coal up the ship and stoke the boilers he would try to steam out at first light for Sumatra. This we did and sailed at first light. At 11 am we were attacked by a Japanese 'plane but suffered no damage. The following day we reached Sumatra and docked at Palembang in the late afternoon.

On reaching the shore we learnt that Jap paratroops were fighting on the outskirts of the town and we were advised, along with many others, to make our way by train to the south of the island. After an overnight journey we reached Medan and managed to board the last ferry to Oosthaven in Java where we were told that most R.A.F. personnel had made their way to Batavia. After several days on the road we reported to the Queen Wilhelmina School in Batavia only to be told that 36 Squadron had been there but had moved on.

From the Dutch we obtained the location of a number of airfields so we commandeered an army truck and, along with an Australian officer, set off in search of the Squadron. After being bombed and machine gunned several times we eventually found one with several unserviceable Vildebeests scattered around together with some Dutch aircraft. We had a brief consultation and decided to destroy the petrol and bomb dumps and, when we left, the base was burning fiercely."

[Editor's note. At this stage the stories of 36 Squadron and 100 Squadron survivors begin to overlap. Ground crews from both Squadrons and others were taken prisoner at Kalikmalaya. See below.]

Meanwhile, on the 15th February, the remnants of 100 Squadron were joined by their ground crews but their spares and equipment and, in fact, the Squadron silver, had been lost at Ootshaven so the only spares they had were those carried in the evacuation from Singapore. The remaining twelve Vildebeests deteriorated through lack of spares and one was cannibalised to supply parts for the rest. The torpedoes were discarded in favour of 250 lb. G.P. bombs and Dutch 40 kilos. Singapore and Sumatra fell on the same day – just one day within the General Staff's estimate of 70 days to send out reinforcements to repel an invasion – and the men were told that the last evacuation ship had left Java and the Squadron was to remain as a token force for the Dutch. One of the lucky ones to get away on this last ship was Sergeant Eric Redshaw, a Squadron fitter, who managed to get back to the U.K. to join the new Lancaster squadron at Waltham.

On the 27th the Squadron was ordered to Mandeong and refuelled for an attack on a Japanese convoy of 57 ships off the north coast of Java. This was to be, in fact, the prelude to the Battle of the Java Sea. In January the Allies had set up a combined command of American, British, Dutch and Australian forces (ABDA) under the command of General Sir Archibald Wavell. At Mandoeng the Squadron met up with an American Fortress squadron briefed for the same mission. Eight Vildebeests and one Albacore

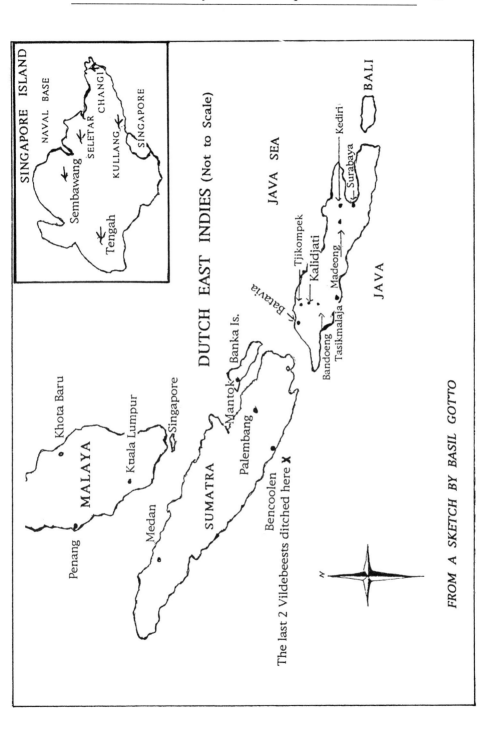

SINGAPORE ISLAND

NAVAL BASE

Sembawang

SELETAR

CHANGI

Tengah

KULLANG

SINGAPORE

DUTCH EAST INDIES (Not to Scale)

JAVA SEA

BALI

Kediri

Surabaya

Tjikompek

Kalidjati

Madeong

Bandoeng

Tasikmalaja

Batavia

JAVA

Khota Baru

Kuala Lumpur

Singapore

Penang

MALAYA

Medan

Banka Is.

Mantok

Palembang

SUMATRA

Bencoolen

The last 2 Vildebeests ditched here X

N

FROM A SKETCH BY BASIL GOTTO

made up the R.A.F. contingent and there were about four or five Fortresses. Cloud base was around 2,500 ft. and the Vildebeests went in at 2,000. Nine enemy vessels were sunk – an average of one for each aircraft. The Forts bombed from 8,500 ft. so, in view of the cloud cover, it is unlikely they made any hits. Returning to base, after scoring a direct hit amidships,the engine of Basil's Vildebeest cut out and he crash landed in a paddy field. The crew were uninjured and eventually made their way back to Mandoeng. The Allied naval force, under the command of Rear Admiral Karel W.F. Doorman, lost its sole light aircraft carrier, the Langley, so the fleet had no air cover or reconnaissance capability. The Japanese also had a 'secret weapon' , a long range torpedo, and the fleet was decimated. Enemy landings were made on the north coast the following day and, a week later, the Dutch East Indies Government surrendered unconditionally.

The rest of Basil's story is a saga in itself and can only be briefly referred to here. News came through of the Japanese landings 60 miles from Mandoeng and the base was to be evacuated and demolished. The Americans were loading their Forts for Australia and gave Basil the choice of a Buffalo or a Dauntless dive bomber. Sergeants Barnes and Toohey, his W|Op|AG and Navigator, commandeered a lorry and loaded it up with supplies, radio,two .5 machine guns and ammunition with the aim of reaching A.H.Q. at Bandung.

After thirty minutes instruction in the hangar, on a completely strange, modern aircraft, Basil took off ahead of the Americans and, after a three hour, hair-raising flight, landed at Tijikampok to find a burnt out Vildebeest, Hurricane and Albacore and one, apparently undamaged, Albacore. The base was deserted. Two traumatic days of walking and hitch hiking eventually brought him to Bandung where he met up with the surviving members of the Squadron.

On the 4th March Basil and Reg Lamb set off in a lorry for Tasikmalaja with a load of bomb detonators. The remnants of the Squadron were on ops that night and were to return to Tasikmalaja.The following night the three remaining serviceable *Vildebe*ests attacked the Japanese base at Kalidjati destroying one building and four Japanese aircraft. Sergeant Appleby was killed although his crew managed to escape. Kalidjati had been an important Dutch air base from which the R.A.F. and R.A.A.F. operated. The Japanese made a surprise attack with motor-cycles and light trucks gunning the aerodrome. The crews managed to get a number of their aircraft away in the confusion.

On the 7th March it was learned that the Dutch had decided to surrender Java. The Squadron Commander, Squadron Leader Wilkins had been killed earlier so Flight Lieutenant Allanson and Flying Officer Lamb, the two most senior surviving officers, persuaded Air Commodore Staton to allow them to take the two remaining Vildebeests and fly as far as possible and ditch in the sea off the west coast of Sumatra with the vague hope of getting hold of a junk in which to cross the Indian Ocean. Lots were drawn to make up four occupants for each aircraft. (The normal crew was three). Remaining personnel, who were armed, would attempt to hold out in the hills inland.

The crews of the last two Vildebeests were:

K6393 Flight Lieutenant Allanson, Flying Officer Taylor, Pilot Officer Tommy Lamb, Flying Officer Gotto.

K6405 Flying Officer Reggie Lamb, Pilot Officer Gallick, Warrant Officer Peck,Sergeant Melville.

At 01.45 hrs. on the 8th March, 1942, loaded with whatever supplies they could gather, the last two Vildebeests took off on their final flight. By 06.30 hrs. the fuel gauges were on red and the pilots searched for a suitable place to ditch off Bencoolen. All four in Basil's 'plane survived and eventually reached a sandy beach. Their last sight of the Vildebeest "was the red, white and blue tail fin riding the blue waters of the Bay." Making their way inland they reached a wooded glade to be greeted by twenty armed Japs and taken prisoner.

Some time later they were joined by Sergeant Melville, the one known survivor from the other Vildebeest. Flying Officer Reggie Lamb, Flying Officer Gallick and Warrant Officer Peck were drowned.

In the words of Lord Trenchard,, over twenty years earlier, 100 Squadron "had kept it going." They had "kept it going" to the very last 'plane and the very last man.

Of the remaining survivors in Java it is possible that some managed to escape on a hospital ship to Ceylon. Former Sergeant Pilot Claude Thompson, a New Zealander who joined 100 Squadron in Singapore, takes up the story of the rest.

"About ten aircrew and 150 ground staff remained and we decided to go up into the hills and fight. We were armed with .303 rifles and took what supplies we could. I also took my parachute cords and some of the silk. On the 8th March we set off in convoy for the hills but we did not get very far. At Garoet we were stopped by an army of Dutch and compelled to stack our arms and proceed with them to a camp and await the Japs. Most of us threw away our rifle bolts which made the Dutch very angry indeed. All along the route the Dutch were wearing white armbands and waving white flags."

Claude goes on to describe the trek to a tea plantation where they were told they would stay for the duration. At the time, the prospect didn't look too bad as they were to "plant gardens and make themselves comfortable." On the 19th March, however, orders came that they were to be moved – it seems to have been into captivity at Tasikmalaya. Claude, with three others decided to make an escape bid,get to the coast and, hopefully, escape by sea although many of the other prisoners had warned them that it was impossible. The warnings proved all too true and Claude's narrative "Into the Sun" relates his experiences as a Japanese P.O.W. travelling 3,000 miles in indescribable conditions to camps in Java, Singapore, Sumatra and the Moluccas.

Perhaps, some day, the story of the air war in Singapore, Malaya and the

Dutch East Indies will be told in full. It is an epic of very brave men flying their obsolete machines, until there were none left, against two enemies: the one, a ruthless, superbly equipped foe, the other, a lethargic, incompetent and inept administration which, like a 20th Century Nero, seemed to fiddle whilst Singapore burned.

[AUTHOR'S NOTE. Copies of Basil Gotto's Diary, "Into the Sun", Bob Hampson's and Tom Lamb's Diaries are deposited in the Squadron's archives. I have been fortunate to see the first two and hope that all of them can be published in the near future. Air Commodore Henry Probert has recently completed a History of the Air War in the Far East.]

Meanwhile, back in Australia, Squadron Leader A.W.D. Miller had taken command of 100 Squadron ("Q" Flight) at Nhill, Victoria. His task was to establish operational training facilities for the Squadron as agreed between Australian Air Board and Air H.Q. Far East. From David Vincent's research it appears that Squadron Leader Miller was far from satisfied with the situation. There was the problem of serviceability, referred to above, and, by the 14th January, there were only three Beauforts on strength. He also felt that a station near the coast was essential for torpedo training and it should also be close to the source of production.

The rapid sequence of events in Malaya, however, quickly overtook deliberations in Australia. Australia now found herself under threat and placed an embargo on the export of "any aircraft materials or equipment of any kind." At the end of February, following the fall of Singapore, it was decided that the R.A.F. would have to relinquish the 90 Beauforts on order although only 20 had, as yet, been delivered. The last days of 100 Torpedo Bomber Squadron are documented as follows in the 100 Squadron R.A.A.F. Operations Record Book.

### RICHMOND 1/3/1942
On the authority of AFCO 24|42 dated 28th February, 1942 No. 100 Squadron R.A.F., which had been employed as an operational training unit, on loan to the R.A.A.F. became, w.e.f. 25|2|42, No. 100 Squadron R.A.A.F. stationed at R.A.A.F. Station Richmond.

The unit's role was designated as G.R.(T) being equipped with Australian-built Beaufort aircraft. An establishment of aircraft (12 I.E. 6 I.R.) and personnel was issued by Airboard and postings of R.A.A.F. personnel against the establishment commenced.

### 7th MARCH, 1942
At this date the unit was commanded by Wing Commander A.W.D. Miller, 33171, and officered by the original members of 100 Squadron R.A.F. 38 R.A.F. airmen who formed the nucleus of the maintenance personnel were

at first supplemented by a number of R.A.A.F. personnel attached from No. 2 Aircraft Depot, Richmond. About this date the Squadron strength of aircraft was twelve. Due to lack of adequate maintenance personnel and facilities the task of organising the Squadron as an operational unit was retarded.

(NOTE. In a report sent by Thomas J. Scully, a former R.A.A.F. pilot, we learn that in addition to the R.A.F. personnel mentioned there were four R.A.A.F. and three R.N.Z.A.F. officers on strength together with, about, a dozen R.A.A.F. N.C.Os and two R.N.Z.A.F. N.C.O.s. Hudson crews were also training at Nhill but, we learn, most of the Beaufort crews "were waiting . . . waiting." Ed.)

Flying activities at this stage (approximately first week) were hampered due to the heavy unserviceability of aircraft occasioned by the lack of personnel and facilities already mentioned. A limited amount of operational training was done and daily operational patrols, usually by two aircraft, were carried out. During the second week of March additional ground personnel were posted to the unit and difficulties occasioned by lack of maintenance crews were somewhat alleviated.

### 13th MARCH, 1942

Following requests for advice regarding state of Squadron training methods and progress weekly reports on training carried out to be submitted to Southern Area and S|Ldr. Kirby. F|Lt. Mitchell proceeded to Laverton to confer with W|Cdr. Balmer on these matters.

So it was, then, that between 8th February and 24th February, 1942, 100 Torpedo Bomber Squadron R.A.F. ceased to exist as an operational unit. The remaining Vildebeests had been incorporated into 36 Squadron and "Q" Flight's Beauforts formed the nucleus of 100 Squadron R.A.A.F. At some time in April or May the R.A.F. personnel at Richmond were either repatriated or posted to Ceylon. A small number of these, amongst them Eric Redshaw, eventually rejoined 100 Squadron when it was re-established at Waltham.

[AUTHOR'S NOTE: There are still some gaps in the story – amongst them is the question of what happened to Wing Commander McKern, who was spoken of so highly by Michael Britten, Eric Hallam and others who served under him. In his book,"Half of my Service – Singapore – The Great Illusion," R.H.B. (Bob) Hampson makes a brief reference to Wing Commander McKern. Like all the others who served under him Bob expressed his admiration for "a pukka regular Air Force Officer and a gentleman." Somewhere along the line Wing Commander McKern had returned to the U.K. and taken command of a Beaufort squadron and, in some manner, had been involved in support for the Russians. At the time of meeting up with Bob in 1944 he was bringing his squadron to 1674 H.C.U. at Beaulieu for conversion to B 24 Liberators. And what happened to Wing Commander Miller who commanded the Squadron in Australia until its incorporation into the R.A.A.F.?]

The story of 100 Squadron R.A.A.F. is beyond the scope of this book and can only be briefly referred to here. The Squadron adopted the 100 Squadron (R.A.F.) badge although it was never officially recognised by the R.A.A.F. It is also interesting to note that the new squadron incorporated the "Q" in its identification letters making it "QH". Teething problems with the aircraft were soon overcome and, after they had been converted to carry torpedoes, the Squadron moved to the Atherton Tablelands in May, 1942, under the command of Wing Commander Balmer, where it took part in the Battle of the Coral Sea. It performed with distinction against enemy shipping along the coasts of New Guinea and New Britain but at a high cost to aircraft and crews. Wing Commander Balmer took the Squadron to Papua and operated from Port Moresby Goodenough Island, Lai and Aitape.

Wing Commander Kessey, D.F.C., succeeded Wing Commander Balmer and paid tribute to the Squadron's performance in the roles of torpedo bombers, army support, medium level bombing, anti submarine patrols and naval patrols. Stan Dannam, another pilot with the new squadron writes of the atrocious flying conditions experienced by the Beaufort crews which were aggravated by inadequate maps of regions where mountains topped 17,000 ft. Rain and humidity played havoc with maintenance and Stan pays tribute to the ground crews who worked in appalling conditions to keep the 'planes flying.

It is with a feeling of deep satisfaction to record that 100 Squadron's offspring, 100 Squadron R.A.A.F., flew the last operation of the war in the Pacific as Stan Dannam writes:

"Whilst in New Guinea with 100 Squadron (R.A.A.F.) the war finished on 15th August, 1945. On this day 100 Squadron was due to take off at 09.00 hours – the actual time of the cessation of hostilities. We continued and bombed our target. Other Squadron Beauforts, however, were airborne after us but were recalled and so did not bomb. This makes this strike by 100 Squadron the last of World War 2." As a Wireless Operator exclaimed over the radio:

"Listen out you blokes! The f...... war's over!"


### THE MALAYAN TRAITOR

A book, "The Worst Disaster – The Fall of Singapore" (Newark UN Delaware, 1977) refers to an R.A.F. officer detected signalling to the Japanese. Captain P.F.C. Elphick R.N. (retd.) backed by Sydney Tavender, Chairman of the Cotswold branch of the Far East Prisoners Association, has researched the following article which appears in a new book on the campaign, "Clipped Wings – the Collapse of British Air Defence, Malaya." by Australian Philip Rivers.

'Fifty years after the fall of Singapore details have emerged of a, previously, unpublicised spy in the British forces who is believed to have played a crucial part in the Japanese victory. The traitor has been identified as a New Zealander serving with the Indian Army. Captain Patrick Stanley Vaughan Heenan, of the 16th Punjab Regiment, who was on attachment to an Air Intelligence Liaison Unit was arrested on December 9th as he tried to hide a radio transmitter he had been using to pass information to the invading enemy.

Soon after dawn on the previous day Japanese aircraft had begun taking out British airfields in Northern Malaya. Within five hours they had all but achieved their objectives. Sydney Tavender, who served in the A.I.L. unit with Heenan says the Japanese aircraft always seemed to know the correct recognition codes, despite the fact that they were changed every twenty four hours. By the time the enemy aircraft could be recognised visually it was always too late.

Heenan was caught during an air raid. "When we discovered he wasn't with us in the slit trenches we became suspicious," Mr. Tavender says. "We went to his quarters and discovered the radio which was still quite warm. That was the last we saw of him. He was arrested."

But it was too late. Left with little air support, the Allied ground forces began to fall back, spending the next 70 days until the capitulation of Singapore on February 15th, 1942, in a long and ignominious retreat down the Malay peninsula. The Heenan affair was covered up and all official details are still protected under government restrictions preventing disclosure for 100 years.

Nevertheless, rumours quickly spread, at the time, of an Irish officer in the R.A.F. who had spied for the Japanese in sympathy with the Irish Republican cause. Although Heenan was neither in the R.A.F. nor an Irishman, the combination of his Irish name, the information he betrayed and the secrecy in which the whole affair was shrouded, led to a popular misconception over his identity and the motives behind his treachery.

Born in Stratford, North Island, in 1910 and brought up in Burma where his father was a mining engineer, Heenan was sent to Cheltenham College for a formal education. By the time he joined the Indian Army in 1935 Heenan was a bull of a man, 6ft.1in. tall and weighing around 13 stones. Heavyweight boxing champion of India in 1936 and a keen rugby player, his fellow officers found him intimidating and disliked him intensely.

Mr. Tavender remembers him as "a heavy drinker, a loner and a man detested by all – he upset a lot of us." Women took a different view. Heenan was good looking and had the tanned skin of a Far East veteran. He was a ladies' man and this provides what is, perhaps, the best clue to his motives for, in 1938 he is known to have formed a liaison with a local girl whom he met on holiday in Japan.

There are a number of theories as to how and when he was recruited by the Japanese. Possibly the Japanese holiday was cover for training. Alternatively, he may have been approached during his time there or afterwards because of his relationship with the Japanese girl. Whatever the circumstances of his recruitment by the Japanese, it appears to have been a stunningly successful operation.

By the time he was captured the damage had already been done and the battle for Singapore was effectively lost. As the Japanese closed in there was not time for a court martial and Heenan was held in prison, no doubt anticipating his release by his advancing friends. It was not to come. The records of Cheltenham College state that Captain P.S.V.Heenan was posted missing, presumed killed, in Singapore on February 15th, 1942, the day of the surrender. But this appears to have been merely a useful device to cover up the scandal of the betrayal and the real circumstances of Heenan's death.

On the morning of February 15th a young British officer was exercising a number of prisoners. Among them was Heenan. The Japanese troops were pressing in on the tired and demoralised defenders of Singapore. Growing ever more arrogant as he thought that freedom loomed Heenan turned to the officer and said: "Tomorrow I shall be free and you will all be dead or prisoners."

The officer took out his service revolver and shot him dead. Within hours Singapore had fallen.'

# CHAPTER NINE

## Bomber Command – The Waltham days from
## St. Nazaire to Berlin

No. 100 Squadron was officially reborn on 23rd December, 1942, when No. 1 Group Admin Instruction No. 11 ordained that the Squadron was to be equipped with sixteen Lancaster IIIs, with two in reserve, and to be based at Waltham, a satellite of Elsham Wolds. Officially, the base was "R.A.F. Waltham" until September, 1943, when it was re-named "R.A.F. Grimsby" but to all who were stationed there it was, and always will be, "R.A.F. Waltham." To gain experience of the Lancaster, ground crews were attached to 101 Squadron, Holme on Spalding Moor ("A" Flight) and 103 Squadron at Elsham Wolds ("B" Flight). On the 30th January, 1943, they were back at Waltham to greet their own Lancs and crews flown in from 1656 Conversion Unit at Lindholme.

Of all the North Lincolnshire wartime airfields Waltham was, perhaps, the most comfortable. Formerly Grimsby's civil airport, it was requisitioned in 1940 when building work began to turn it into a purpose built bomber base. Unlike many other wartime bases it was completed with wooden accommodation huts, instead of the cold and draughty Nissens, connected by paved pathways before its population of 1500 or so airmen and airwomen moved in. Not only was it spared the mud of later airfields in their course of construction but it was also sheltered from much of the snow on the exposed Wolds although it did experience some chilling North Sea winds.

An added bonus, for off duty airmen, was a regular bus service to Grimsby and Cleethorpes. More important was the strong affinity between the Station and the people of Waltham, Holton le Clay, Grimsby and Cleethorpes when they began to regard 100 Squadron as "their Squadron". This affinity was particularly strong with the villagers of Holton le Clay and has lasted to the present day. When the short runway was in use the main A16 Grimsby|Louth Road was closed by a barrier and traffic was halted until the Squadron had taken off. Waiting travellers would watch and wave as the Lancasters cleared the boundary trees and often see the crews wave back. One local inhabitant, who would sit on top of a pig sty at the bottom of his garden said: "It was marvellous. As soon as one aircraft had lifted off the tarmac another was coming down the runway and this went on until all the aircraft had taken off. Even if there was an air raid they kept on going. They came back about four in the morning."

Eddie Mawer was a young lad of nine at the time. A favourite pastime was to cycle, with his friends, from Grimsby to Holton le Clay. Once there they would leave their bikes at the side of the Louth Road and crawl through the hedge to watch the armourers loading bombs into a nearby Lancaster. "I can still conjure up the picture of the sky over Grimsby during the war when we used to watch Lancs from Waltham circling for height as they set off on their bombing missions. The sky seemed full of Lancasters and the noise of those Merlin engines will live with me for ever. On one occasion, whilst heading for Louth on a tandem with a friend, we were traversing the notorious Cordeaux Corner when we came across some nine or ten bombs scattered across the road. They had fallen from an R.A.F. lorry which was pulled up at the side of the road. The driver was stood in the middle of them wondering, perhaps, what the hell to do next!"

Many Squadron and Station personnel met and married their partners at Waltham and made their post war homes as far away as Canada. Others, like Jon Prochera from Poland and Jimmy Flynn from Eire, made their homes in, or near, Waltham.

In short, Waltham was a happy Station. An all-ranks club provided a homely venue where air-crews, ground-crews and Station personnel could get together informally; an enterprising local came with his mobile van selling newspapers, rock buns and the occasional cigarettes; the N.A.A.F.I. van would dispense unlimited mugs of tea at all hours of the day and night; just outside the main gate was "The King's Head" and the bus to the "Gaiety" and "Lifeboat" in Cleethorpes. All this, together with two worthy Station Commanders, Group Captains R.A.C. Carter and Ian Newbiggin, contributed in no small way to the high morale of both Station and Squadron where the two worked in perfect harmony.

The story of 100 Squadron from January, 1943, to the end of the war in Europe cannot be separated from the rest of Bomber Command or, more particularly, from 1 Group. 1 Group's motto, "Swift to Attack" was appropriate enough although its prefix, "Maximum Effort", to almost all its operational orders, would seem more apt.

It is not possible, in the scope of this book, to detail every operation flown by 100 Squadron but it is true to say that the experiences recorded here can be echoed by any of the 15,000|16,000 crews that made up Bomber Command in World War 2. Most surviving aircrew will have been asked at some time or other,"What was it really like?" The question is very difficult to answer. In one sense it is easy to describe that initial sinking feeling at briefing for what looked like being a particularly dicey trip; there was the tension on the run up to the target through probing searchlights and a barrage of flak; there was that sense of awe at the sight of fires, exploding bombs and shell bursts and the sickening, tightening of the guts in the vicious 'corkscrews' to evade enemy fighters.

Then there was the sheer boredom, for many crew members, of flying hour after hour for up to 2,000 miles in company with a few hundred other 'heavies' and the strain of constant look out for enemy fighters and friendly aircraft alike. Attuned to the roar of four Merlins there was, sometimes, a feeling of detachment from the world below to be followed by a sense of driving along a badly rutted road as the 'plane bumped and rocked as the skipper took it through a flak barrage. It is highly unlikely that any crew, fortunate enough to complete a tour of operations without injury, did not return from, at least one operation, without their aircraft peppered and holed by exploding flak.

The above description applies to those who made it through a tour of thirty operations. A few even managed three or four tours. On the other hand, out of 110,000 aircrew in Bomber Command, 55,000 were killed and many more injured. 8,953 aircraft were lost. 100 Squadron's share of the bill was 593 killed and 113 Lancasters.

A remarkable feature of Bomber Command crews, and, indeed, all aircrew, was their youth. It was not exceptional for a lad of eighteen to have completed a tour of operations before his nineteeenth birthday. It is even more remarkable that a teenager would be taught to fly and be entrusted to take thirty odd tons of heavy bomber, with its cargo of bombs, hundreds of miles to Germany when he hadn't even passed a test to drive a car!

As in World War 1 100 Squadron was quite a cosmopolitan bunch with members from Australia, New Zealand, Poland, Argentina, Canada and South Africa. Of these the Canadians were the most numerous constituting up to 30% of the Squadron strength at one time. Some crews would consist of six Canadians with the one R.A.F. flight engineer whilst others would have a full mix of pilot, navigator, bomb aimer, wireless operator, gunners and flight engineer from the R.A.F. Although most of the young R.A.F. pilots, navigators and bomb aimers had been trained overseas, in Canada, South Africa or America, this new, close contact with men from Commonwealth cities, prairies, forests, gold mines and sun soaked beaches opened up new horizons. Many who survived the war started new lives in the countries of their former crew mates and many of the links forged in the '40s are as strong today in the '90s.

Wing Commander J.G.W. Swain took command of the Squadron on 26th December, 1942, and on the 4th March eight Lancasters started the Squadron's operational career with Bomber Command on a mine laying mission to St. Nazaire U-boat base. Although the operation itself was successful it was at the cost of one Lancaster lost on the operation and another written off when it crashed in Nottinghamshire. During the course of the operation the weather at Grimsby had closed in and the remaining six Lancasters were diverted to other airfields. Four days later the Squadron sent six Lancasters to join 329 other heavies on its first bombing raid on Nurenburg. Wing Commander Swain led the Squadron bombing at 23.30hrs. The target area was obscured by haze and so the bombing was not as concentrated as hoped. Nevertheless it was reported that 600 buildings were destroyed and 1400 damaged including railway installations, the M.A.N. and Siemens factories.

This was the beginning of a new type of war for 100 Squadron – a war of attrition – with the sole aim of destroying German cities, factories, ports, communications and the morale of the German people. Very gradually, with developments in radar, tactics were improved to give greater accuracy in searching out and marking the target. In 1942 'Gee' was navigating main force to the Ruhr and new channels extended the range. From 1943 'Oboe' and 'G-H' guided an increasingly effective Pathfinder Force and a more refined 'H2S' enabled individual navigators to keep their 'plane on track and on time. "Fishpond" provided an extra pair of eyes for the wireless operator to detect enemy fighter aircraft.

But, as ever, each new measure brought counter measures by the enemy. 'Gee' was jammed and 'H2S' could give away an aircraft's position to the enemy so its use was restricted until well over Germany. Millions of strips of foil, "window", were thrown out of the bombers to foul up the German radar; 'ABC', or 'Airborne Cigar', was carried by 101 Squadron to broadcast engine roar on German fighter control frequencies and 100 Group operated further radar counter measures. Secondary raids and feints, sometimes using trainee aircrew from O.T.Us and Conversion Units, were laid on to divert German defences from the main force.

However effective the tactics were, they could always be upset by the weather. German fighter pilots described main force bombers, flying above cloud on a moonlit night, "like flies on a table cloth". Below cloud, caught in searchlights, they were "flies on the ceiling". A target obscured by cloud meant bombing sky markers; unforeseen adverse winds could play havoc with the timing and concentration of main force and icing could bring 'planes down. Fog and low cloud led to numerous crashes near base after an, otherwise, successful operation with the loss of many a crew. Such was the scenario for 100 Squadron and the hundred or so other squadrons of Bomber Command until the end of the war.

Between March and July, 1943, 100 Squadron gained its first Battle Honour of World War 2 in Europe, The Battle of the Ruhr, although, in April, it managed to fit in two operations to Italy to Milan and Turin. Most major West German industrial cities appeared night after night on the battle orders: Stettin, Hamburg, Frankfurt, Stuttgart, Mannheim, Duisburg, Dortmund (see Battle Order p116) and Essen. On the 16th April the Squadron took part in a low level attack on the Skoda works at Pilsen. Four nights later it joined a force of 330 other aircraft for a highly successful raid on Stettin where 100 acres in the town centre were devastated. There was a price to pay, however, as twenty one aircraft were lost including two from

4th March, 1943.

NO 100 SQUADRON BATTLE ORDER

SERIAL NO. I.

OFFICER I/C NIGHT FLYING.... W/CMDR. SWAIN.
AERODROME CONTROL PILOT.... SGT. SPICER.

| DISP. | A/C | A/C NO. | CAPT. | F/E. | NAV. | B/A. | W/OP.AG. | M.U. GUN. | R.GTR. | Beacon Cc. Ht. | Remarks. |
|---|---|---|---|---|---|---|---|---|---|---|---|
| 27 X | D | ED 559 | F/L.CURLE. | SGT.HART. | P/O CRAIG. | P/O CHALLONER. | P/O RILING. | SGT.GOOCH. | SGT.DURDIN. | 160 1500 | 7.1. |
| 26 | H | " 564 | P/O HARVEY | " BARR. | SGT.MANDER. | SGT.CRAIK. | SGT.WOOD. | " CANNINGS | " METEAR. | 190 1750 | 8.1. |
| 24 | J | " 609 | F/L.S-BOTHOM. | " TYPER. | P/O TOWERS. | F/O WEST. | " NUNN. | " HUN. | " PASCOE. | 200 2000 | 7.1. |
| 20 | G | " 563 | SGT. OVERTON. | " CABLE. | SGT. CLEMENTS. | SGT DAVIES. | " ARGARL. | "SUNDERLAND" | " BARRATT | 210 2250 | OPERATIC |
| 24 lo | V | " 587 | S/L. BARKER. | " EDWARDS. | " WALKER. | " MORGAN | " BROCK. | " MILLAR. | " SALVAGE | 220 2500 | IS 8 |
| 7 | Y | " 557 | F/O JONES. | " LING. | P/O HERRIN: | " WALKER. | " COOPER. | " HODGES. | " HOUSTON. | 230 1600 | ORDERED. |
| 8 | S | " 549 | SGT. AVEY. | " HALLETT. | SGT.SPENCE. | " CUMBERBATCH | " ROBINSON | " DAVIES. | " LANDRY | 240 1850 | 8. |
| 2 | U | " 583 | F/L.MC GRATH. | " WILKIE. | P/O WRIGHT. | P/O JOHNSON. | P/O PACEY. | " PROCHERA. | " AITKEN | 250 2100 | 6.4 |
| 28 | A | " 555 | RESERVE. | | | | | | | 260 | |
| 25 | O | " 556 | | | | | | | | 270 | |

AIRCRAFT TO RETURN TO DISPERSALS AFTER LANDING.

AIRCRAFT.    D - J - S - U - O   to carry   1,'850 galls. petrol.

           H - G - V - Y - A   to carry   2,068 galls. petrol.

NAVIGATORS & BOMB AIMERS BRIEFING..............13.45 Hours.

MAIN BRIEFING............................14.45 "

TRANSPORT TO COMMUNAL SITE..........15.45 "

OPERATIONAL TEA.........................16.00 "

TRANSPORT FROM COMMUNAL TO TECHNICAL SITE.....16.30 "

TRANSPORT CREWS TO AIRCRAFT...........17.15 "

(J.G.W. SWAIN)

Wing Commander, Commanding, No. 100. Squadron

100 Squadron Battle Order No. 1

Waltham. Intelligence reports from returning crews, on this operation, summarise the dangers and hazards referred to earlier and provide a good example of what bomber crews regularly faced:

Three reports of enemy aircraft on approach to Stettin; moderate heavy flak and light flak with twelve to fifteen searchlights coning; 0116hrs aircraft seen to explode and disintegrate at 9,000ft; 0108hrs.aircraft exploded at 10,000ft.; 0109 hrs. aircraft hit by flak and falling to ground in flames and held by two searchlights; 0006 hrs. aircraft flying at 100ft. hit by light flak from ship and flew into water; 0331hrs. aircraft flying at 200ft. seen to catch fire and crash in sea; 0018hrs. aircraft seen to explode in air emitting shower of green T.I. markers; 0015hrs. aircraft shot down by light flak after dropping bomb load. Seen to explode on ground. The above are a few of eighteen separate reports on one operation.

On the 24th April, 1943, Wing Commander R.V. McIntyre, D.F.C., took over from Wing Commander Swain and, on the 13th May, led the Squadron in an attack on Bochum. His 'plane was badly damaged by flak over Cologne but, with two engines on fire, he continued to bomb the target and returned to crash land at Coltishall. He was awarded an immediate D.F.C. His wireless operator, Flight Sergeant Renno, had received shrapnel wounds in the abdomen and thigh but continued at his post without informing his captain of his plight and obtained a number of radio fixes to assist navigation back to base. He was awarded an immediate D.F.M.

By June the Squadron could put up 25 Lancasters a night and on the 11th it joined another 760 'heavies' on a massive raid on Dusseldorf causing extensive damage. The price was two Waltham Lancasters amongst the 38 aircraft lost by Bomber Command. Eight further raids were made on the Ruhr during the rest of the month when the Squadron lost nine more aircraft with many others returning badly shot up by flak.

A less serious incident, in mid 1943, is recalled in John Carson's cartoon when a Squadron Lancaster was in conflict with a steam roller. Flt.lSgt. Eric Redshaw, a Squadron fitter, wrote: ' . . . One day I chanced to look across the airfield and there, some 300 yards down the peri-track, came a steam roller chuffing away merrily, the clank of its motion carrying clearly across the airfield. As this registered so did the sight of a taxying Lanc – not too far behind. The scene just held me – like a tableau – whilst I thought:

"Strange! Going at some lick with all four props running!"The Lanc was gaining on the 'roller and the driver must have just become aware as was shown by the quickening puffs from the 'roller's chimney. Evidently he thought he had to get somewhere quick and pull off the peri-track. Some seconds later the steam roller came to a stop but the Lanc came inexorably on. Whether the pilot judged that his port wing tip would clear the 'roller I can't say but, suddenly, the 'roller driver leapt frantically down from his controls and ran off.

In the next few seconds the Lanc's port outer prop chewed into the 'roller's rooflcanopy scattering the wood like confetti. In an instant the prop jerked

"The Lanc. and the Steam-Roller. Waltham, Summer 1943
Cartoon by John Carson (550 Squadron)

to a stop and the Lanc lurched to a halt as the pilot braked hard with the other three props still running fast. The 'tableau' seemed to hang in time whilst I saw no more action or no-one move or get out . . . It seemed that I was the only onlooker and, in the hustle and bustle of daily dispersal routine no-one else mentioned the incident. I never did discover the sequel.'

July was the month of the Battle of Hamburg which began on the 24th. Prior to this, on the 12th, the Squadron was part of a 1 and 5 Group force which attacked Turin. This was the most effective of the ten raids on Turin but the Squadron lost two of the 13 Lancasters reported missing. The four raids which devastated Hamburg took place between 24th July and 3rd August when almost 800 heavy bombers attacked the city and port on each raid. On the first of these raids "window" was used for the first time although it had been available since April, 1942. Middlebrook and Everitt state that, by confusing German radar, its use probably saved 120|130 aircraft and could have saved many more of the 2,200 lost in the previous year. Another feature of the Hamburg raids was that H2S was used for marking.

The most effective of the attacks on Hamburg was the second, on the night of 27th|28th July, which created the firestorm in which 40,000 people died. Flight Sergeant John Game, Flight Engineer in Pilot Officer Andrew's crew, still remembers with awe the sight of the blazing inferno he saw when dispersing 'window' down the flare chute. The last of the raids, on the 2nd/3rd August, was a failure when main force encountered heavy thunderstorms. Of the 30 aircraft lost it is estimated that at least four were due to icing, lightning or turbulence. 130 aircraft were lost on the four raids – one of them from 100 Squadron. It was on the last of these raids that twelve of the Squadron's aircraft could not take off because of an accident on the runway. Of the thirteen which did make it one was attacked by a night fighter over the Dutch coast when two of the crew were killed and a third, Sergeant Poucher, detained in Louth hospital.

Bomber Command suffered its heaviest losses of the war to date on 23rd August when 727 aircraft attacked Berlin and 56 were lost. Although only a partial success much damage was caused in the south of the city and Gauleiter Goebbels was reported "to have gone nuts." This was a bad night for the Squadron when it lost three aircraft. Jim Noble, Bomb Aimer in Warrant Officer Preston's crew, told of the crew's fate when shot down over Holland. He and three others were prisoners in Stalag 4B, the Rear Gunner "walked home"(!) but the Pilot and Flight Engineer were killed and are interred in North Bergen, Holland. It is interesting to note a typical Commonwealth "mix" in this crew: Skipper, Warrant Officer F.A. Preston, RAAF, Flight Engineer Sgt. H. Chadwick RAFVR, Navigator Sgt. E. Gardini RAFVR, Bomb Aimer Sgt. J. Noble RAFVR, Wireless Operator Sgt. A.E. Henry RAFVR, Mid Upper Gunner Sgt. Adelstein RCAF, Rear Gunner Sgt. M.R. Fiddler RAFVR. Their regular aircraft, "J Johnny" had a picture of a jumping kangaroo painted on its nose.

From Jim Noble we have an account of the Italian raids to Turin, Milan and Genoa. One of the targets on the Turin raids was a factory complex just outside the city but the main objective was the railway network carrying supplies from Germany to Northern Italy for onward transportation to the south to meet the Allied invasion of the toe of Italy. Jim describes the long, lonely haul across France on the first of these raids until they reached Lake Bouget where they altered course for the climb over the Alps. "Suddenly the sky was full of Lancasters . . . Streaks of light flashed over the snow as villagers dashed out of their houses to see what was going on." At this point the pitot head froze up rendering the A.S.I. and altimeter u/s so the pilot continued flying on engine revs and artificial horizon to Turin when the pitot head thawed out. On the return flight a number of Halifaxes were reported to have been shot down by flak as they strayed off track over the Le Havre defences.

Communications and dock installations were, again, the target at Genoa. The bomber stream crossed Southern France under a full moon for the run up to Genoa and Jim asked the pilot to take the aircraft down a few thousand feet to have a good look at the target. This was done and, after making one orbit, the bombs and leaflets were dropped and course set for home. On the way out of the target area a CR 42 appeared

"J-Johnny" – Lost on Gelsenkirchen, 26th June 1943

| John Adelstein | Bert Henry | Max Fiddler | Jim Noble |
|---|---|---|---|
| (Mid Upper) | (W/Op.) | (R. G.) | (Bomb Aimer) |

Warrant Officer Preston      Harold Chadwick
(Skipper)      (Flt. Engineer)

*Jim Noble*

from the rear but kept out of range. On instructions from the gunners the skipper reduced revs but the enemy aircraft refused to take the bait and turned off and disappeared. The route back took them over the Bay of Biscay and Jim describes "the wonderful sight of hundreds of Lancs flying 50|100 ft. over the sea to avoid possible attacks by Ju 88s." The returning bomber force was met by a Spitfire escort but, with their short range and running short of fuel, "it was a strange sight to see Spitfires and Lancasters jockeying for position to land at Predannack." (Predannack, near Start Point was a Coastal Command Station. Ed.)

After breakfast and refuelling the crew took off for Waltham where it was found that three 4 lb. incendiaries were lodged in the fuel tanks. "We had brought them back from Genoa and, needless to say, that was the last time we bombed below the briefed bombing height!" As is known, it was the practice to paint a bomb on the nose of an aircraft after every raid. "Because of the lack of action on the Italian trips they painted an ice cream cone instead!"

On the 31st 622 aircraft attacked Berlin again with heavy losses of 47 aircraft. The raid was not a success. Flight Sergeant Game described the ring of searchlights ringing the city but the marker flares fell 28 miles away. "Lord Haw Haw" made a bit of propaganda out of the raid

The graves of Warrant Officer F. A. Preston, RAAF, and Sergeant Harold Chadwick, RAFVR, at Bergen, Northern Holland
*J. Noble*

by commenting on the number of cows killed in the fields. Seven more aircraft were lost during the rest of August including one on the 18th when Bomber Command lost 40 aircraft on a special raid on the 'V2' research establishment at Peenemunde. This raid was notable for a number of reasons: it was the only precision raid, in the second half of the war, carried out at night on such a small target by the whole of Bomber Command; it was the first full-scale raid under the control of a master bomber (Group Captain J.H. Searby); there were three aiming points; it was the first raid in which 6 (Canadian) Group operated Lancasters and it was the first night on which the Germans used the new 'Schrage Musik", twin upward firing cannons, mounted in Me 110s. John Prochera, who had escaped from Poland in 1939, was a 100 Squadron rear-gunner on this raid. Hit by flak on the return flight John was wounded in the face by flying perspex; he went on to complete 97 operations and was awarded the 'Virtui Militari', the Polish equivalent of the Victoria Cross, by the Commander in Chief of the Polish Airforce.

And so, through the rest of August and September, battle orders came and went: Munich, Hanover, Bochum, Mannheim. In October 100 Squadron spawned its second offspring when "C" Flight became 625 Squadron which, later, moved to Kelstern. A month later yet another offspring, 550 Squadron, was produced to make its home at North Killingholme.

It was sad enough for the Squadron to lose crews on operations but the shock seemed greater when a tour-expired skipper was killed on a training flight. On 4th October Captain Morgan, an American pilot on the Squadron, took off with a crew of fairly new arrivals on the Squadron on a familiarisation flight and altitude test. Lancaster ED583 "M" exploded over North Thoresby.

'Ground observers heard a crackling sound and, looking up, saw bits of Lancaster falling all over the sky. The engines landed in an orchard near Gainsby and a large section of the wreck landed on the Methodist Chapel at North Thoresby partly demolishing it. Mr. M. Grantham was feeding his hens when he heard the crack and saw the Lancaster falling to pieces. He also heard a whistling sound and ended up with pieces of wireless equipment crashing into the ground quite near to him' (Lincolnshire Air War – 1939 – 1945. S. Finn.)

For the rest of the year the Squadron's losses began to rise again partly because of enemy action over targets as distant as Berlin but, in many cases, from atrocious weather conditions. The Squadron had a foretaste of the latter on 20th October on the way to Leipzig when it encountered 10|10 cloud between 12,000 and 16,000ft with attendant icing and electrical storms and one aircraft was lost. On the same raid Warrant Officer G.E. White brought back his aircraft after it had been on fire for four hours. An engine caught fire near Bremen on the way out but White flew on and bombed sixteen minutes after the main force penetrating heavy defence belts. When the bomber landed he remained at his post directing the fire fighting party until the flames were extinguished. After a particularly successful raid on Kassel on 22nd the Squadron lost another Lancaster when it crashed into high ground, near Louth, on its return. The Pilot, Pilot Officer Andrews and three crew members were killed in the crash but the Flight Engineer, Flight Sergeant John Game survived after spending a year in hospital. Another survivor was Pilot Officer Barrett, Rear Gunner, who, a year later, started a second tour only to be lost on a training flight.

# CHAPTER TEN

## Berlin – November 1943 to March 1944

Although there had been earlier raids on "The Big City", the main Battle of Berlin, where the Squadron gained its next Battle Honour, took place between the 18th November, 1943 and the 24th March, 1944 in sixteen major raids. Not only was Berlin the most heavily defended target in Germany but the battle took place in the worst flying weather in the year. Time after time crews returned with fuel reserves down to 100 gallons after battling against icing and adverse winds often finding their own base closed down by fog and low cloud.

The first raid took place on the 18th November when 400 Lancasters attacked. Bombing results were inconclusive as the target was covered by 10|10 cloud and nine Lancasters were lost. One of these, ED991-H, was a 100 Squadron aircraft which crashed at Salzwedel. Flight Sergeant R.B. Doughty and his crew survived as prisoners of war. The Squadron joined a much bigger force four nights later without loss and, again, the target was obscured by cloud. The raid, however, was considered successful with large areas of damage and 175,000 people bombed out of their homes . Barely awake from the previous night's operation crews were called to briefing again for Berlin on the 23rd. Amongst others, Jack Hamblin's crew were amazed to see a deep red glow, many miles ahead on the approach to Berlin, caused by fires still burning from the previous night's raid. Hamblin described being coned by searchlights and trying to hold the aircraft steady as 'it bucked like a bronco' after being hit on the port side by heavy flak. There was a heavy smell of cordite and noise from exploding flak. In another Squadron aircraft Rear Gunner, Sergeant Jimmy Flynn's turret failed and he lost his oxygen supply. The last thing he remembered was, "Bomb doors open!" He was rescued from his turret by the wireless operator, Johnny Macananey and awoke to see the target burning behind him.

Warrant Officer Leman's crew had to bale out when their Lancaster was attacked on the way to Berlin by a fighter. The navigator, Flight Lieutenant James Lake landed in a field and, after hiding his 'chute and 'Mae West' walked several miles and met up with his bomb aimer, Flight Sergeant Jefferies, who had injured his back. Unable to walk they gave themselves up to a farmer and were eventually taken to a prison camp where they met their skipper again. The engineer, Sergeant Daniels, was also taken prisoner but the rest of the crew, Sergeants Fuller, Lloyd and Chandler were lost.

The Squadron lost four aircraft on three separate raids on Berlin between 27th November and the 3rd December but it was the weather that caused the greatest tragedy on the 16th/17th. Seventeen Squadron Lancasters returned safely from Berlin only to find Waltham closed in by low cloud and nil visibility. With no diversions available it seemed a case of 'every man for himself'. The Commanding Officer, Wing Commander D.W. Holford, D.S.O.,D.F.C., crash landed "N" at Kelstern and, shortly afterwards, Flying Officer Proudfoot crashed at Barnolby-le-Beck. Circling Waltham, searching for a break in the cloud, were "Q" and "F" who collided in mid air just south of base. Of the four crews, 28 men, only six survived. An enquiry into the improvement of safety in such conditions led to the "Waltham Circle", an arrangement with local searchlight units to guide in bombers during bad weather.

Just before Christmas, on the night of 23rd/24th December, Jimmy Flynn had another memorable visit to Berlin. The 'plane was hit by flak just as they bombed although there was little visible damage. Skipper Bill Brooke threw the Lanc into relative darkness and proceeded on the homeward flight only to stray off track over Emden."Without warning searchlights coned the aircraft and a box barrage opened up. Bill threw the Lanc into turns and dives that Jimmy had not thought possible. Despite this the aircraft was held in the beams so he put the bomber into a screaming dive from 21,000 feet down to 4,000 feet. He yelled to Vic Condell, the flight engineer, to use the trimmer as he was unable to pull out of the dive but Vic spun the trimmer a little too sharply as it nearly pulled the wings off. They managed to leave the area with the searchlights left still probing the piece of sky they had been in. Inspecting the aircraft on their return, after over eight hours flying, they counted 40 holes in the wings and fuselage." [Bombers Over Berlin – Alan W. Cooper. (William Kimber)]

On the eighth raid of the main offensive, on the 29th/30th December, Flying Officer Cyril Barton bombed on the markers and a large explosion was seen, despite the clouds. On the return flight the compass went haywire and their position had to be fixed by astronavigation. Almost out of fuel "Cy" managed to land near Grimsby. After leaving 100 Squadron Flying Officer Barton was awarded the Victoria Cross posthumously on the Nurenburg raid in March, 1944.

Although the Squadron had less than a year's service with Bomber Command the end of 1943 saw it holding second place in No.1 Group for the number of successful missions completed and first place for the least number of losses. Such attainments, together with a spell of 700 sorties without loss in 1944, gave 100 Squadron the reputation of being a 'lucky squadron' but this, to the writer, seems a somewhat facile reason for its successes. Any luck that was involved came from first class leadership from Station Commander downwards, through Squadron and Flight

Commanders, Section Leaders and team work within crews. It came from the dedication and the quality of ground crews who worked in the open in all hours in all kinds of weather. The Lancasters were their aircraft – just as much as they 'belonged' to the crews that flew them – and they knew them like the back of their hands.

Another feature of 100 Squadron was in-service training. Most crews would find their operational sorties regularly punctuated with bombing practices, H2S cross countries, and fighter affiliation and this went on throughout a whole tour of ops. Experienced crew members would accompany new crews on their training flights and pass on valuable tips they had learnt themselves. Although the gunners were regarded as the 'eyes' of the crew, in one sense, all crew members were exhorted to look out and search the skies from take off to landing. A good skipper would insist upon strict intercom silence except for the obvious reason when a crew member needed to pass on an operational instruction. Idle chatter could drown a vital "Corkscrew" or warning of another, dangerously near, aircraft. Section Leaders diligently checked the logs of navigators, flight engineers, bomb aimers and flight engineers and commented, advised and, if merited, played hell! Encompassing all this was the overall morale of a happy Station. Perhaps the inspiration came from Station Commander Group Captain Ian Newbiggin's exhortation at the end of every briefing:
"Good luck! Good bombing and no early returns!"

The Squadron started the New Year with yet another attack on Berlin losing Flight Sergeant R.W. Chinnery and all his crew in JB740-R and, on the following night, JB 549-C with Pilot Officer G.W. Henderson and his crew failed to return probably shot down by fighters over Berlin. There was a respite from Berlin until the 21st January when the Squadron attacked without loss. Miraculously, it seems, the Squadron also survived the next three raids without loss but disaster struck on the 30th when the crews of Warrant Officer J.A. Crabtree, Flying Officer R.M. Parker and Warrant Officer K. Ives were lost. Of these 21 men only Flight Sergeant R.G. Fenton, of Ives's crew, and Sergeant J.W. Knight, of Crabtree's crew, survived as prisoners. On the previous night Jimmy Flynn completed his first tour. He recalled seeing three Lancasters going down in flames and "the lovely sight of a Me 109 hit over the target area."

The Squadron lost another Lancaster on the night of 19th February when Flight Lieutenant George Sidebotham and his crew were shot down whilst attacking Leipzig. All the crew escaped from the aircraft but were taken prisoner and moved to Stalag Luft 3 in March where they met up with another Waltham flyer, Flying Officer McEwan, a Canadian Bomb Aimer. The two officers helped in the organisation of an escape and a number of them got out through a tunnel. Subsequently, in reprisal, 50 officers were shot. This incident has been the subject of many books and the film, "The Great Escape."

The last operation of the Battle of Berlin took place on the 24th March and is remembered as 'the night of the strong winds' which carried the force of 811 bombers south at every stage of the flight, even as far as the Ruhr. 72 aircraft were lost and, amongst them, 100 Squadron's ND 642-H. The following crew members were buried in Berlin: Flying Officer A.J. Jenkins,Sergeant W.J. Moore, Flight Sergeant G.A. Saunders, Sergeant G. Pearson, Sergeant R. Ross, Sergeant D.G. Harris, Sergeant F.A. Farr.

But Berlin was not the only target for Bomber Command in the first quarter of 1944. Brunswick, Magdeburg, Leipzig and Stuttgart were attacked with losses of between 7% and 9[1/2]% of main force on each raid. Returning from Stuttgart on the 21st February Flight Sergeant Wadge's Lancaster collided with a German twin engined night fighter coming in from the port beam at the very moment the mid-upper gunner was rotating his turret to starboard. The Lanc fell out of control from 22,000ft. to 19,000ft. and Flight Sergeant Wadge ordered his crew to prepare to bale out. In the event, with excessive engine vibration, part of the port wing missing, the fuselage holed, a shattered mid-upper turret and damaged rudder Flight Sergeant Wadge found he could maintain control by holding the control column hard to starboard and the rudder well to port. On checking with his crew over the intercom all responded except the mid-upper who had facial injuries and was preparing to abandon the aircraft having lost his intercom. Fortunately he was restrained by the wireless operator who then went to the aid of the rear-gunner who was trapped inside his turret with his oxygen supply cut off. Although the wireless operator managed to free the doors the rear-gunner refused to leave his post and remained there until the aircraft managed to land at Ford.

Ground inspection revealed: six feet of the port wing tip torn off, the mid-upper turret had been stove in, the top eighteen inches of the starboard fin and rudder had been bent outwards at right angles, twelve inches of one tip of the port outer propeller was missing and all the other blades were damaged. The navigator's window had been smashed, all the aerials torn away, the rear-gunner's oxygen pipe severed in three places, the rear turret door was jammed, there were numerous holes in the fuselage and the fuel jettison trunk was released on the port side. For his incredible feat of bringing the Lancaster home Flight Sergeant Wadge was awarded an immediate D.F.M.

Four nights later Flight Sergeant Wadge and crew took off for an attack on Schweinfurt at 18.30 hrs. but returned early with the Captain feeling ill. He was told to jettison fuel over the sea but returned saying the jettison facility would not function. At 21.45 hrs. he was ordered out to sea again to jettison his bomb load but he, his crew and aircraft were never seen again.

Still rather tired from their Schweinfurt operation the previous night Flight Lieutenant Crowley-Smith ("Bish") and crew took off on the 26th for the thirteenth operation of their tour to Augsburg.

"We were stooging along at 23,000 ft. over the Black Forest and in the

And they landed it back in England!

Flight Sergeant Wadge, DFM, and crew with the battered "J-Jig". Part of the
enemy aircraft was still embedded in "Jig"
*"Bomber Squadrons of the RAF" Philip Moys. (McDonald)*

distance, on the port side, we could see the glow from the fires at Augsburg. We suddenly caught a heavy burst of very accurate flak under our belly. The aircraft became virtually uncontrollable and the bomb aimer, who was down in the nose, trying to get a pinpoint was badly hit. We were on fire and losing height rapidly. I told the crew to bale out and when they had all gone I myself jumped. Almost immediately the aircraft blew up at about 5,000 ft.

I remember no more until I found myself sitting on my parachute in my socks, in two feet of snow, trying to light a cigarette. Out of the darkness came a group of soldiers in coal-scuttle helmets and I thought, 'Oh hell. Stalag Luft, here I come!' But the first word they said was "Schweitz" and when I looked more closely I could just see that they had red arm bands with a white cross. Apparently I had landed on a frozen lake. They carried me up the bank and helped me across a long bridge with one soldier keeping my hands in his greatcoat to avoid frost-bite. To my amazement, there, on the other side of the bridge, was a very attractive cafe, all lit up, and as I was helped through the door, I saw, there on the counter, a large display of English cigarettes.

The cafe was run by three pretty young ladies who treated me with great kindness while the soldiers, who turned out to be elderly "Home Guards",looked on with interest. I was wrapped up in blankets with pink knitted slippers on my feet and seated in an armchair. I was then given hot rum and water followed by ham and eggs. Considering that our exploding aeroplane had broken almost every window in the valley, including those in the cafe, I would not have been surprised if I had had far worse treatment. I was given a bed for the night in a cottage used by the soldiers and the next day,after my flying boots had been found and returned to me,I was taken by car to Dubendorf, near Zurich."

A few years ago "Bish" called on one of the three pretty girls, now over seventy, and they had 'a great reunion.'

# CHAPTER ELEVEN

## March to December 1944

On the 15th March the Squadron was briefed to join nearly 900 bombers for an attack on Stuttgart. The following account describes a young crew's first operation with one of the R.A.F.s most memorable characters, Air Commodore Arthur Wray, DSO, MC, DFC, AFC, No.12 Base Commander at Binbrook.

"It was March 15, 1944. I was a young Sergeant Pilot with only seven hours flying time on Lancasters, posted a week earlier to 100 Squadron at Waltham, a windswept airfield near Grimsby and one of three bomber stations making up 12 Base under Wray's command. That morning we had been told: 'You're flying on your first operation tonight with the Base Commander.'

We were standing nervously round our Lancaster. "J" Jig when he drove up, a stocky figure with iron grey hair and a blaze of medal ribbons on his battledress. Arthur Wray was then 47; we were all 20 and my first impression, as he limped across the tarmac was that he was so old. None of us seven sergeants had ever seen such an officer before. But this one had a warm, friendly smile and relaxed manner that put us at ease. We took to him at once. The target that night was Stuttgart, one of Germany's most viciously defended cities. For a crew as green as ours it was a daunting prospect but Arthur Wray appeared totally unconcerned. When I walked with him round "J" Jig to inspect the aircraft before take-off he chatted away as cheerfully as though we were going on a joy ride.

We had been flying for an hour, with the Air Commodore at the controls, when one of our gunners spotted the dark shadow of a Lancaster sliding beneath us, crossing our path. A few moments later another crossed above. Wray immediately suspected that we were straying from the bomber stream. As we flew on alone it transpired that the navigator had misread the flight plan and given the wrong course.

'Now I can't get a fix Sir,' he reported, 'our radar's being jammed.'

'All right,' said Wray, mildly, 'work out a course by dead reckoning.' There was a long silence, then:

'Sorry, Sir. but we're lost. We'll have to turn back.' With a crisp, 'Turn back be damned!' the Air Commodore helped us plot an approximate course and we flew on across Germany towards Stuttgart.

We arrived fifteen minutes late to find ourselves the only Lancaster over the city and began our bombing run through an intense barrage of flak. But Wray was dissatisfied with our approach. To impress on us the need for accuracy, he coolly circled back over Stuttgart and began a second run through the flak. To me those few minutes seemed interminable but Wray set an example in the heat of action which no training school could hope to match. Bombs gone, we turned away with searchlights probing for us and he gave me another invaluable lesson – flinging "J" Jig around the sky in the gut wrenching "corkscrew" evasive manoeuvres which would help defend us against searchlights and night fighters.

As we neared the coast of England after eight hours in the air he said: 'I'm a bit tired now. You'd better take over.' In the Lancaster's cramped cock-pit it was a real struggle for Arthur Wray, with his lame leg, to leave his seat. I realised for the first time that if he had been hit he would have been trapped with no hope of baling out and admired all the more his courage in choosing to fly with a raw crew." (From 'The RAF's Unforgettable 'Father' Wray by Squadron Leader Douglas Sutton, DFC as told to Peter Brown.)

The most disastrous raid of the war for Bomber Command took place on the night of the 30th|31st March, 1944, when 795 aircraft were despatched to attack Nuremburg. Main Force lost 96 aircraft, mainly to fighters, as it battled to and from the target. Miraculously, all 100 Squadron aircraft returned safely although a 'sister' squadron, 101, at Ludford Magna lost eight. Part of the scene was described by Flight Lieutenant D.F. Gillam: "We started leaving contrails at the height we had been ordered to fly, 19,000 ft. but we were an experienced crew and I decided to disobey orders and get as much height as possible. We got up to about 22,000 ft. which was as high as we could get fully loaded. From there I could see a mass of contrails below us; they were like a formation of American daylight bombers.

"I watched a Lancaster flying about 2,000 ft. below us and about two miles off to my starboard. It had a dirty great contrail out to the back. I watched, fascinated, as a twin engined German type overtook him, approaching just under the contrail. I could see everything perfectly clearly but we couldn't help. The German got underneath the Lancaster and fired straight into his belly with an upward firing gun. The bomber took no evasive action at all. There was an explosion and it blew clean in half. There were no parachutes. My stomach turned over and we tried to get even higher. By then I was feeling very cheesed off with the powers that be for sending us out on a night like that." [This should have been a moon stand-down period but the raid was planned on forecast high cloud cover on the outward flight with the target clear. Although a Met. Flight Reconnaissance Mosquito reported that the protective cloud was unlikely to be present and that there could be cloud over the target the raid was not cancelled. (Middlebrook & Everitt, Bomber Command War Diaries,)]

On the night of the 10th April Pilot Officer Mortimer and his crew were on a mining operation in the Gulf of Danzig when they were attacked by a Me 410 and the 'plane caught fire. The attack injured the rear-gunner and put his turret out of action. Other cannon shells hit the port outer engine, damaged the elevators and put the trim tabs in the fully UP position. In a steep dive the Lancaster's airspeed indicator registered 410 knots and a Verey cartridge from the dinghy pack ignited leaking hydraulic fluid. With the help of the Flight Engineer, Pilot Officer Mortimer finally pulled the 'plane out of its dive after falling 14,000 ft. Meanwhile the wireless operator had struggled against the "G" forces and managed to extinguish the fire and repair the intercom whilst the mid-upper extracted the wounded rear-gunner from his turret. As the 'plane levelled out the Me 410 came in to attack again and the mid-upper opened fire as the Captain managed to fly into the comparative shelter of a cloud. The pilot was finding it impossible to control the aircraft against the damaged trimmers so two cords were removed from the navigator's life jacket and tied to the top of the control column from where they passed from behind the pilot's seat to the bomb aimer who took up much of the strain for the rest of the trip. In this manner, with one engine feathered the aircraft returned to base where undercarriage and flaps were lowered by emergency air pressure and Pilot Officer Mortimer landed it using all his strength.

Fifty years later John B. Raper DFC, the navigator recalled this operation in another context – the "Jinxes":

"After joining the Squadron in January 1944, when nightly losses were already high, it suddenly became apparent that whenever an NCO pilot was commissioned he and his crew went missing on the next operation. This happened on six consecutive occasions. On 22nd March we were briefed for a trip to Frankfurt and, shortly afterwards I ran into the Adjutant who told me our Skipper's commission had come through and his kit would be moved over to the Officers Mess while we were flying. After reminding him about the sequence of losses he agreed not to tell 'Monty' Mortimer or move his kit until we had returned. The fatalistic spell was broken!"

Referring to the mining operation, above, he went on to say: "Not long afterwards another pattern appeared when a crew returned with a 'plane badly shot up. If they were given a brand new replacement Lancaster they went missing on the next operation and, again, this happened on five or six occasions. On the night of 9th April 1994, we flew to Gdynia carrying a magnetic mine which was dropped in an attempt to disable a German pocket battleship anchored in the harbour. We were severely shot up on the return trip with a badly wounded reargunner. The Medical Officer, Doctor Marshall, on learning that our 'plane, "U Uncle", would be under reparis for over two weeks and we would get a new aircraft, decided to hospitalise the whole crew saying that none of us was fit to fly. A week of sick leave followed and then back to operations in our old 'plane. Another unaccountable jinx was broken."

As Wing Commander Brookes remarked it was sorties like these, rather than headline making raids such as the Dam Busters, that typified the life – and death – of such units as 100 Squadron in Bomber Command. One grieves at Bomber Command's losses but when one considers the spectacle of many hundreds of bombers, from airfields in Yorkshire, Lincolnshire and East Anglia converging into a narrow stream, flying hundreds of miles over heavily defended enemy territory, in every kind of weather, concentrating their bombing into a spell of twenty or thirty minutes and then flying home again it is a miracle that losses were not much greater.

Sergeant Boden (R.C.A.F.) and his crew were killed when their aircraft was shot down over Belgium whilst returning from an attack on Karlsruhe on the night of the 24th|25th April. They are buried at the Commonwealth War Cemetery at Heverlee, near Leuven, and the local people remember, with gratitude, the sacrifices made by the R.A.F. in the liberation of their country.

On the 3rd May 100 Squadron joined the rest of No. 1 Group and No. 5 Group on a precision night attack on Mailly-le-Camp. Eleven aircraft were despatched but one returned early with engine failure. Two other crews were attached to No. 1 Group's Special Duties Flight (SDF) with orders to mark the Special Target. Leading the S.D.F.s was a 100 Squadron Flight Commander, Squadron Leader H.F. Breakspear.The general target was a large German military camp seventy five miles east of Paris and the Special Target was a tank depot.

Confusion arose when the Main Force Controller found he couldn't broadcast instructions because his VHF set was being drowned by an American Forces broadcast and during the delay German fighters caused heavy casualties. When the main attack eventually started under the direction of the Deputy Controller, Wing Commander L.C. Deane, 1500 tons of bombs were dropped with great accuracy. 114 barrack buildings, 47 transport sheds and ammunition buildings were hit. 102 vehicles, including 37 tanks, were destroyed on the Special Target and 374 German soldiers were killed or injured. There were no French casualties on the raid but some were killed when a Lancaster crashed on their house. Six 100 Squadron crews bombed the Special Target whilst the remainder attacked the barracks.

For No. 1 Group in general the cost was high: 28 out of 173 aircraft were lost, including six from 460 Squadron at Binbrook, but, again, 100 Squadron was 'lucky' and all aircraft returned safely.

On the 14th April General Dwight Eisenhower,the Supreme Allied Commander,assumed overall command of the United States Army Air Force and Bomber Command in preparation for 'Operation Overlord'.Although it maintained its strategic role, Bomber Command was to be occupied, more and more, with tactical targets in support of the Normandy invasion. Initially these, as in World War 1, were concentrated on the railway system in Northern France. By "D Day" Bomber Command had dropped 42,000 tons of bombs in 8,800 sorties on these targets. Intermingled with these attacks the Squadron also attacked concentrations of enemy armour, as at Mailly, and "V"-weapon sites and helped to open "Overlord" by bombing German gun emplacements on the Normandy coast at 23.35 hrs. on 5th June.

About this period a Lancaster crashed on take off from Waltham. Fortunately, the crew managed to escape from the 'plane before it exploded. The navigator is reported to have said, "Blast it! There go my 3H pencils." Peter Burnett, R.C.A.F., the bomb aimer, still sports one of his flying boots at his home in Ontario. " I left the other in the kite," said he.Debris was scattered all over the village of Holton le Clay; windows were shattered, ceilings brought down and, even, locked doors blown open. One large piece of white hot metal sliced into an apple tree denuding it of its leaves and shrivelling up the apples on its branches.

Peter also recalls another example of the close links between the Squadron and local villagers. Living with her parents in a little cottage near the "King's Head" in Waltham was a young girl called Sally Lancaster. She was a great knitter and would sit outside the cottage for hours knitting little dolls which she gave to airmen to bring them luck. Peter swears they did just that.

On the 20th June 100 Squadron completed its 100th operation against Germany and, in that month, had dropped 1197 tons of bombs followed by 1206 tons in July. Between the 10th and 30th June the Squadron lost five aircraft in attacks on the railway network. On the 11th Flying Officer Lambert was wounded and baled out over the English Channel. He swam half a mile to the shore where he had to walk through a minefield to reach Allied forces. On the 30th 118 No. 1 Group Lancasters attacked railway yards at Vierzon, near Orleans,using its own marking flight. Bombing was described as being very accurate and a success for the markers. Losses were high – 14 Lancasters, 12% of the force, including one from Waltham. Another Waltham Lancaster, "M"-Mike, was intercepted by a twin engined fighter. The pilot put his aircraft into a steep turn to port with 85 degrees of bank when it hit its own slipstream and the starboard wing turned right over the top. The bomber was on its back for fifteen seconds before the pilot regained control, having dropped from 12,000 ft. to 4,000 ft., and landed back at Waltham without ailerons.

Throughout July and August attacks continued against railway centres, 'V' weapon sites and some strategic targets. At the end of July during an attack on Stuttgart the bomber stream was intercepted over France in bright moonlight: 38 Lancasters were lost including one from the Squadron. On August 7/8 a big attack was mounted against five enemy positions in front of Allied forces in Normandy and, on the 14th, over 1,000 heavy bombers struck at German night fighter bases in Holland and Belgium in preparation for a resumption of raids on German targets. On one of the first of these against Kiel, on the 27th, the Squadron lost another aircraft.

Another example of the regard held for the R.A.F. in its battle to liberate Europe comes from Denekamp in Holland. On the night of the 13th August Flight Lieutenant Paston-Williams's Lancaster, LM 658 "W", was shot

RAF-GRIMSBY (WALTHAM) 1941-1945
TO FIGHT FOR OUR FREEDOM AND TO
END THE NAZI TYRANNY. YOUNG PEOPLE
FROM ALL OVER THE WORLD CAME TO
THIS AIRFIELD TO SERVE AND TO FLY
THE WELLINGTONS AND LANCASTERS
OF 142 & 100 SQUADRONS.
OVER 1000 BRAVE YOUNG MEN CAME
THROUGH THIS ENTRANCE —
NEVER TO RETURN. MANY MORE WERE
❖ SHOT DOWN AND CAPTURED ❖
WE WILL REMEMBER THEM
AND SALUTE ALL WHO SERVED HERE.
F.W.B. 1987.

Plaque erected at old guard room entrance to RAF Waltham by ex-Corporal
Fred Bury, 1987

Three Waltham Lancasters leading a "Gaggle"
"L Leather" "Jug and Bottle" "Able Mabel"
*(From Original Painting by Graham Wragg)*
*Winnipeg Air Museum*

down by a night-fighter of the German Squadron 11 NJG 1 and crashed at Bergentheim, near Hardenberg. Flight Lieutenant Paston-Williams, Sergeant Downie, Flight Engineer, and Flying Officer David (R.C.A.F.), gunner, managed to bail out and were captured but the rest of the crew were killed. Amongst these, however, was the Navigator, Flying Officer G. Hood, who had managed to bail out and was, apparently, sheltered by a young, Dutch Resistance worker.

Both Hood and the resistance worker were captured by the Germans and shot and were buried in a lonely wood. The Germans put a bomb on top of the graves. Five months later the bodies were re-interred in a graveyard. The actual site of the killings is now marked by two memorials and the local inhabitants regard the spot as a sanctuary which, for almost fifty years, has been decorated with flowers daily. After the war the German officers responsible for the killings, Scheinberger and Sandrock, were captured by the Dutch and hanged.

The combined assault by Bomber Command and the American 8th Air Force was, by this stage, beginning to overwhelm the German air defences and to compel the withdrawal of fighter squadrons from their westerly airfields. Thus, during the summer months, Bomber Command was increasingly able to mount daylight raids in support of Allied forces in France, later in Holland and, eventually, over Germany itself. There would continue to be losses and Luftwaffe success as with the Me 262s against B 17s, but a new phase was developing in the Bomber Offensive.

The pattern was for squadrons and groups to collect together in a 'gaggle' behind a 'vic' of three leaders. This was far different from the Americans' strict formation flying and, from the American point of view, must have looked very haphazard and undisciplined! Flying Officer 'Doc' Watson, R.C.A.F., bomb aimer in Flight Lieutenant Lynn Bell's crew recalled an amusing incident when returning from a 'daylight' over Germany. Also returning from another target was a formation of U.S.A.A.F. Fortresses (B.17s): Lynn edged his Lancaster alongside one and waved to the pilot. Keeping station Lynn then feathered an engine and, with a concerned look at the pilot, pointed to the idle prop. He then feathered another and a third holding his hands up in despair indicating the three idle props to the American who, by now, was himself looking worried. Lynn then pulled away on all four motors with a grin and a wave to the Fort.

Such attacks as these, by day and night throughout the rest of the year, brought the Squadron two more Battle Honours – 'Fortress Europe' and 'Normandy'.

An innovation on the Squadron at this time was introduced by Squadron Leader George Pirie, D.F.C., Squadron Navigation Officer. This was the attachment of a small camera to the P.P.I. tube (Plan Position Indicator) of the H2S set. Navigators would take photographs of the P.P.I. at set intervals on the bombing run, at 'Bombs Gone' and the actual time of impact. This gave a check on the normal bombing photograph with which it was compared.

"Hellzapoppin"
The only Lancaster to return from an operation with more bombs than it took
off with! (Left to right: Jack Wadsworth – F/E, Bill McGough – Mid-upper,
Henry Brown – Skipper) "Hellzapoppin" crashed at Ghent after the Cologne
raid of 2nd March 1945
*J. S. Metcalfe*

It also gave navigators a bit of extra practice in making a 'mock' bombing run of their own because, occasionally, navigators themselves would bomb on H2S.

The last major Bomber Command raid on Frankfurt took place on the 12th/13th September when the Squadron lost another aircraft with all the crew killed. There ensued a remarkable period of, over three months, until Christmas Eve, during which the Squadron flew 700 operational sorties without loss. For most of the rest of September attacks were concentrated on the Channel Ports and gun batteries in support of Allied forces which, by now, had broken out of the Normandy beach-head moving rapidly east to Holland and the Rhine. Walcharen, which guarded the port of Antwerp, and Breskens were repeatedly attacked in an attempt to clear the way for British and Canadian forces. Two other enemy strongpoints, Cleve and Emmerich, were taken out in the advance to the Rhine.

From both these towns the enemy could threaten Allied forces near Nijmegen after the failure at Arnhem. 100 Squadron joined the rest of No. 1 Group on the daylight attack, with fighter escort, on Emmerich. The town was obliterated. Squadron Leader Dave Robb, R.C.A.F., and his mixed R.C.A.F. and R.A.F. crew were on their fourth operation on the 7th October flying "H-How". "H" was the 'plane regularly used by Flight Sergeant Harry Brown and his crew who were on leave at the time. They had named it 'Hellzapoppin' after a popular musical of the time and Bomb Aimer, Stamper Metcalfe, had spent hours painting the name on the aircraft.

Just as Flying Officer "Mo" Mosure, R.C.A.F., released the 4,000 lbs. 'cookie' the 'plane was hit by eleven incendiary bombs from an aircraft which had crossed, crab-like, above. One of the incendiaries crashed through the cockpit wrecking the airspeed indicator and altimeter, rolled down into the bomb aimer's compartment and ignited.

"We're on bloody fire!" bawled Mo, "Where's all the goddam fire extinguishers?" Flight Sergeant 'Poker' Gamble, flight engineer passed down the first and Flight Sergeant Ron Brown, wireless operator passed forward all the spares until Mo's smoke blackened faced appeared in the tunnel and, with a grin, announced, "It's out!"

Meanwhile the other 340 aircraft and their escorts had turned for home whilst "Hellzapoppin" was still heading east. Navigator, Sergeant Art White, not fully aware of the instrument damage up-front, gave Robbie a course direct for base and the 'plane gingerly turned to the west but all on board had a feeling of nakedness as they surveyed the empty sky. Settled on the new course the crew surveyed the damage and Sergeant Monty Kerr, R.C.A.F., the mid-upper gunner, whose turret had just been missed by another incendiary, reported smoke coming from both wings. The Skipper had increased speed to get over friendly territory when 'Poker' identified the smoke as fuel vapour escaping from the tanks. Speed was reduced to conserve fuel and, with the navigator regularly calling out heights and airspeeds from his duplicate panel, finally landed at Waltham almost 30 minutes late still carrying its load of incendiaries.

Waiting at dispersal was a reception committee headed by Squadron Commander, Wing Commander Hamilton, D.S.O., D.F.C. Ground crews and airmen examined the stricken Lanc whilst Robbie's crew described their experiences, fully expecting Robbie and Mo to get an immediate D.F.C. It was a come down to hear Wing Commander Hamilton say,

"Well, Robbie, maybe next time you'll look up!"

Other damage to the aircraft included partly severed rudder and elevator control rods which were hanging on by a fraction of an inch. "Hellzapoppin" was taken away to the maintenance unit whilst the crew was ribbed by other crews for being the only crew in history which landed with more bombs than it took off with. Others remarked,

"Well, what did you expect with a name like that?"

Returning from leave Harry Brown's crew demanded to know what we had done with their Lanc."Where's our golliwog?" asked Stamper Metcalfe. The mascot had been with them on every trip but, although they searched the aircraft at the M.U. it was never found. After completing their tour both Robbie and Mo were awarded the D.F.C.

The 14th October saw the opening of "Operation Hurricane",a series of concerted attacks by Bomber Command and the U.S.A.A.F. on industrial cities in the Ruhr. Twenty 100 Squadron Lancasters, each carrying 15,000 lbs of high explosives, took off at 06.45 hrs. to join 1,000 other heavy bombers, with fighter escort, for an attack on Duisburg. Flak over the target was intense and crews reported Lancasters and Halifaxes exploding in the sky in palls of black smoke. Fourteen aircraft were lost. Returning, around noon, crews were de-briefed, had some lunch and retired for a few hours sleep. Somewhere around tea-time the Squadron was again called to briefing for another attack on the city taking off at midnight.

Fires from the previous attack were visible 100 miles away and, again, over 1,000 'heavies' smashed the city. In the two attacks Bomber Command had dropped 9,000 tons of bombs on Duisburg and, on their return from the night raid over 1,000 American 'planes were taking off for the same target. At 1500 hrs. the Squadron was called, yet again, for a third operation – this time to Wilhelmshaven which was carried out successfully without loss. That was three major operations within 48 hours and, in the rest of the month, the Squadron was to attack Bochum, Cologne, Stuttgart and Essen.

November began with attacks on Gelsenkirchen and Wanne-Eickel when Allied bombing priorities had shifted to German oil refineries but an outstanding tactical daylight raid, in which the Squadron took part, was on Duren. The town was one of three to be attacked between Aachen and the Rhine in the path of the American advance. The actual aiming point was a cross roads and crews could hear the Master Bomber, calling over the R/T, "Oh! beautiful bombing chaps, beautiful bombing but spread them around a bit!" One wag remarked that they were all going down the same hole! The town was wiped out but, it was later learned, the American tanks were bogged down and the advance was slow and costly.

Karlsruhe, Essen and the oil refineries at Leuna were targets in early December and, on the 15th, Flight Lieutenant Jack Playford D.F.C. returned to the Squadron to take his old 'plane "Able Mabel" to Ludwigshafen on its 100th operation. Christmas Eve brought no respite for the Squadron when it was briefed to attack Cologne. Sadly, Flight Lieutenant Griffiths and his crew failed to return.

So ended 1944 with the Allies verging on the banks of the Rhine although it was to be another three months before it was crossed. Nevertheless 100 Squadron was to play a full role in Bomber Command in clearing the way, by day and by night, for the ground forces to the very end of the war.

Battle Order – Duisburg

# CHAPTER TWELVE

## From Bombs to 'Manna'

The New Year opened badly for the Squadron. "L"-Love, popularly known as "'ell for Leather", inexplicably crashed in The Wash while on a training flight and fighter affiliation exercise with Flight Lieutenant Weatherall and his crew. "L" was one of the few Lancaster B 1s on the Squadron in 1944 with Rolls Royce Merlins – one flight engineer described her as "being able to belt down the runway like a scalded cat" – and had just returned to 100 after a major overhaul. Three days later Flying Officer Barker's aircraft was lost over Hanover.

Although Arctic weather curtailed operations in January the Squadron still managed to keep flying, a great tribute to the ground crews working in the open, often, in sub-zero temperatures. On the 7th the Squadron was briefed for one of its longest operations – to Munich – a return flight of over nine hours: in case of delays on take off bowsers were standing by to top up fuel tanks. On route navigators found the forecast winds had veered 90 degrees with speeds between 90 and 100 knots with the result that 'planes were skirting the Swiss border. One rear-gunner reported seeing Swiss searchlights pointing vertically upwards and, as his Lanc edged closer to the border, they pointed like fingers of light, north, towards Germany!

Attacks on oil refineries were resumed on the 14th when the Squadron joined another 550 Lancasters for a raid on Leuna, near Leipzig. Although intense flak was encountered Albert Speer described this attack as one of the most damaging raids on the synthetic-oil industry carried out in this period. (Middlebrook and Everitt.) Two nights later the Squadron, supporting PFF, opened the attack on oil refineries at Zeitz where, again, heavy damage was inflicted despite the intense flak.

Another loss, on this raid, brought home to the writer that feeling of gloom and sadness when a crew was reported missing. About a week earlier a grinning Canadian Flight Lieutenant had come into the hut and asked if his crew could 'bunk down' with us. Of course, there was plenty of room and we looked forward to meeting new faces. Strangely, we hardly saw each other as either the crews would be flying at different times or, perhaps, leave might have intervened. On the 16th January Flight Lieutenant Quigley and his crew failed to return from Zeitz. On the 17th a sober faced officer and two clerks from the Orderly Room came into the hut and, quietly, removed all the young Canadians' possessions. We never even knew their names.

The month ended with a raid on the Bosch works at Stuttgart and the Squadron suffered its third loss of the year on operations when, on 1st February, Flight Lieutenant Conn and crew failed to return from Ludwigshaven. The Squadron Commander, Wing Commander Ian Hamilton, D.S.O.,D.F.C., led the Squadron on an attack on the oil refineries at Bottrop, defended by intense flak, when over 100 searchlights were seen. It was on this operation that the Squadron lost one of its most popular crews – Flight Lieutenant Ordell, R.A.A.F. and his Australian crew. What was probably Bomber Command's most effective raid of the war took place on the night of the 13th|14th February when it opened 'Operation Thunderclap' – attacks on targets in Eastern Germany agreed by Churchill, Roosevelt and Stalin. Wing Commander Brookes writes:

"The Squadron offered 19 aircraft for an attack on Dresden, now an important evacuation centre for Government departments from Berlin and a vital point for the transportation of troops to the Eastern Front." Quoting the Squadron Operations Record Book he goes on:
'Our aircraft, 18 of which finally took off, attacked on the second wave and found fires still burning as a result of the earlier raid by No. 5 Group. Marking was satisfactory and the Master Bomber had complete control of the attack throughout. All our crews bombed on definite instructions and, in the opinion of experienced crews, the whole effort was the best in which they had participated for a long time. The glow of the fires was visible for over 200 miles on the return journey. Photos, including colour pictures, confirmed their optimism showing intense fires over the whole of the city. One aircraft was lightly damaged by flak over Germany on the homeward trip but none of the others had any adventures at all apart from four which had to land away from base through shortage of fuel. A very successful trip. "Crews were now even confident enough to dismiss the threat posed by Me 163 and Me 262 jet fighters." (But they still had a healthy respect for flak! Ed.)

796 aircraft had attacked Dresden in two separate waves. On the 23rd February half that number created proportionally more havoc on Pforzheim when 83% of the town was destroyed although this attack, probably the most effective single raid of the war, received but a fraction of the publicity of the other two raids.

Pforzheim lay midway between Stuttgart and Karlsruhe, both heavily defended cities. At briefing its importance was described as being the centre of production of precision instruments. 100 Squadron was amongst No. 1 Group Lancasters to open the attack at 20.00 hrs.,after the Master Bomber had brought the force down to 8,000ft. One navigator described the scene a minute or so before the attack opened:
"Ahead and below I saw a perfect circle of yellow flares like a golden

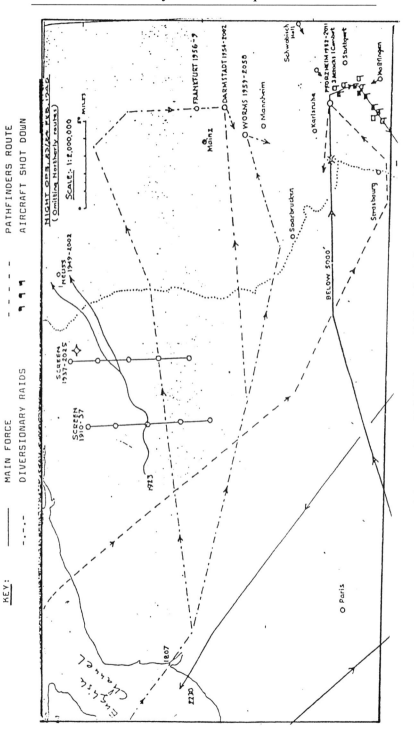

Night operations 23/24 February 1945 – Pforzheim

A Glimpse into Hell
Two Lancasters over Pforzheim, 23rd February 1945
(Note cascades of glowing target indicators)
*I. W. M.*

ring ringing the town and, within seconds, a cluster of green target indicators started to go down into the centre."Within twenty minutes the town was virtually annihilated at the cost of twelve Lancasters. For most crews Pforzheim was just another 'op' out of the way and it was many years before its full significance became known to them.

At some time in the '60s the whole town was bull-dozed away to remain as "The Hill" at the edge of the new town. A German lady, Ursula Moessner, now living in California, researched the raid and said that another reason for its attack was that it lay in the path of advancing American forces. When she heard of the navigator's description of the markers she wrote telling him that Pforzheim was the pre-war centre of the German jewellery industry and the town's symbol, embossed on all official notepaper, was a gold ring.

It was on the Pforzheim raid that Bomber Command gained its last Victoria Cross of the War. Captain Edwin Swales, D.F.C., a South African pilot on No. 582 Squadron, Pathfinder Force, was the Master Bomber responsible for the meticulous marking. He supervised the whole raid despite two attacks by a German night fighter which damaged the rear turret and put two engines out of action. Returning to base in turbulent weather he was eventually unable to maintain height and ordered his crew to bale out but he, himself, left it too late and crashed in Belgium. He was found dead at the controls

Throughout the Spring Bomber Command flew a number of daylight sorties in support of British, Canadian and American forces on various fronts. Sometimes this meant that bomb loads had to be changed at the last minute because an intended target had been overrun by the Allied advance. It was in those circumstances that Waltham armourers, as Fred Butler writes, formed the 'Waltham Yo-Yo Club.' As one lot of bombs was winched down another lot was winched up!

There was more to the armourer's and airframe fitter's job, however, than sheer physical exertion. It was not uncommon for an aircraft to return with damaged hydraulics or electrical circuits and with part or all of its bomb load which it had been unable to jettison. This was the time when the armourer's skill, nerve and courage were stretched to the utmost because the bombs had to come off. Corporal Ken Drury was an airframe fitter with 97 Squadron at Bourn in 1943 and gave the following account of one such incident.

"One day, when I had just bought my tea and a wad, 'Chiefy', Warrant Officer Haines, came up to me and said: 'Ah, Corporal Drury, there's a Lanc at Braintree, an American station. She's boomeranged with a full bomb load and they can't get the bomb doors open so I've volunteered you to get them open so they can remove the bombs.'

'O.K. Chiefy,' I said, 'but why us?' 'Because we are the nearest and they are from up Grimsby way,' he replied.

We set off in a small canvas-topped van, a junior armourer officer and

Flt. Sgt. Bill Greenslade, RCAF, with crew and ground-crew Waltham 1944
Standing far left – Fred Butler of "Yo Yo Club"

*Bill Greenslade*

driver in front and two erk armourers and me in the back. We arrived at the aircraft and the armourers removed the camera flash "bomb" which was housed in a chute at the rear of the 'plane. I accompanied the officer to the bomb aimer's spot in the nose only to find that an attempt had been made to jettison the bomb load of a 4,000 pounder, 500 lb. H.E.s and several cases of incendiaries.

The jettison lever had been forced through the safety gate but the bombs would not drop unless contact was made between the bomb-door micro-switch and the bomb release gear. I was left with the instruction to climb on the main-plane and wave my cap when I had the bomb doors open whilst the rest of the party shot off in the van to the communal site. All American aircraft were out of sight and I was nearly dying of loneliness and fright. There were no oil leaks from the kite so I tried the selector – "bomb doors open" – pumped two or three strokes on the hand pump and broke the hydraulic lock which opened the 33 ft. long bomb doors about an inch.

It was then possible to put your chin up against the fuselage, fingers in the crack and pull the doors open. I was doing this when there was a CRACK! I ran thirty yards at speed and dived into a tractor-made rut in the dried mud and lay there sweating and praying. With no further action or sound from the aircraft I finally made my way back to find a packet of leaflets which the bomb aimer had stuffed through the inspection panel in the bulkhead of his compartment.

Well, I pumped the bomb doors open, making sure I didn't open them to their full extremity because, being ignorant of anything electrical, I didn't want to make any hazardous contact. I then climbed on the mainplane and waved my cap in true Airforce manner.

The team returned and I was taken to the dining hall and given a good meal and I gathered that hundreds of Yankees had been watching from a distance having been told she might well go up. It was then that I recalled, as we left Bourn, Chiefy had said, 'Have a care Corporal!'

The young officer promised to pay for the beer if we got back to Cambridge in time so the MT driver gave us a demonstration of low flying and the officer was as good as his word. The next morning Chiefy came up: 'O.K. yesterday Corporal?'

'O.K. Chiefy.'

'Good! Take the rest of the day off.' "

The tension, implicit in Corporal Drury's story, was relieved by one further incident as he goes on to say:

"On the way back to a Cambridge pub at speed we stopped to pick up a chap I recognised as the "Dame" in Ralph Reader's "Gang Show." He climbed into the van and one of the erks moved off the box containing the camera flash and onto the floor. The speed really put the breeze up our passenger and he soon expressed his concern. I asked him if he was really scared.

'Of course I'm scared,' he said.'You would be if you knew what you are sitting on,' and I told him what it was and that it exploded to light up the bomb strikes. He shot off the box to the other side of the van and the erk said, 'It'll reach thee there mate!' He got out at the next crossroads with the retort: 'You're mad – the lot of you!'"

March opened with an attack on Mannheim followed, on the 2nd, by a daylight attack on Cologne by 858 aircraft. For the previous few months there had been rumours of 'scarecrows' – black, oily explosions amongst the flak – which, crews were led to believe, were an enemy device to simulate exploding bombers and thus deter crews from bombing their aiming points. This raid was filmed by a R.A.F. film unit and subsequently shown on cinema news reels. Part of the sequence shows a pall of thick black smoke described, by the Imperial War Museum, over forty years later, as a 'scarecrow'. By a remarkable coincidence Flight Sergeant 'Poker' Gamble and his wife saw the news-reel at a cinema and he identified his own 'plane on the raid flying between two others just underneath the pall of smoke.

In the mid '80s the writer managed to borrow a copy of the film from the I.W.M. and pointed out the 'scarecrow' to 'Poker'."Scarecrow be damned!" snorted Poker as he watched the film. "That was a Lanc and I had been watching it like a hawk until it disintegrated right in front of my eyes. Half the bloody undercarriage fell just in front of us and it's a miracle it didn't hit us. That Lanc got a direct hit but whether from flak or another aircraft I don't know. One thing's for sure – it wasn't a bloody scarecrow!" (Note. Germany has always maintained that it never had 'scarecrows'. Ed.)

The Americans entered Cologne on the 6th – the same day that the Squadron joined Main Force for the second of the 'Thunderclap' raids on Chemnitz. Kassel, Essen and Dortmund*, which suffered the heaviest attack of the war by 1108 aircraft, followed in quick succession. 100 Squadron suffered its last casualties of World War 2 when Flying Officer Vale and his crew were lost on the final attack on Nuremburg.It is salutary to consider that, even at this late stage of the war, No. 1 Group could lose 24 Lancasters, 10.4% of its force on one target most of the losses, apparently, inflicted by enemy fighters on the way to the target.

"Operation Thunderclap" continued on the 5th March with an attack on the East German city of Chemnitz. The raid was followed, on the 7th, by an attack on Dessau when Flight Lieutenant Hoyle's aircraft was twice attacked by a Ju 88.

The 2nd April, 1945, was a day to remember for 100 Squadron and the villagers of Holton le Clay and Waltham. In mid-afternoon the sound of Merlins could be heard all round the airfield as 24 Lancasters taxied from their dispersals to the perimeter track to form a queue for take-off. Watched by dozens of villagers the Lancasters took off, circled the airfield and, one by one, roared in at low level to 'shoot up' the control tower to the accompaniment of wireless ops firing off Verey cartridges of every colour. In such a manner 100 Squadron said "Farewell" to Waltham, its home for over two, memorable years. The bonds between R.A.F. Grimsby and 100

Squadron, together with a glimpse of the minutiae of Service life, are admirably illustrated in the Station Commander's final Station Bulletin.

[*This was the largest number of aircraft ever despatched and the heaviest tonnage ever dropped (4,851 tons) by Bomber Command on one target in one day.]

### STATION BULLETIN
### No. 21. NOT TO BE TAKEN OFF THE STATION. 31st March,1945
### SPECIAL EDITION
### MESSAGE FROM STATION COMMANDER

It is with the greatest regret that I have to confirm the news that is now general knowledge. The Squadron is moving out on Monday, 2nd April and the Station will close down almost immediately afterwards. Although a care and maintenance party will remain, everyone, except personnel of 5015 Artisan Flight should anticipate early posting and prepare themselves accordingly.

The business of packing up affects everyone. Individually, personnel, particularly Inventory holders, should see that they are properly cleared before leaving the Station. Failure to get your clearance chit signed by the Adjutant causes a good deal of trouble and is likely to result in 664B action where anything is missing. Not only should individuals get their personal affairs shipshape and tidy but Squadron Commanders are under an obligation to see that all their quarters are left clean and in good order. There will be a 'marching out' inspection of every building before it is vacated.

Before saying goodbye I should like to thank everyone on the Station for their whole-hearted loyalty and support. We are disbanding now because we have done our job, and done it so well that the Hun has been broken sooner than anyone ever dared to hope, even a year ago.

I am well aware that many of you, like myself, leave Grimsby with great regrets but, when you go, you can justly take pride in the fact tha t you have made a very real contribution towards the achievements of the Station and thus to win the war.

Where all have done so well it would be invidious to mention any section or person by name but to say goodbye without mentioning the Squadron would be unpardonable.

100 Squadron is a great Squadron because it has the right spirit – a great fighting spirit when on ops and a friendly, co-operative spirit when at home. 100 Squadron has always identified itself with the Station; it has supported the Station in everything; it has encouraged the Station to support it in everything. We are happy to have had 100 as our Squadron and, in saying goodbye, I know I am joined by every member of the Station in wishing it: GOOD LUCK, GOOD BOMBING, AND NO EARLY RETURNS.

To all the others I have been privileged to command during the past year,

I confess I am sorry indeed, to have to leave you before the war is won. I thank you again for good work and your co-operation and sincerely hope fortune favours you in the future.
IAN S. NEWBIGGIN.
G|Captain.

After a day or two to settle into its new home at Elsham Wolds, together with a few training flights, the Squadron took part in the attack on the German naval base at Kiel with some crews detailed to mine the harbour. It was a successful raid with the "Admiral Scheer", "Admiral Hipper" and "Emden" badly damaged. A massive, daylight raid on the naval base at Heligoland on the 18th left the target area "like a crater-pitted moonscape". (Middlebrook & Everitt.)

". . . The approaching bombers must have been seen, or heard, from miles away and hundreds of boats of all shapes and sizes left the island in all directions as the bombers approached. The wakes radiated out like the spokes of a bicycle wheel . . . there was every colour of smoke and flames from the explosions." (Flight Sergeant A. Gamble.)

In keeping with its remit of a generation ago 100 Squadron "kept it going" to the very end joining 350 other Lancasters for the last, major, operation of the war – Berchtesgaden – Hitler's 'Eagle's Nest' and S.S. Barracks. It was symbolic that this, final raid should destroy the last vestige of Nazism which had subjugated Europe for a decade.

### OPERATION MANNA

Between the 26th April and the 7th May the Squadron took part in "Operation Exodus" which repatriated some 75,000 British prisoners of war from Belgium. In the same period an operation was set up to bring relief to the people of Western Holland who were still under the German yoke and, literally, starving to death. This was "Operation Manna".

The winter of 1944|45 had been particularly severe. People ate crocus and tulip bulbs using all their ingenuity to make them more palatable – one method was to cook them in engine oil. Men, women and children roamed the countryside on tyre-less bicycles in an attempt to trade cherished possessions, clothes, linen, blankets, for a few kilos of potatoes. Repeated requests had been made to the German Commander in Western Holland, as early as January to, raise the rations to subsistence level at least. Towards the end of April the Dutch Government in exile, through Churchill, Roosevelt and Eisenhower, managed to arrange a truce so that Bomber Command and the U.S.A.A.F. could drop food supplies in selected areas. The Germans made it a condition that the bombers crossed the coast at 50 feet climbing to 500 feet for the drop.

100 Squadron "Nose Art" (1)
Flt. Lt. Lloyd Davis, DFC, and crew with the Spanish version of "S" Sugar
(Flt. Lt. Lloyd Davies came from Chile and was an instructor in the USA
before joining 100 Squadron)
*George Vickery*

Back: Flg. Off. Bert Sandberg    Flt. Lt. Owen Lloyd Davies DFC    Flt. Sgt.
Vic Vickery
RCAF Bomb Aimer RAF Pilot         RAF Rear Gunner
Front: W. Off. Stan Porter        Flg. Off. Robbie Robinson
RCAF Wireless Operator            RCAF Navigator

● At the time of the unveiling of the statue of Sir Arthur Harris, you were kind enough to publish my letter which drew attention to the Germans who mostly supported the total war waged by the Hitler regime.

It is now ironic that they wish to celebrate the launching of their first V2 (Vergeltungswaffe) rocket which was produced at the cost of thousands of lives of prisoners and slave labourers and resulting in death and destruction to the civilian population in this country.

It is not generally known that we also had a V2 produced in this country by a loyal and dedicated workforce and I had the honour to serve as navigator in the Lancaster Bomber HW V2 (pictured) of 100 Squadron which attacked targets across Germany in 1944/45 from bases in East Anglia.

It seemed appropriate to name our aircraft Vergeltungswaffe (vengeance weapon).
STANLEY C R SAVAGE,
Parkway, Gaywood,
King's Lynn

100 Squadron "Nose Art" (2)
100 Squadron's reply to the "V2"
*Published in "Eastern Daily Press"*

At briefing bomber crews were aghast and angry at the conditions for the drop – at those heights the Lancasters would be sitting ducks for the German defences. It was with some trepidation, then, that crews took off in the new role of 'mercy flyers'. In the event the Germans did not break the truce and "Operation Manna", "Bread from Heaven" caught the imagination of every crew that flew upon it. In addition to packages of flour, dried egg, spam, tinned stew, biscuits, chocolate, coffee and countless other items of foodstuffs and supplies dropped from their bomb bays, crews threw out their own rations of sweets, chewing gum, chocolate and cigarettes. This description by a Squadron crew typifies the 2,000 plus Lancaster "Manna" sorties:

"On the 2nd May we took off in "M-Mike 2" at 11.50 hrs for the 90 minute flight over the North Sea to our dropping point near Rotterdam. It was an exhilerating experience skimming 50 feet over the waves at 150 knots. Crossing the Dutch coast we climbed to 500 feet and, looking down through his perspex 'bulge', the flight engineer could see rifle-bearing German soldiers on the flat roofs watching the procession of Lancs roaring in. As we turned for the dropping zone we just managed to clear a church steeple. On the ground were hundreds of Dutch people cheering and waving flags, handkerchiefs and, even, bed sheets as the Lancs came in low over their heads. The dropping zone was a patch of open country just outside Rotterdam which had been marked by Pathfinder flares. There was time for only one run and we dropped our load and descended to 50 feet again for the flight home. It was a most moving and heart-warming experience."

And so, on the 8th May, came "V.E. Day" – the war in Europe was over but there was still uncertainty about the future as some crews prepared themselves for possible action with "Tiger Force" in the Far East. On the 29th May the Squadron, like many others in Bomber Command, took its ground crews on a "Cook's Tour" of the Ruhr to see some of the devastation they had helped to inflict on Germany. When the euphoria of victory had subsided there was time to examine the balance sheet

One cannot separate the achievements of 100 Squadron, or any other Squadron, from those of Bomber Command as a whole: their collective contribution to the final victory was immense, the Official History calls it "decisive". Equally it is difficult to make comparisons with other squadrons, indeed to do so would be odious. Nonetheless, the records show that in its 25 months of operations in Bomber Command 100 Squadron flew 3,984 sorties on 280 separate raids in which it dropped 18,108 tons of bombs and a large number of mines. On their own these figures do not tell us a great deal viewed in the overall context – Bomber Command Lancasters flew over 130,000 sorties and the whole Command dropped almost one million tons of bombs.

If, however, one assumes that the main offensive began with the Cologne raid in May, 1942, and, comparing 100 Squadron's Lancaster strength with other squadrons, a different picture emerges: on any reckoning, in any "League Table", 100 Squadron emerges, as it did in World War 1, as one of the truly great squadrons. During those twenty five months Squadron personnel were awarded two D.S.O.s, one C.G.M.,94 D.F.C.s, 85 D.F.M.s and one Polish equivalent of the Victoria Cross. The cost was high: 593 young men died; 92 aircraft were lost on operations and a further 21 were destroyed in crashes. [See also Appendix 2. Ed.]

Of more than 7,000 Lancasters built during World War 2 only 28 survived to complete more than 100 operations. 100 Squadron had the remarkable distinction of flying five of these great veterans: EE139 HW-A, 'Phantom of the Ruhr', which completed 121 sorties after "C" Flight was hived off to form 550 Squadron; ND644 HW-N which was lost on Nurenburg on 16th March, 1945, after completing 115 sorties, "F Fox", HW-E "Take it Easy" and ND 458 HW-A, 'Able Mabel'. 'Able Mabel' took Jack Littlewood and

Plt. Off. McQuaid    Flt. Sgt. Nelson                    Flt. Off. Jones
Sqn. Ldr. Scott    Flt. Sgt. Johnson                 Flg. Off. Sanderson
                          Flt. Lt. Harwood

100 Squadron "Centenarians" – "Able Mabel"

Skipper Flt. Lt. Jack Playford shaking hands with Sergeant W. Hearn, NCO i/c Ground Crew.

Left to right: LAC J. Cowls, fitter/airframe; Cpl. R. Withey, fitter; Sgt. Hearn; Flt. Lt. J. Playford DFC, RCAF; LAC J. Robinson, fitter/engines; A. C. J. Hale, fitter/engines. "Able Mabel" completed 132 operations

his crew through a complete tour in 1943 and, a year later, was cherished by Flight Lieutenant Jack Playford, R.C.A.F. and his crew who took it on its 100th operation to Ludwigshaven. 'Able Mabel' went on to complete 132 operations and ended her days at Bomber Command Instructors' School in 1947.

Almost fifty years later, little remains of 100 Squadron's 'home' at

100 Squadron "Centenarians"
EE139 "Phantom of The Rhur"
100 Squadron shares the honours with "Daughter Squadron", 550.
"Phantom of the Ruhr" completed 121 operations.
*Roland Hardy*

Waltham: a crumbling control tower, dilapidated 'Ops' Room, an old hangar, a few broken huts and cracked, pot-holed runways gradually succumbing to weeds and grass. Where airmen once lived and laughed there are now modern bungalows. Soon there will be workshops and, even, a golf course. Yet, just beyond the end of the old short runway, there is a simple granite memorial, erected by the Royal Observer Corps. It is set in a small patch of land bordering the A 16 near the point where 'they used to close the road when the Lancs were taking off.' Holton le Clay Parish Council has adopted the land and planted saplings around the site whilst local villagers have made a little garden around the memorial itself. The people around there think a lot about the Squadron. They have their memories which they have passed down to a third generation and they have private ones – like the mysterious lady who makes her own private pilgrimage to plant a seedling beneath the Squadron Crest.

Another Memorial to the 'Waltham Days' stands at the old guard room

100 Squadron "Centenarians"
"F" Fox – "Press on Regardless"
Another shared honour with 550 Squadron. "F" Fox takes off for Dusseldorf to
complete her century of operations with best wished from RAF and WAAF
personnel at North Killingholme.

entrance to the Station at the other end of the airfield. It takes the form of a
commemorative plaque and was commissioned by Mr. F.W. Bury in 1987.
During the war Fred was a corporal in the Intelligence Section. The
inscription on the plaque reads:
'R.A.F. GRIMSBY (WALTHAM) 1941-1945.
To fight for our freedom and to end the Nazi tyranny, young people from all
over the world came to this airfield to serve and to fly the Wellingtons and
Lancasters of 142 & 100 Squadrons.Over 1,000 brave young men came
through this entrance – never to return. Many more were shot down and
captured.
WE WILL REMEMBER THEM AND SALUTE ALL WHO SERVED
HERE.
F.W.B. 1987.'
    A short walk down the Louth road from the Memorial brings one to "The
Jug and Bottle" – a new pub built on the dispersal site of another Waltham

100 Squadron "Centenarians"
ND644 "N NAN"
Flt. Lt. H. G. Topliss RCAF, shaking hands with Sgt. H. W. Williams NCO
i/c Ground Crew
Left to right: A. C. F. Turrell, fitter/engines; Flt. Lt. Topliss; L. A. C. J.
Atkinson, fitter/engines; Sgt Williams; L. A. C. B. Gorst, fitter/engines.
"Nan" was lost on the Nurenburg raid 16/17 March 1945 after completing 115
operations with 100 Squadron.
*Roland Hardy*

Lancaster, PA 177, HW-J. Jointly flown by Squadron Leader Dave Robb,
R.C.A.F. and Flight Lieutenant Wally Nobes, R.C.A.F.and their crews the
aircraft was named "Jug and Bottle" after the out-sales bar in a Doncaster
pub. The walls in the lounge bar are covered with photographs of 100
Squadron crews and aircraft, 142 Squadron and No. 1 Group airfields in
North Lincolnshire.

For a few years, now, former Waltham flyers have met with villagers
and serving members of 100 Squadron on Remembrance Sunday to join in
the Memorial Service. Weather permitting they are fortunate enough to see
a fly past of 100 Squadron aircraft paying their tribute to their own airmen
of an earlier generation.

The Old and the New
Pub built on dispersan site of "Jug and Bottle"
Sqn. Ldr. D. Robb, DFC, AFC, RCAF (Retd.) and Flt. Lt. Wally Nobes, DFC, RCAF (Retd.)

Photos –

# CHAPTER THIRTEEN

## From Lancasters to Lincolns

The summer of 1945 saw the beginnings of a peacetime contraction of the R.A.F. and hundreds of the much loved Lancasters were gathered at airfields up and down the country to be scrapped within a couple of years. As with the Fe 2B, thirty years earlier, it justifiably merits the accolade that no other aircraft served its country so well as this – the finest bomber aircraft of World War 2.

Back at Elsham Wolds 100 Squadron and its sister squadron, 103, took part in another form of 'Exodus' making a number of flights to repatriate 8th Army forces from Naples. On the 15th December the Squadron moved to Scampton where it began to convert to the Avro Lincoln, the Lancaster's 'big brother'. The Lincoln, a larger and much improved Lancaster, as Wing Commander Brookes describes it, had a maximum speed of 319 mph and a ceiling of 30,500 ft. Over its enhanced range of 1470 miles it could carry a bomb load of 14,000 lbs. Re-equipped with Lincolns the Squadron moved to Lindholme in 1946 from where it took take part in two tours 'showing the flag'.

The first of these was to the Prague Flying Display in September where it competed with its American rival, the B 29 'Super-Fortress'. The newspaper, "Svobodne Noviny", reported:'Sensational starts were made by the biggest existing warplane, the American Super Fortress, and the British Lincoln took the risk to show the public that he can put out three of his four motors and still carry on to fly.'[Shades of Lynn Bell!([Ed.)]

The second tour, to Valparaiso, took place in October. Flight Sergeant Frank Ockerby described the visit: "I joined Squadron Leader Bretherton's crew as wireless operator in October, 1946, and on the 25th boarded Lincoln GB-A bound for Chile for the inauguration of President Gonzales Videla. Canadian born Wing Commander G.J. Bell was in operational control of the three Lincolns and Group Captain Lloyd, officially representing the R.A.F.,also accompanied us. Ground crews flew in each aircraft and spares were carried in the bomb bays.

. . . It was a flight to remember: the Sahara, the wide expanse of the South Atlantic, Copacabana Beach, Sugar Loaf Mountain and the 20,000 ft. peaks of the Southern Andes. I shall never forget the sight of the scuttled

## NO. 100 SQUADRON BATTLE ORDER.
### SERIAL NO. 49.

OFFICER I/C NIGHT FLYING: W/CDR. McINTYRE
AERODROME CONTROL PILOT: SGT. NAIR

| A/C LTR. | A/C NO. | CAPT. | P/2 | NAV | B/A | WO/AG | M.U. GUNNER | R. GUNNER | REMARKS |
|---|---|---|---|---|---|---|---|---|---|
| G | ED 815 | P/O HAWLEY | SGT. BARR | SGT. WANDER | SGT. CRAIK | SGT. WOOD | SGT. CANNINGS | SGT. MEHAR | |
| F | ED 561 | SGT. THURLOW | SGT. PYLE | SGT. THOMPSON | SGT. WALTERS | SGT. JARMAN | SGT. MISNER | SGT. NORMAN | |
| D | ED 973 | SGT. WHITE | SGT. MARTIN | SGT. DOWDELL | SGT. WEST | SGT. BASHFORD | SGT. FRANCISCONE | SGT. SMITH | |
| J | W 4998 | SGT. MOORE | SGT. WILKINS | SGT. STONE | F/O COVENTRY | F/S WOOD | SGT. KEOGH | SGT. MAUNSELL | |
| A | ED 688 | SGT. WILDEN | SGT. TARVER | SGT. COLE | SGT. MATHESON | SGT. AGLAND | SGT. SIMMS | SGT. HARBOUR | |
| H | ED 647 | F/S. CRACKNELL | SGT. DONDALL | SGT. FRECKLETON | SGT. COOK | SGT. HARVEY | SGT. STERICKER | SGT. REILLY | |
| K | ED 991 | W/O. HAYWOOD | SGT. WEEKS | SGT. ELSEY | SGT. MARTIN | SGT. SMITH | SGT. EDWARDS | SGT. B.SSERS | |
| B | ED 556 | SGT. EDWARDS | SGT. FORDER | P/O. MULLINGER | SGT. C.G.DAN | SGT. MALTHOUSE | SGT. HARRISON | SGT. BROCKLEBANK | |
| P | ED 786 | S/LDR.MANAHAN | SGT. LONGSTER | P/O. COLLINS | SGT. McVITTY | SGT. MITCHELL | SGT. WATTS | SGT. MARTIN | |
| U | ED 583 | P/LT. McGRATH | SGT. WILKIE | P/O WRIGHT | F/O JOHNSON | P/O FACEY | SGT. PROCHERA | SGT. AITKEN | OPENT |
| N | ED 562 | SGT. SLATER | SGT. SINCLAIR | SGT. JOHNSON | SGT. BROWN | SGT. FAIRCLOUGH | SGT. DAY | F/S. CAMPBELL | |
| Q | LM 349 | SGT. BERRY | SGT. MAGILL | SGT. HOWELL | SGT. BRADBURY | SGT. JOHNS | F/S. EVANS | SGT. WATSON | AS |
| V | ED 750 | SGT. MORGAN | SGT. GILES | P/O JONES | SGT. SHYBA | SGT. WILSON | F/S. PAQUETTE | F/S. WOODS | |
| O | ED 749 | F/O GERBEROWSKI | SGT. PEARSE | F/O. FLEMING | SGT. PEAKE | P/SGT PERRY | SGT. STEINBERG | SGT. ROBERTS | ORDER |
| S | ED 609 | SGT. McGILL | SGT. COLLINS | F/O. BERG | SGT. BRADLEY | SGT. GLOVER | SGT. LAKE | SGT. STEPHENSON | |
| H | ED 976 | SGT. THOMAS | SGT. VICKERS | SGT. REILLY | SGT. EVANS | SGT. WINN | SGT. HILL | SGT. DAVIES | |
| J | ED 988 | SGT. PRESTON | SGT. CHADWICK | SGT. GARGINI | SGT. NOBLE | SGT. HENRY | SGT. BOLTON | SGT. FIDLER | |
| C | LM 320 | S/LDR. TURGEL | SGT. WINN | B/O. PETTS | P/O. RUSSELL | P/O. MARNOCH | P/O. HARVEY | SGT. HUDSON | |
| H | ED 705 | F/LT. HOWGILL | SGT. HOWE | SGT. BEST | SGT. CHRISTIE | SGT. FOX | SGT. R.VEN | SGT. GARDNER | |
| A | ED 821 | SGT. TOWNROW | P/O. FITCHETT | P/O. BISHOP | P/O. SHORT | P/O. BOLDERSON | SGT. COSGROVE | P/L. MURPHY | |
| D | LM 317 | SGT. FLETCHER | SGT. CLARKE | SGT. FRANEY | SGT. COOPER | SGT. JACKSON | SGT. MANWEATHER | SGT. McCRAE | |
| E | ED 362 | F/S. NAILE | SGT. CONNAH | SGT. MERSTEAD | P/O. REYNOLDS | SGT. DILLON | SGT. PORRITT | SGT. BENNET | |
| G | W.4999 | SGT. PICKLES | SGT. MARSHALL | P/O. CRUM | P/O. BLACKIE | SGT. MITTON | SGT. MACKIE | SGT. FORSHER | |
| F | W.4989 | SGT. T - ROOKE | P/O ENSOR | F/O. CRAWFORD | SGT. HILTON | SGT. LAMBERT | SGT. STANDFIELD | SGT. ROGERS | |
| F | 553 | SGT. SMITH | SGT. BROWNLOW | SGT. GLADMAN | SGT. BRADBURY | SGT. TANDY | SGT. SPENCE | SGT. BROWN | |

¶ TO DISPERSALS AFTER LANDING
1700 GALLONS.
" MAXIMUM EFFORT"

The Squadron put up 25 Lancasters for
Dortmund. 23rd May, 1943.

| | |
|---|---|
| MAIN BRIEFING................................ | 1700 hours |
| NAVIGATORS AND BOMB AIMERS BRIEFING.......... | 1730 hours |
| TRANSPORT TO COMMUNAL SITE................... | 1550 hours |
| OPERATIONAL TEA.............................. | 1330 hours |
| TRANSPORT FROM COMMUNAL TO TECHNICAL SITE.... | 2000 hours |
| TRANSPORT CREWS TO AIRCRAFT.................. | 2115 hours |

R. V. McINTYRE
Wing Commander Commanding, 100 Squadron.

German warship, Admiral Graf Spee, in the River Plate. We were given a wonderful reception and enjoyed the hospitality of many British families in Santiago. Thousands of Chileans were shown over the Lincolns and, on the 8th November, we provided an air display over the Chilean and American fleets in Valparaiso harbour.

The splendour of colours and uniforms at the President's inaugural ball outshone any Hollywood production and other brilliant functions were held at the Santiago British Legion and the Prince of Wales Club. We began our return flight on the 12th and arrived back at Lindholme on the 19th having covered 20,000 miles on the tour in 80 hours flying time."

From November, 1946, until March, 1950, when it moved to Waddington, the Squadron was based at Hemswell taking part in Group and Command bombing and training exercises. These included cross country flights using astro-navigation, bombing practice at various ranges and fighter affiliation for the benefit, apparently, of Meteor crews. There were also exercises with

A Lincoln crew after a sweep of the Malayan Jungle
Left to right: Flt. Sgt. R. Sacree; Sgt. K. Reakes; Flt. Lt. J. Mackay (Signals Leader); AVM Wragg (AOC); Wg. Cdr. R. Jell, DFC (Squadron Commander); Flt. Lt. J. Richards (Engineer Leader); Flt Lt. H. Lister (Navigation Leader); Flt. Lt. T. Chandler DFC (Radar Bombing Leader)
*Wg. Cdr. R. Jell DFC, AFC, RAF (Retd.)*

the Royal Navy using H2S 4a to show that the bombers would be able to pick them out. Shortly afterwards a detachment of three Lincolns joined 57 Squadron at Tengah, Singapore, for 'Operation MUSGRAVE', the war against Communist rebels in Malaya. After three weeks of strikes against the rebels, during which the detachment gained experience of the tactics, the rest of the Squadron arrived from Waddington and 57 Squadron returned to the U.K. At this time the Squadron was commanded by Squadron Leader Danny O'Brien who handed over to Squadron Leader Ronnie Jell in July. From Wing Commander Jell, DFC, and Flight Lieutenant Barnie Collen, DFM, we have a detailed account of the operations in Malaya.

Concealed in camps in the featureless jungle Malayan 'bandits' would make forays against plantations, road and rail communications and ambush the ground forces of the British Army. The original technique, to flush out the bandits, was for the Squadron to fly in a box formation with a lead aircraft putting down smoke bombs for the main formation to bomb some two minutes later. The target areas were determined by the Army and Police beforehand and crews were briefed by an Air Liaison Officer of the 'Black Watch'.Target areas would be surrounded by troops during the attack hence, very precise bombing was essential. Wing Commander Jell improved on this method by changing to a timed run from a precise smoke pin-point provided by the Army – Hampshires and Green Jackets – in forward positions. This removed the need for a lead aircraft's smoke bombs which were replaced by a full load of high explosives. The method worked so well that night operations could also be mounted by using a vertical searchlight instead of the smoke. The only variation from day attacks was for aircraft to attack singly with an "H"-Hour timing on target for each aircraft. As a result of this new mode of attack operational manuals for jungle warfare were amended accordingly.

The bombing kept the enemy on the move and they now found it was they who were walking into ambushes laid by the surrounding troops. On some occasions individual crews were given solo strikes. Flight Lieutenant Collen described one occasion when he and his crew were briefed 'to destroy anything that could be associated with the enemy.' After delivering single bombs from minimum height they dropped down to examine the results and repeated the process until they had hit the target.Following the bombing attack the aircraft would fly over at low level with the gunners strafing the jungle.

Another 'hairy' operation was the nightly escort of trains, from Singapore to Kuala Lumpur, which had been frequent targets for the Communists. "As the train entered 'Bandit country' a 100 Squadron Lincoln would start the sequence by dropping flares ahead at regular intervals. When the Lincoln had exhausted its supply of flares another Lincoln, from No. 1 Australian Squadron, would take over and continue until the train was out of the danger zone." (Flight Lieutenant Barnie Collen). On one occasion Barnie's wireless operator, Di Sacree, picked up an S.O.S. from an Australian Lincoln where

"Bombs Away" – over the Malayan Jungle 1950
*Flt. Lt. Collen DFM, RAF (Retd.)*

"In the Box" – Malaya 1950
*Flt. Lt. Collen DFM, RAF (Retd.)*

a flare had jammed in the fuselage and was burning away aft of the H2S. With the aid of Di's WT link the Australian crew landed safely at Tengah.

On daylight sorties crews always returned to Tengah at low level and 'buzzed' the homes of the plantation managers en route – a great morale boost for the managers. When able to get away to Singapore for a few days leave some managers would attend Mess parties and express their appreciation of the sight of friendly aircraft in the remoteness of their up-country homes.

High temperatures and thunderstorms made flying dodgy at the best of times when every ounce of power was needed to get a fully laden Lincoln airborne. On one occasion Flight Lieutenant (then Flight Sergeant) Collen's port inner engine cut out at lift off.

"His skill enabled him to hold the aircraft straight and to build up speed at very low level and, subsequently, to climb and join up with the formation orbiting base . . . Landing back on three, after a successful operation, was no less difficult compounded by high temperature, thunderstorms and only one runway out of wind. It was a complete demonstration of crew courage, skill and devotion to duty to be worthy of full and lasting recognition."

"On a Strafe" – Malayan Jungle 1950
*Flt. Lt. Collen DFM, RAF (Retd.)*

(Wing Commander R. Jell). Flight Sergeant Collen was awarded the D.F.M.

During its six months in Malaya the Squadron made over 100 attacks and dropped over 2,000 tons of bombs on the bandit infested jungle. Wing Commander Jell paid tribute to the high morale of the Squadron at Tengah and was particularly proud of an average serviceability rate of 98% in an adverse tropical climate far away from U.K. main servicing and supplies – yet again, a tribute to the ground crews. The Squadron returned to Waddington in January, 1951, and was specially photographed for an article in "Tatler" and Wing Commander Jell received a M.I.D. For the next sixteen months the Squadron took part in more Command and Group night bombing exercises and in May, 1951 it was despatched overseas again, to Shallufa in the Suez Canal Zone.

After the overthrow of King Farouk in a military coup led by General Neguib, Egypt became politically unstable and the new dictator made threats to British occupancy of the Suez Canal Zone. Air Vice Marshal Sir Hugh Lloyd, C-in-C Bomber Command, visited Waddington and announced that 83 Squadron would take 100 Squadron's fully serviceable and up to date Lincolns to Egypt within seven days. Wing Commander Jell protested in the strongest possible terms but was told to mind his own business. However, two days later, the order was rescinded and, four days after that, 100 Squadron proceeded to Egypt for "Operation ALACRITY."

On arrival at Shaluffa the Squadron found the runways covered in sand, there were no support facilities, no N.A.A.F.I. or Padre and a doctor was bussed in as required. The control tower contained a pack R|T set operated by an officer and air traffic assistant sent to see the Squadron in. Wing Commander Jell's first task was to keep up morale and keep everybody busy. To these ends he flew aircraft to collect mail from BFPO and instituted an 'aircraft cleaning competition' in the endless battle against sand. The winning crew had the assistance of a Company of the African Rifles the following week which put the prize for the cleanest aircraft further beyond the reach of other crews! This was so effective that when the Squadron eventually returned to Waddington its Lincolns were the cleanest on the Station!

The Squadron's brief, should military operations occur, was to provide air cover for the Second Infantry Brigade by taking out any points of resistance and Egyptian Army barracks in the path of an Army move on Cairo. In the event the situation didn't develop. Wing Commander Jell also received a visit from the A.O.C. 204 Group, Air Vice-Marshal David Atcherly, who flew into Shallufa in his Meteor. The A.O.C. told him the Navy were worried about the coastal guns covering Alexandria and asked for plans to be made to eliminate them. Air Vice Marshal Atcherly then boarded his 'plane, took off for Nicosia and was never seen again. The Squadron made a continous search of his route at low level but no trace was ever found.

The Squadron's three months detachment to Shallufa was extended to

100 Squadron at Eastleigh, Nairobi 1954
Photo – Squadron Leader G. M. Bailey AFC, RAF (Retd.)

five during which it made many training flights and dummy runs on the barracks at Heliopolis and the guns at Alexandria. It seems like a re-run of the Waltham "Yo-Yo Club" as the unfused bombs were unloaded from a trip to Heliopolis and winched up again for another visit to Alexandria. Relief from the 'attractions' of Shallufa, where everywhere seemed to be out of bounds, came with the treat of a trip to Cyprus laden with ground crews. On one occasion the Squadron was "raided" by Vampire pilots from Deversoir who raided the store and and stole the Squadron's flag. The Squadron retaliated the following day when three Lincolns 'bombed' their base with toilet rolls just before their A.O.C.s inspection. "This action quickly drew a surrender telephone call from their Station Commander and our flag was ceremoniously returned together with a case of whisky." (Wing Commander Jell.)

One of Wing Commander Jell's last duties, before he handed over command of the Squadron to Squadron Leader Alexander, D.F.C., was to select the Battle Honours for the Squadron Standard although it was to be another four years before the Standard was presented to Squadron Leader Kunkler. On the 15th July, 1953, six Squadron aircraft led the fourth formation of Lincolns in the Queen's Birthday Fly Past at Odiham and, a month later, the Squadron moved to Wittering.

January 1954 brought another overseas detachment for "A" Flight to Kenya where it was based at Eastleigh, Nairobi, to take part in strikes against the Mau Mau terorists. During the next two months 53 attacks were made over strips of heavily wooded country which shielded Mau Mau hideouts. Wing Commander Brookes describes the method of attack:'A pair of Lincolns would rendezvous with a marker aircraft known as "Eagle Red" which would then pin-point targets "1" and "2" with either air or ground markers and the first Lincoln would deposit ten 500 lb. bombs on each. "Eagle Red" then marked targets "3" and "4" for the benefit of the second Lincoln and, afterwards, both bombers would carry out low level strafing runs using front and rear turrets. If the targets were adjacent, both Lincolns would fly over together to widen the area of destruction. On one occasion Flight Sergeant Collins received the D.F.M. for retaining formation, despite the sudden loss of two engines, until the bombing run was complete. All these attacks were known to have caused considerable casualties and were instrumental in breaking up large bands into small, ill-organised groups. A Mau Mau simi knife now hangs in the Squadron crew-room as a memento of these times.'

Within weeks of returning from Kenya the Squadron began to re-equip with the Canberra B2. It was the end of the piston age and the dawn of a new era.

# CHAPTER FOURTEEN

## Jets

The writer first saw an English Electric Canberra at a Yorkshire airfield in the early '50s. It was parked at its dispersal, partly concealed from the road by a row of trees. Painted black it gave an impression of sleek, powerful – even wicked – deadliness. Over thirty years later he saw a whole squadron of them painted in standard camouflage and was treated to a flying display which still demonstrated this aircraft's power but, also, gave a sense of beauty and versatility one would never associate with a bomber.

Conversion from Lincolns to Canberras at Bassingbourne took three months and the Squadron was back at Wittering and operational for the

A modified "AV" Canberra, Wittering – mid-50s
*Flt. Lt. J. P. Barker RAF (Retd.)*

Air/Sea Rescue trials, Wittering – mid-50s
1 & 2 Shackleton arrives and releases airborne lifeboat

3 Down she goes . . .

4. Paddling for it!

5 Heave to!

6 All aboard!

7 Sailing home!

Duke of Edinburgh's visit in July, 1954. For the crews concerned the change over must have seemed traumatic. Gone were the wireless operators, bomb aimers, flight engineers and gunners of the Lancaster and Lincoln days leaving only selected pilots and navigators to man the new aircraft. The Official Records stated: "The Squadron is a Main Force Squadron of Bomber Command selected, equipped and manned for trials work with the Bomber Command Development Unit." but in effect the Squadron was really a trials unit performing whatever Canberra test flying was required by the B.C.D.U., which was also based at Wittering.

Squadron Leader H.B. Hunt, DSO ,DFC, AFC, who succeeded Squadron Leader Alexander, DFC, did not allow his men to consider themselves in any subordinate role. He continually reminded them that 100 Squadron was an integral part of Bomber Command and that its work with BCDU was of the utmost importance to the Command as a whole. The Canberra was the first of, what would be, an all jet bomber force and would soon be followed by the Vickers Valiant "V" bombers of 138 Squadron at Wittering.

In 1955 the Bomber Command Armament School was also re-located at Wittering to cater for the 'special weapon requirements' of the new "V" Force. One example of the Squadron's trials work was the determination of 1,000 lb. GP bomb behaviour on release. The higher speeds of the jets led to unpredictable ballistic characteristics causing unacceptable bombing errors and a few seconds delay following the activation of the bomb release. Trials to iron out these problems took place over Heligoland where hundreds of bombs were dropped singly or in clusters of six until German objections finally ended the tests.

Another important set of trials was the development of aircraft flight patterns to avoid detection by hostile fighter Air Interception (AI) radar. In this context the Squadron operated newly developed, high sensitivity, passive radar receivers and antenna horns mounted in the tail of the Canberras which provided a pictorial display for pilot interpretation. The sensititivity of the receivers was three or four times the effective range of AI detection radar and so it was possible to determine, after a short time, the enemy flight path, take avoiding action and stay out of range.

The trials covered many aspects of Canberra operations including tests to overcome heating problems with the Avons and difficulties with re-starting at altitude; landing trials on snow covered runways and co-operation with night fighters from Coltishall. The photo-sequence illustrates another kind of co-operation with Coastal Command's Air|Sea Warfare Development Unit where a 'ditched' crew in a dinghy had to recover an airborne life-boat dropped, by a Shackleton, and sail it back to port.

Squadron Leader C.P. Kunkler wrote:

"I regret that during my period of command the Squadron did not achieve great heights. This was not because we did not have some first class chaps doing an excellent job, but simply because the Squadron had the role of the Bomber Command Development Unit and one did not compete with the glamour boys of the Command with high bombing scores etc." (Quoted by Wing Commander Brookes.) Nevertheless, if individual crews make up a team called a squadron, individual squadrons – whatever their role – make up the team of Bomber Command. This was best illustrated by the Commander of a Station which was the home of a Tornado squadron in the '80s when he said:

"If it wasn't for 100 Squadron we wouldn't be able to do our job." At that particular time the Squadron was engaged in a training facilities role with Strike Command and N.A.T.O. forces – still flying Canberras!

The Squadron's big day came, after a very long wait, on the 21st October, 1955, when it finally received its Standard for which it had actually qualified, after 25 years service, in 1943. The Standard was presented by Air Marshal Sir George Mills, K.C.B., D.F.C., the AOC-in-C Bomber Command. Sir George, in fact, had served with 100 Squadron between 1927 and 1929 – back in the Horsley days at Spitalgate and Bicester. The Battle Honours represented on the Standard were: Ypres 1917, Somme 1918, Independent Force and Germany 1918, Malaya 1941-1942, Fortress Europe 1943-1944, Ruhr 1943-1945, Berlin 1943-1945 and Normandy 1944. Other Battle Honours, not depicted on the Standard are: Biscay Ports 1943-1945, German Ports 1943-1945, Baltic 1943-1945, France and Germany 1944-1945 and Walcheren.

Regretting that he was unable to attend the Standard Presentation Ceremony Lord Trenchard wrote to Squadron Leader Kunkler:

"I look upon 100 Squadron almost as one I have been in myself. I seem to have been connected with the Squadron most of my service life and I always remember the good work done by members of it."

It was in this period that the Wittering Wing received the Freedom of the Borough of Stamford and 40 and 100 Squadrons began to carry the blue and gold chequers of the Stamford coat of arms on the tail fins. 100 Squadron retained the chequer-board until the very end of the Canberra era but it still, proudly, displays the skull and cross-bones. At some later date, probably in the mid '80s, some enterprising flyer invented the 100 Squadron cocktail which also commemorates the Stamford colours. It consists of Blue Bols floating on top of a raw egg. For the more squeamish the egg can be substituted by Advocaat!

More changes came in 1956 when Valiant squadrons arrived at Wittering. In August 100 Squadron was divided into a Trials Flight at Wittering and a Reconnaissance Flight at Wyton. The former continued its work with B.C.D.U. flying Canberra B 2s, 6s and B (I)8s; the latter operated the long-range Canberra PR7s, with crews drawn mainly from the disbanded 82 (PR) Squadron, in preparation for high-level meteorological work for the forthcoming hydrogen bomb tests at Christmas Island in the Pacific. In March, 1957, four PR7s were sent out to the Pacific to join detachments from 58 and 76 Squadrons where they were to provide daily met reports for the Station Meteorological Officer. Later, air-burst photography and

100 Squadron Canberras over Wittering 1955
*Squadron Leader G. M. Bailey AFC, RAF (Retd.)*

100 Squadron receives its Standard
The Standard Parade at RAF Wittering 21st October 1955
*Squadron Leader E. Brewin RAF (Retd.)*

collection of air samples were added to their tasks. "D" Day for this momentous occasion was 15th May, 1957. From Squadron Leader John Clubb RAF(Retd.) and "Christmas Island Cracker" by Air Vice-Marshal Wifred Oulton, we have been able to gather more details of the hazards of this operation.

The aircraft were specially equipped for the task of navigating long distances over the bare expanse of the Pacific Ocean using 'Green Satin' navigation which worked on the Doppler principle but the drawback of the system was its failure to "lock on" when surface winds were calm. With the Decca system closed down for part of the operations this could cause serious problems. The aircraft also carried long range HF radio, radio compass and side facing F.24 cameras.

The Met role was to fly pre-drop sorties twelve hours and four hours beforehand and one near Valiant take-off time to calculate wind velocities between 40,000 and 50,000 feet downwind of the drop zone. The 'bonus task' was to determine wind velocities, air temperatures and cloud cover at the Valiant's bomb release height of 45,000 ft. The wind data was used to predict fall-out patterns and to feed into the Valiant's bomb-aiming equipment. An added photographic task after bomb release entailed the pilot trying to fly level with his eyes closed carrying out flat turns at 25 second intervals in order to keep the fixed camera pointing in the right direction during the early stages of the development of the cloud. In true navigator fashion Squadron Leader Clubb writes that the pilots flew more accurately with their eyes shut than with them open! The method of setting up the fixed camera was devised by Brian Cocker, one of the young pilots, who, sadly, died in a mid-air collision on 13th June, 1957. The camera was aimed by sighting along two chinagraph marks on the canopy. Another task involving 76 Squadron was to fly through the mushroom cloud to collect air samples in special wing-tip containers which were swiftly relayed back to the U.K. This was the task of 58 Squadron who were the couriers and were posted along the route home in order to get the air samples to Aldermaston as quickly as possible. "The atomic clouds looked a thousand times more frightening than any cumulo-nimbus I have ever seen." (Squadron Leader Clubb.)

This pattern of operations was followed throughout the series of tests but it was nothing like as straight-forward as it appears. Torrential rain flooded runways where the water level had to be checked by a Land Rover before the aircraft could take off. From "Christmas Island Cracker" we learn that strong turbulence and icing were encountered in climb and descent in both cloud and clear air with temperatures below -70 degrees C. Squadron Leader Clubb also writes of one occasion when a mission had to be aborted when cumulo-nimbus was encountered at 52,000 feet with air temperatures of -80 degrees C.The extreme cold often caused engine surge or 'flame out' which could also occur with a small, abrupt change in aircraft attitude. On one occasion large ice

Britain's First "H" Bomb Test
Christmas Island
15th May 1957
*Sqn. Ldr. G. M. Bailey AFC, RAF (Retd.)*

crystals damaged both engine's impeller blades necessitating a double engine change.

A radio failure almost brought disaster to Squadron Leader Hammatt, Officer Commanding the 100 Squadron detachment, returning from a 6½ hour Met sortie to the Carolines. Flying on instruments in, or above, cloud for 80% of the time he and his navigator found that the radio compass was out of action, probably because of the intense cold, when about 500 miles from base. They also found they couldn't contact base on VHF because, with hindsight, of a radio blind spot below and behind the Canberra, but the main factor was the temporary shut down of the high-powered VHF transmitter on Christmas Island for maintenance. The transmitter had been replaced by a stand-by which was only suitable for local flying. By sheer chance Squadron Leader Hammat heard a 76 Squadron aircraft on the R|T. Group Captain Giles, Officer Commanding Flying Wing, was just taxiing out for some local flying when he heard the PR7's transmissions and appreciated the problem immediately and took off in pursuit of the aircraft.

To conserve fuel Squadron Leader Hammat shut down one engine and, through contact with Group Captain Giles,eventually picked up a weak signal from ground control – 200 miles away. He glided down from 40,000 ft. and arrived over Christmas Island at 4,000 ft. with just over 800 lbs of fuel remaining. Squadron Leader Hammatt reported: "After landing we checked the navigation plot but failed to locate the 'lost' 300 miles. I think, that in flight, we had met a southerly jet stream or very strong wind at a time during which 'Green Satin' had unlocked perhaps without showing the red indicator light warning the operator to switch to manual operation."

On returning from 'sample collection sorties' the aircraft taxied to the decontamination centre and the containers were immediately packed into heavy lead cannisters and loaded into the bomb bay of a waiting Canberra for immediate despatch to England. The crews, themselves, were carefully extracted making sure they did not touch the outside of their aircraft. They were then stripped, thoroughly showered, dressed in fresh clothing and checked by Geiger to ensure they were clean of any contamination. The aircraft were washed down with high pressure hoses which stripped off the barrier paint and the engine intakes and turbines received similar treatment. The effluent was carefully disposed of to avoid later contamination of personnel.On one occasion a young member of the decontamination squad had a most traumatic experience. Taking over from a colleague he had misunderstood instructions regarding the part of the wing that had been cleaned and carried on, as he thought, from where the other had left off. When he returned to decontamination he was shocked to discover that the Geiger counter 'went off the clock' in the vicinity of his bottom! He had to submit to repeated scrubbings of his nether regions before he received the "All clear". Waiting for his equipment to continue the decontamination process he had rested on the untreated part of the wing and then re-washed the rest of it.

Canberras of 58 and 100 Squadrons also had the task of flying the samples back to the U.K. Within minutes of the cannisters being loaded after the first test a 58 Squadron PR7, WT503, crewed by Flight Lieutenants Taylor and Bruce-Smith,took off on the first leg to Hickam in Hawaii closely followed by Flight Lieutenants Langdon and Batchelor of 100 Squadron in WT 504. The latter were to act as back-up in case of problems at Hickam. After refuelling 503 took off for the 5½ hour leg to Travis, San Francisco. Waiting at Travis, to take over for the next two legs were Flying Officers Marman and Evans and another 58 Squadron Canberra, WT 790, crewed by Pilot Officer Loomes and Flying Officer Montgomery acted as reserve aircraft.

The next leg took them to Namao, Edmonton, where 503 rapidly refuelled and left for Goose Bay. There was a delay in refuelling the second aircraft resulting in Loomes and Montgomery taking off half an hour later. The first aircraft made the 4½ hour flight without incident only to find that the weather forecast received en route was old and inaccurate and that Goose Bay was closed in by a heavy snow storm. Communication with Goose Bay was difficult but Flying Officer Marman managed to let down through thick cloud on the beacon when G.C.A. picked him up for the final approach. Three times he was lost by G.C.A. and, by now experiencing severe icing and with insufficient fuel to reach the alternative at Seven Islands, he made a fourth attempt. Taking his aircraft below the normal limit, in heavy snow, Marman sighted the runway and landed safely. The aircraft was quickly refuelled and the next 'slip crew' took off to deliver the samples in the U.K. within the required time.

Meanwhile, Loomes and Montgomery had arrived over Goose Bay but the weather had deteriorated further into blizzard conditions. Again, three approaches were made with no success and, overshooting from a fourth attempt, nine miles beyond the runway, the aircraft crashed into the muskeg killing both crew members instantaneously.

On their return from the Pacific 100 Squadron Reconnaissance Flight handed over its Canberras to 58 Squadron whilst the Trials Flight continued its development work with new equipment and techniques. At that time the Squadron shared Wittering with a Valiant Squadron but much of the trials work was carried out in development work for the "TSR2". Flight Lieutenant J.P. Barker, R.A.F. (Retd.) described some of the Squadron's tasks in this field with modified Canberras.

At this stage of the 'Cold War,' another period of measures and counter-measures, new tactics and bombing patterns had to be devised which entailed penetrating at 250 ft. in an attempt to get below enemy radar. One method known as 'Low Altitude Bombing' (LAB) or 'Toss' bombing entailed releasing the bombs in a 50 degree dive pulling out in a half roll into the opposite direction. A variation of this was to go in low and release the bombs in a vertical climb and "toss the bombs over the shoulder". No doubt this was most exhilerating for the crews concerned but it also could be very 'hairy'! The Squadron was also involved in radar bombing trials for the TSR2 but, although hundreds of millions of pounds were spent on the TSR2, it never went into production. Nevertheless the Squadron's work was not wasted. The new techniques would later prove valuable to the new "V" Force and, later still, to the Tornados. These few examples of trials work with BCDU give an insight into the importance of 100 Squadron's contribution to the security and defence of Britain and, although it worked behind the scenes, it certainly was not in a 'backwater'.

Off duty the "100 Squadron Boys" have always shown initiative: we have heard of World War 1 flyers popping off in an Fe 2 B for a pint with American news-men; it was 'old hat' in World War 2 to leave muddy foot-prints on the Mess ceiling; bicycle races were held on the flat roofs at Shallufa and we hear of 'Jousting contests at Wittering in which opposing contestants mounted on bicycles, charged at each other wielding broom-sticks. However, the incident which demolished a Nissen hut was not deliberate. Gathered together for a Poker game one cold winter's night the players couldn't get the wood-burning stove to function – until someone soaked the wood in petrol!

As the youngest officer it was Flight Lieutenant J.P. Barker's duty to parade the Squadron Standard through Stamford to St. George's Chapel where it was laid up when the Squadron was disbanded on 31st August 1959. It was to be over two and half years before the Squadron was to take to the air again: when it did, it was in its well proved role as one of the R.A.F.s strategic bomber squadrons in Strike Command flying another Handley Page aircraft, the Victor B2.

# CHAPTER FIFTEEN

## The "V Force" Era

The post-war years can generally be described as the period of the "Cold War" with the major industrial nations divided between the communist East and the capitalist West. In military terms this led to the formation of two opposing alliances known as "The Warsaw Pact" countries of Eastern Europe, dominated by the Soviet Union, and the "North Atlantic Treaty Organisation" – N.A.T.O. – in which the United States and Canada joined with thirteen States of Western and Southern Europe in a defensive alliance. The central feature of this period was the enormous build up of nuclear weapons by both sides. There was a progression from atom bombs to hydrogen bombs, with 'conventional delivery' by long range bombers, to inter-continental ballistic missiles which could obliterate whole cities within minutes of being launched.It is true that the 'temperature' of the "Cold War" varied considerably in the forty years or so after the end of World War 2 with periods of 'peaceful co-existence' and 'detente' leading, in the late '80s, to limited disarmament and, finally, to the break up of the Warsaw Pact itself.

To many people the '60s were the 'Roaring Sixties' – the 'Beatles' era, a time of 'I'm alright Jack' and a time of 'never having had it so good.' Perhaps this feeling was partly induced by peoples' reaction to the threat of nuclear war. As a forward base for N.A.T.O. Britain was particularly vulnerable and the population in general openly speculated about the practicality of a 'four minute warning'. The basic philosophy of defence against nuclear or conventional attack was the threat of instant retaliation against the aggressor with nuclear weapons. The average man-in-the-street drew some comfort from his knowledge that "we" had a formidable force of "V" bombers, the Victor, Valiant and Vulcan which could inflict an unacceptable level of destruction on a would-be aggressor – the nuclear deterrent.

On 1st May, 1962, 100 Squadron was reformed once more at Wittering, alongside 139 (Jamaica) Squadron, equipped with the Handley Page Victor 2 bomber. It formed part of the R.A.F.s "V" Force which then carried the responsibility for the United Kingdom's Strategic Nuclear Deterrent and provided the major part of the U.K.'s contribution to N.A.T.O.s Retaliatory Strike Plan.

The Victor B 2 had a splendid performance – .93 Mach at well above 40,000 ft. and able to carry up to 35 1,000 lbs. bombs although its principal weapon, from inception, was the free fall nuclear bomb. In 1964, to counter the increasingly dense and formidable air defences of the Warsaw Pact, the Victor was modified to carry the 'Blue Steel' missile, with a much more powerful warhead, which could be launched well away from heavily defended targets. The original, white anti-flash paint was replaced by camouflage on top surfaces, and tactics and training were changed to penetrate enemy defences at 200 ft. – or below.

['Blue Steel' was originally built for the Vulcan and was modified for the Victor. It weighed 16,000 lbs. and was rocket propelled using Hydrogen Peroxide and Kerosene and guided by an inertial navigational system which was updated in flight from the mother aircraft's navigation system. Range at high level was 110 miles and, at low level, 35 miles.]

For the first two years of its new existence the Squadron had its own aircraft and groundcrew but, by the end of 1964, in conformity with Command policy, aircraft and groundcrew were transferred to centralised servicing leaving the flying squadrons with eleven five-man crews. The new policy may have been more economical in manpower but it was not popular and many groundcrew continued a warm association with their former squadrons.

100 Squadron Victor-2 with 'Blue Steel', Wittering 1964
*Air Vice Marshal W. J. Herrington CB. RAF (Retd.)*

The 'modus operandi' of the "V Force" was designed to defeat the threat from a growing inventory of Soviet long range, ballistic missiles targetted against the United Kingdom: it had to ensure that the bombers could get airborne and clear of the effects of nuclear explosions on their airfields in the very limited warning time available from the American Ballistic MIssile Early Warning System (BMEWS), a maximum of 15 minutes, possibly less.[Note.Enemy strategy was designed to remove the threat of retaliation by a first strike against U.K. airfields.(Ed.) Unlike the U.S.A.F., with its B 52s of Strategic Air Command, the R.A.F. did not conduct airborne alert although all "V Force" aircraft were equipped for in-flight re-fuelling."]

To counter a posssible surprise attack each squadron maintained one aircraft and crew on 'Quick Reaction Alert' (QRA) at all times. QRA aircraft were maintained at constant readiness parked close to the end of the runway with groundcrew in attendance: aircrew were rostered on alert duty of two to four days working and living as a team, ready to respond instantly to any emergency. To ensure its effectiveness the QRA force was frequently tested at no notice by Bomber Command Headquarters; there was always an element of inter-squadron rivalry as crews raced to be first in the cockpit, with engines running ready for take off, by day and night.

To reduce the vulnerability of the Force in times of tension, aircraft were dispersed in twos and fours from main bases to specially prepared airfields throughout the U.K. A hostile attack would thus have to take out 40 or 50 airfields to destroy the entire force. Once dispersed, aircraft were positioned on readiness platforms with crews in the cockpit if an attack was thought imminent. The entire force could then be "scrambled" by a single command from the Bomber Controller and all aircraft could be airborne in under two minutes.The "scramble" procedure was often practised and demonstrated to visiting V.I.P.s and Defence Colleges to illustrate its effectiveness. Moreover, if one engine failed to start during the simultaneous start sequence the aircraft would take off on three engines as, indeed, crews were trained to do in a real crisis.

The Alert procedures were tested frequently to check the Station and Squadron recall system and the ability to generate aircraft and weapons to meet the prescribed NATO readiness requirements. This was deterrence at work.

Such was the way of life for the crews of 100 Squadron during this era – periods on QRA, meeting training critereia in the air and on the ground and constant updating and study of each crew's discreet targets which were part of a vast, integrated strike plan involving American bombers, land based missiles and submarine-based systems.

[The problems and risks of re-fuelling with hydrogen peroxide and kerosene, a highly volatile 'cocktail', and then fitting a nuclear warhead are glossed over. In another context AVM Herrington described an occasion on QRA when two days continuous rain short circuited the release for two underwing fuel tanks containing 2800 gallons of kerosene leaving the Victor and its weapon sitting on a lake of aviation fuel. Ed.]

Overseas training flights, where crews serviced their own aircraft, and participation in air displays in the U.S.A., Canada and New Zealand were welcome breaks from the normal routine. Morale was high and crews liked the Victor which provided an excellent weapons platform. In April, 1966, the first live drop of a 'Blue Steel' by an operational squadron was carried out by Flight Lieutenant Austin and his crew over the weapons range in Cardigan Bay. The unarmed missile functioned perfectly and splashed down very close to its target.

In March, 1967, the Squadron achieved the rare distinction of winning the Bomber Command Bombing Competition outright for which Rolls Royce presented a unique silver trophy depicting the "Winged Lady" surmounting a symbolic representation of a bomb and inscribed:

*"FOR EXCELLENCE"*

Circumstances, however, were conspiring against the "V Force" and against the Victors in particular. First, the responsibility for the British Deterrent was transferred to the Royal Navy's Polaris submarines. Second, recurrent fatigue problems with the main spar, brought on by low flying, necessitated a major engineering programme to retain the Victor in front-line service which was no longer justifiable. The aircraft were gradually withdrawn and the Squadron was disbanded on 30th September, 1968.

This brief period of the Squadron's history, unlike much which preceded it, was unspectacular, of necessity unheralded and was dedicated to keeping the peace rather than fighting wars. But at no time has 100 Squadron's role been more critical or demanding on its crews and their families for, if the deterrence which they helped to maintain had failed, the consequences, a third world war, would have been cataclysmic. There would have been no bases for the bombers to come home to.

# CHAPTER SIXTEEN

## The Second Canberra Era

Over three years later, on 1st February, 1972, 100 Squadron re-emerged at West Raynham – the start of the second Canberra era. The story for nineteen of the last twenty years has been about a remarkably beautiful and versatile aircraft which, even in 1972, was 23 years "old". It was flown in a surprising variety of roles by 100 Squadron which was to expand into one of the largest units in the Service. Derek Tuthill* writes that the Canberra was no ordinary aircraft having established 22 FAI world records,some of which still stand: a PR3 won the London – New Zealand Air Race in 1953; a B2 was the first jet aircraft to cross the Atlantic without air – to – air refuelling or an intermediate stop and a Canberra carried film of the Queen's Coronation to the United States – the quickest method of delivery at the time.

On 25th January, 1972, 19 of No. 85 Squadron's 24 Canberras made a farewell fly-past at RAF Binbrook and, during the next few days, moved to RAF West Raynham. On 1st February the Squadron was halved with 12 of its aircraft and 21 aircrew forming the nucleus of the re-emerged 100 Squadron. The only 'new' aircrew were the Commanding Officer, Wing Commander B.M. Burley, two Flight Commanders and one other crew. The Squadron was equipped with the original bomber version of the Canberra, the B2, the trainer T4s and T19s.The latter were B2s modified by the installation of A.I. radar, as T11s, and used for training all-weather fighter crews. Later, with the radar removed, they were designated T19 and used by 85 Squadron as silent targets testing air and ground radar defence units.

*[Squadron Leader Derek Tuthill, RAF (Retd.), who served on the Squadron for a total of twelve years, has carefully researched Squadron records covering the period to 1992 and the author is particularly grateful for his contribution to this section.]

Initially, the two squadrons shared hangar and operations facilities but, with very hard work by aircrew, groundcrew and the Department of Engineering. 100 Squadron moved into its own accommodation on the 8th. On the 23rd February, 55 years to the day since 100 Squadron first came into being, Air Chief Marshal Sir Andrew Humphrey returned the Standard to the Squadron's care.

Flying Canberra B2s and T19s the Squadron operated in pairs for the RAF School of Fighter Control for the training of student fighter controllers. These Practice Interceptions (PIs) accounted for over half of the Squadron's flying whilst much of the remainder was the provision of target aircraft to give live interception experience to student crews of fighter O.C.Us. Wing Commander Brookes describes this role as the provision of realistic opposition for the air defence and radar units of the R.A.F. both at home and abroad. Flight Lieutenant J.A. Barker also refers to deployment in target towing or "playing the enemy" for fighter squadrons at home and abroad with detachments to St. Mawgan, Lossiemouth, Leuchars, Sardinia, Malta and Cyprus. Initially, the banners were 'attacked' by cine-camera guns but, as fighter pilot training progressed, live ammunition was used on the banners being towed 800ft. behind the Canberras. The accuracy of the fighters can be judged by the number of shredded banners!

As the year progressed the Squadron took part in Air Defence Exercises (ADEX) with detachments to Stavanger|Sola in Norway and to Decimonannu, Akrotiri, Leeuwarden and St. Mawgan where banner targets were towed for air-to-air gunnery. In other exercises the Squadron provided the opposition for U.K. and French forces and carried out attacks, simulating missiles or conventional aircraft, on the Royal Navy, United States Navy and the Royal Netherlands Navy – in fact all NATO naval forces. Squadron Leader Tuthill described the evasive tactics of the warships as 'leaving the

100 Squadron Rugby Sevens West Raynham 1973
J. Barker, P. Smith, B. Sands, A. Gebbie
M. Moore, K. Knight (Cap), R. Allison
*J. A. Barker*

Aircrew and Groundcrew Malta detachment, February 1974
*J. A. Barker*

sea criss-crossed in wakes of green and white foam'. These maritime exercises saw the start of an association with Airborne Early Warning (AEW) Shackletons of No. 8 Squadron which was to last for almost two decades. As always there was a price to pay. One crew survived when B2 WH739 struck a hill on final approach in April but, in June 1972, the crew were killed when T19 WJ610 crashed shortly after take-off.

Flight Lieutenant J.A. Barker wrote of the excellent spirit of comradeship at West Raynham under the command of Wing Commander Burley and, from 1974, Wing Commander Harcourt-Smith. On the ground the Squadron's sporting achievements brought esteem when it won trophies for West Raynham's Rugby 7s, Five-A-Side Soccer, Cricket and the Annual Athletics Sports Day events. Social life seems to have been reminiscent of the Waltham days with get-togethers of air and ground crews for darts, beer, barbecues, summer dances and "The Christmas Ball".

This pattern of Squadron operations continued throughout the next two years – the tasks many and various – though there was a 40% reduction in flying for a period following the interruption of oil supplies from the Middle East after the 1973 Arab-Israeli war. There was greater involvement with the AEW Shackletons at Lossiemouth, banner detachments to Akrotiri, to Malta in February, 1974 to provide silent targets for 23 Squadron and to Karup in Denmark operating as the 'enemy' in a major ADEX. In May the Squadron flew a philatelic cover, commemorating the 25th Anniversary of the first flight of the Canberra, which raised over £2,000 for the RAF Museum.

1975 opened with the familiar but demanding round of activities in support of the RAF at home and abroad – detachments co-operating with 8 Squadron and Royal Navy AEW Gannets, provision of communications and navigation assistance for Hunter aircraft in transit between Brawdy and Gibraltar, ADEXes and banner flying. It also participated in the first F4 Armament Practice Camps (APC) with 111 Squadron at Luqa. But this was the year of a major U.K. Defence Review with implications for the RAF in general and for 100 Squadron in particular. 56 Squadron's Canberra Flight in Cyprus was run down: a B2 and a T4 were transferred to 100 Squadron. On the 19th December 85 Squadron merged with 100 and the new unit, under the command of Wing Commander J.D. Harvey, moved to Marham on 5th January, 1976. When 98 Squadron was disbanded its seven Canberra E15s and its flight checking role were absorbed by 100. Thus, by early 1976, 100 Squadron had become one of the largest units in the RAF.

For more than a year the Squadron was accommodated in a collection of ramshackle buildings, fit only for demolition, on the south side of the airfield well away from the main camp and its facilities. Just two days after its move, on the 7th, the Squadron resumed its task flying. The greatly increased number of sorties caused problems for Marham Air Traffic Control accustomed, as it was, to handling the Victor tanker fleet. By the end of February traffic was even heavier with the arrival of 231 OCU and another two E15s from 98 Squadron on completion of its last PLUTO calibration sortie. Five ex-98 Squadron aircrew joined 100 Squadron to provide E15 and flight checking expertise. The E15s originated in the mid 'fifties as the B6 but were modified and operated in Cyprus as B15s. They were further modified with updated navigation and radio equipment for flight checking and designated E15.

June and July saw a detachment to Dharan towing banners for air-to-air gunnery by Lightnings of Nos. 2 and 6 Squadrons of the Royal Saudi Air Force with another detachment based at Luqa, Malta. The main exercise of the year took place in September with the Squadron based at Stornoway. The flying, against NATO shipping is described as "successful and enjoyable although the lack of Scandinavian allowances and the fact that the detachment's sleeping bags had been left at Marham by mistake caused a certain amount of gloom and discomfort."

The Squadron spent another uncomfortable winter in their temporary accommodation but relief came in March with the move into No. 4 Hangar and a modern, purpose-built dispersal nearby. Because of the changes the Squadron's 60th birthday could not be celebrated until May when contact was made with many former members who came along to join in the festivities. Meanwhile the Squadron had a full quota of practice interceptions and ADEXs plus banner detachments in Malta. With the political situation in Malta deteriorating, however, it was becoming clear that the Squadron's days on the island were numbered and matters were not helped when two 100 Squadron groundcrew broke into the Police HQ in Valletta and removed the Maltese flag from the roof. The flag, along with an AEROFLOT sign, made a fine souvenir for their crew-room! At home there was a near-disaster in August when E15 WH 948 caught fire during an air test. The Canberra proved uncontrollable at approach speed and the crew tried to reach the Norfolk coast to eject over the sea. However, the fire spread rapidly and it became necessary to abandon the aircraft near Holt. Fortunately, the crew survived and there were no civilian casualties.

The Squadron "lost" another aircraft at the beginning of 1978 when Canberra T19 WH903 was burnt as part of a fire-fighting demonstration when the Queen visited Marham. Another B2, WJ753, was lost in a spectacular crash whilst landing at Marham yet, miraculously it seemed, all four crew members survived. There were three banner detachments to Malta but, in July, the R.A.F. began its withdrawal from the island. In an attempt to compensate for the loss of this training facility banners were flown from St. Mawgan, Lossiemouth and Marham but success rates were low and it became obvious that an air-to-air firing range in a more amenable climate was necessary. During the summer Marham was closed for run-way re-surfacing and the Squadron operated from the U.S.A.F. reserve airfield at Sculthorpe, half an hour's drive from Marham or four minutes by Canberra. Night flying was, apparently, very popular as the drive back to Marham could include a diversion to the 'Rose and Crown' at Great Massingham.

Wing Commander Peter Le Marquand
Unveils the Squadron Memorial at Holton Le Clay, 7th November 1978

The main NATO exercise in 1978 was flown from Oerland in Norway with low and medium-level simulated attacks on naval targets.

Meanwhile, one day back in 1976, two members of the Royal Observer Corps, Jim Holmes and Roland Hardy, were taking a nostalgic walk round the old airfield at Waltham. The sight of cracked runways and delapidated huts evoked old memories. With a lump in his throat one said to the other, "Wouldn't it be nice if we could do something for those who lost their lives flying from here?" From that moment they decided that something would be done.

Their first task was to ascertain the likely cost. The quote for a memorial in Indian Granite, from Messrs. Leake's Masonry Ltd. of Louth, was £600. The proposal was then put to the Squadron Commander, Wing Commander P.N. Le Marquand, who gave the project his blessing and, through Flight Lieutenant Derek Tuthill, offered all the help the Squadron could give. Permission and encouragement was also gained from the Ministry of Defence so Jim and Rowland then approached Lindsey County Council to seek a suitable site.

As we know, the site chosen was on the lay-by off the A 16 at Holton le

The three Observers of Bravo 3 post Fulstow Royal Observer Corps whose efforts led to the erection of the Squadron Memorial
Left to right: Johnnie Johnson BEM; Roland Hardy; Jim Holmes.
*Roland Hardy*

100 Squadron Cricket Eleven, West Raynham 1972
Umpton; Woodward; Moore; Smith; Fenton; Knight;
Pascoe; Wright; Sykes; Barker; Hoffler.
*J. A. Barker*

Clay. With all the ground work completed the next problem was to raise the money. Donations were received from Grimsby and Cleethorpes Councils, Holton le Clay Parish Council, 100 Squadron, Crosskeys Fulstow R.O.C., the general public, raffles and a social evening at the R.A.F.A. Club Cleethorpes. Credit for much of this work and the organisation of the project goes to Observer 'Johnnie' Johnson, B.E.M., who acted as Secretary, contacted ex-members of the Squadron and handled all the administrative side of the task. It was a blow to all concerned to find that the cost had risen to £700 in the two years the project was under way but, happily, Messrs. Leake's Masonry agreed to make up the balance as a donation and on the 6th November, 1978, they went along to erect the Memorial.

The following day, in a moving ceremony, Wing Commander Le Marquand, accompanied by a contingent from 100 Squadron, unveiled the Memorial as two Squadron Canberras flew overhead in salute. The dedication of the Memorial was made by Squadron Leader Reverend B.H. Lucas, B.A., R.A.F., the Church of England Chaplain at R.A.F. Marham. Whilst wreaths were being laid, after the ceremony, Piper Sergeant G. Taylor, 100 Squadron, played the lament "Flowers of the Forest". The day ended with a tour of the airfield and refreshments at the R.A.F.A. Club, Cleethorpes.

1979 opened with severe blizzards over East Anglia cutting off both Marham and Sculthorpe for several days – the Canberras, in fact, were covered by snow for over a week. Squadron crews greeted the February thaw with delight as the first detachment of the year flew out to the sunshine of Akrotiri for target towing. Akrotiri became a very important A.P.C. base for fighter training and the Squadron's role there has been maintained to the present day. It was usual for the Squadron to have two or three aircraft at the base for eleven months of the year with the crews changing monthly although, later, the change-over took place fortnightly.

Once more, in its 'behind the scenes' role the Squadron played an important part in training fighter crews of both the R.A.F. and NATO forces. The pilots of many Harrier, Phantom, Lightning, Jaguar and, of course, Tornado Squadrons improved their skills "attacking" 100 Squadron Canberras in the sunny Mediterranean. Squadron crews, themselves, enjoyed their own sea-survival exercises in the warmth of the Med and off-duty leisure-time would find crews relaxing at a beach barbeque. In contrast, winter-survival exercises would find them on ski slopes at Troodos with particular attention to apres-ski!

With a long-term future at Akrotiri assured the Squadron purchased an old mini-bus from the Marham PSI and had it flown out to Cyprus by Hercules. Derek Tuthill writes: "Finished in an attractive shade of blue, the 'Blue Bomber' soon became notorious throughout Cyprus and was reputed to be able to find its own way home from the 'Bunch of Grapes' at Pissouri. Eventually, the 'Bomber' was declared to be beyond economical repair and a successor was purchased and flown out to a life in the sun. The process was repeated several times and the current transport is 'Bomber No. 5' "

In March the Squadron carried out a major calibration task for the new Air Defence Radar at Saxa Vord. A feature of the task was the location of 'holes' in the radar cover causing gaps in the system. This work has been described as boring but vital for the accuracy of navigational aids and the Squadron achieved an accuracy of 1|10 degree and 1|10 mile. In May the Squadron returned to Marham and in July operated from Stornoway in an anti-shipping role. It was on this exercise that one crew had a narrow escape when they experienced engine failure on the final approach. They just managed to reach the beach and bounced onto the airfield where they came to a stop by the squadron dispersal. The only damage was a burst tyre and a damaged nose-wheel mudguard. The passenger, who had been briefed that the Stornoway runway was rather bumpy, was unaware that there had been a problem! On a lighter note, Sergeant Geoff Taylor, who had learnt to play the bag-pipes whilst an apprentice at Halton, mentioned the fact in Stornoway one evening. His claim was greeted with disbelief by the locals and one young lady offered to buy him a drink if the 'Sassenach' could play the pipes better than she could. Pipes were produced and, before Geoff had played half a dozen notes, she conceded defeat.

The Squadron operated in its various roles throughout 1980 beginning in January with a detachment to Akrotiri staging via Naples. There were more flight checking tasks including calibrations of Mount Olympus, Neatishead, Llanbedr and Buchan radars whilst banner detachments were sent to Gutersloh and Leeuwarden. During the year the Squadron received more refurbished E15s and the Squadron's, and R.A.F.s, last T19 was sent to Marshall's at Cambridge Airport for disposal. This Canberra, WJ975, is now on display at the Bomber County Museum, Cleethorpes. The major exercise of the year was flown from Lista in southern Norway with NATO warships as targets but the year ended in tragedy. On 7th November Canberra B2 WH667 suffered engine failure whilst taking off from Akrotiri with a banner target in tow. The aircraft crashed and both crew members were killed.

1981 opened with the usual detachments to Cyprus in January but plans were afoot for the further growth of the Squadron, under the command of Wing Commander J.N. Landeryou, as the year progressed. By June it was confirmed that No. 7 Squadron, with its Canberra TT18s, would merge with 100. In view of 100 Squadron's greater seniority and its greater contribution to the new squadron the Chief of Air Staff approved the retention of the 100 Squadron number. No. 7 Squadron's role had been the operation of the 'Rushton Winch' towing a target on 20,000ft. of wire and, with the help of No. 7 Squadron crews, 100 began to train its own crews for a new, and additional, role.

The Rushton Target was used for the training of Army and R.A.F. Regiment Units firing Rapier ground-to-air missiles. The target, trailing on 20,000 ft. of wire, would be engaged by the ground operator who aimed at a flare ignited on the target. Although the Rapier missile was unarmed it was not uncommon for the target to be holed. A Rushton Target was carried on each wing of the Canberra providing a total of 12 engagements.

In addition to its normal tasks of target-towing in Cyprus, radar calibrations, mock interceptions and the assimilation of 7 Squadron the Squadron had to prepare for the move to Wyton in 1982. It was also learned that No. 13 Squadron would be disbanded and that four of its PR7s would join the enlarged squadron. Whilst all this was going on the Squadron flew a major exercise from Ovar, a NATO airfield in northern Portugal, where the Canberras were directed onto their targets by aircraft of the Portugese Air Force. The year ended with heavy snowfalls at Marham but the runway was cleared to allow the delivery of five ex-7 Squadron TT18s which were re-painted in 100 Squadron colours ready for the move to Wyton.

Poor weather prevented a mass formation flight to Wyton on 5th January,

1982 so transit was made by individual aircraft. The Squadron's strength was now 7 B2s, 4 PR 7s, 5 E15s and 7 TT 18s. Former 7 Squadron pilots and navigators joined 100 to provide additional Rushton experience and responsibility for servicing the Rushton Winch, formerly undertaken by civilians at St. Mawgan, was taken over by 100 Squadron groundcrew. On the 25th January the Squadron flew a philatalic cover for the R.A.F. Museum which commemorated the Fe 2b and depicted Fe 2bs of 100 Squadron taking off from Nancy/Ochey in January, 1918. The Canberra carrying the covers retraced the routes flown 64 years earlier. Later, 'special' versions of the cover were signed by ex Lieutenant J. Williamson who had flown Fe 2bs with 100 Squadron in 1918.

In February the Cyprus detachments were resumed. Both crew members survived when Canberra B2 WK116 crashed into the sea whilst returning to Akrotiri after a range sortie. Back in the U.K. the Squadron sent its first Rushton detachment to Kinloss from where the aircraft flew to the Royal Artillery Range, Hebrides (RARH) off Benbecula. The Canberras flew under radar control trailing a Rushton target on 20,000 ft. of wire which was engaged by either Army Air Defence Units or RAF Regiment squadrons firing Rapier ground-to-air missiles. This first detachment was very successful and, from then on, Rushton detachments became as much a part of Squadron routine as the APC detachments at Akrotiri. [One also learns that some very succulent Benbecula salmon found its way to the Mess at Wyton!(Ed.)]

From April onwards 100 Squadron flew a large number of sorties within the U.K. carrying priority freight and passengers associated with the Falklands war. Three of the Squadron's PR7s were prepared for deployment in the South Atlantic but, in the event, they were not required. In September the Squadron returned to Lista for the annual major exercise and the end of the year brought involvement with flight testing of the ill-fated AEW Nimrod. The end of the year also saw RAF Wyton, with its Canberras and Nimrods, transferred from No. 1 Group to No. 18 Group. Just as RAF Wittering, a few miles up the A1, proclaimed itself 'The Home of the Harrier' RAF Wyton, with Canberras 'guarding' the main gate, was now the recognised 'Home of the Canberra'.

# CHAPTER SEVENTEEN

## The Last Ten Years

1983 saw 100 Squadron's training facilities role extended even more, first, with the provision of sleeve targets for the Royal Navy Gunnery School, HMS Cambridge, when TT18s were detached to St. Mawgan to operate on the Wembury range. There was also a new requirement to provide low-level target aircraft for Army Air Defence Units. In the rest of the year the Squadron flew far and wide in a variety of tasks.

In June a detachment was sent to Lajes in the Azores to participate in a maritime exercise – the Canberras were needed to cover a phase of the operation being the only 'attack' aircraft capable of reaching the target without air-to-air refuelling. In the same month an E15 flew to Belize via Keflavik, Gander and Bermuda to carry out a flight check of the Belize airfield radar and TACAN and, in November, another E15, engaged in a flight check of Gibraltar TACAN, diverted to Tangier because of bad weather at the 'Rock'.

By 1983 the RAF was looking for a suitable aircraft to replace the Squadron's Canberras, some 30 years old, but none of the more modern aircraft could match, let alone surpass, all of the Canberra's capabilities. Consideration was given to building a special version of the HS125 but funds were not forthcoming. In the end, it was decided to treat the Canberra with care and extend its life by a further ten years.

The wide range of tasking continued in 1984 with more flying for the Army provided by low-level target aircraft at Manorbier and Templeton. The major exercise was flown from Bergen|Flesland whilst the Belize flight check included an en-route stop at Nassau.

The 14th December was a memorable day for the Squadron, for Roy Shillinglaw, a World War 1 observer with the Squadron, and for a group of Vildebeest and Lancaster flyers from World War 2. On that day they were privileged to see MRAF Sir Michael Beetham present the Squadron with its new Standard. For many, it was the first time they had seen the Standard and there was a certain pride amongst the guests when they recognised their own contribution to its Battle Honours.

Flying activity was curtailed in 1985. The year started with ice and snow and, although the Cyprus and Kinloss detachments took place as usual, fuel

The Aircraft depicted, Canberra E15 WH983 flew the 100 Squadron FE2B
commemorative covers on 25th January 1982
*(Cover, Photographs and Explanatory Notes Courtesy of Squadron Leader Derek
Tuthill RAF (Retd.)*

economies reduced the level of routine tasking. There was a detachment to
Warton in March and April for trials with the Tornado F2 but from April to
October the Squadron operated from the USAF base at Alconbury whilst
the Wyton runway was re-surfaced. The crew of B2 WK162 had a narrow
escape when the A.S.I. failed on take off. The take off was abandoned but
the aircraft over-ran the runway and caught fire. Further large scale exercises
took place from bases at Skrydstrup in Denmark, Lista and Stornoway.
The Akrotiri detachment flirted with the U.S. Navy providing banner targets
for air-to-air gunnery by Tomcats from USS Nimitz.

1985 provided another landmark in the history of 100 Squadron with
the inauguration and first reunion of the 100 Squadron Association.
(See Appendix 4). About 100 former members and their guests, some
from as far away as Canada and Australia, joined Wing Commander M.
Purdie and his Squadron at Wyton on the 19th October. The highlight of
the day was a visit by the BBMF Lancaster, 'City of Lincoln'.
Accustomed to the whine and whistle of jets for almost 40 years the
unforgettable sound of Merlins brought quite a few misty eyes to the
onlookers. An added bonus was the privilege of being allowed to actually
climb into the Lanc when former crew-members showed their wives and
friends 'where they used to sit'.

The following day brought another sense of 'belonging' to former 100
Squadron flyers when the Old Standard was laid up in the Parish Church of

## Squadron Leader J.C.WILLIAMSON MBE RAF (RETD)

James Colney Williamson was born at Oswestry on 17 April 1898. After education at Oswestry Grammar School, he joined the Artists' Rifles in February 1916 and transferred to the RFC in May. Following a course at No. 1 School of Aeronautics, Oxford, he went to Wyton Aerodrome in September 1916 for flying training. After conversion to FE2bs at Dover early in 1917 he joined his first squadron, No 38 at Buckminster for night anti-Zeppelin patrols.

He was posted to 100 Sqn at Ochey, France, in January 1918 and carried out 31 night raids until the night of 17/18 May when his aircraft was hit by anti-aircraft fire. By a combination of skill and good luck, 2/Lt Williamson landed the stricken FE2B safely in a forest clearing where an inspection revealed that its engine was beyond repair. With his observer, Lt N.F. Penruddock, he set fire to the aircraft to prevent it falling into enemy hands – unfortunately the fire revealed their position to enemy troops and they were captured. The remainder of the squadron, returning to Ochey, saw the fire and when Williamson and Penruddocks failed to return assumed they had been killed in the crash – however, next morning a German aircraft dropped a message at Ochey aerodrome advising that the crew were safe. Williamson and Penruddocks escaped twice during the next few weeks and were finally sent to Danholm, a camp for difficult prisoners, where they remained until repatriated in December 1918.

'Willie' Williamson remained in the RAF on flying duties until 1926 when he left due to family commitments. Rejoining in 1935 he was appointed to Balloon Command, Stanmore. In 1940 he went to Kenya for flying instruction duties and later to South Africa where he was promoted to Sqn Leader and made an MBE. From 1944 he was on Air Attaches' Staffs in Cairo, Baghdad and Ankara. In 1947 he carried out Administrative duties at Lyneham and spent his last 4 years service in the Air Ministry before retiring in 1953.

Since leaving the RAF he has been a Parish, District and County Councillor in Essex. Today he still lives in Essex with his wife Veronica, is an active member of the Magic Circle and the Maldon Operatic Society, and maintans contact with his old squadron.

RAF BB

F.E.2b

The first British Squadron formed specifically for night bombing: No.100 Squadron

1 February 1917

F.E.2bs of No.100 Squadron leaving Ochey for a raid on Trier. January 24th 1918.

SQN LDR J C WILLIAMSON MBE RAF (RETD)
(FORMERLY 2/LIEUTENANT, 100 SQN RFC)

FLOWN IN CANBERRA E15 WH983 OF 100 SQN FROM
RAF WYTON ON 25 JANUARY 1982. THE FLIGHT
RETRACED THE NIGHT BOMBING ROUTE NANCY/
OCHEY TO TRIER OF 24/25 JANUARY 1918.

PILOT: WG CDR J N LANDERYOU RAF—OC 100 SQN
NAVIGATOR: SQN LDR D E TUTHILL MBE RAF
FLIGHT TIME: 2 HOURS 15 MINUTES.

Officer
Commanding
No. 100 Squadron
Royal Air Force
Wyton
Huntingdon

CERTIFIED COPY   N⁰    95    OF 1500

SQN LDR D E TUTHILL—PROJECT OFFICER

"So now, Young Hawk, it is your turn . . ."
*100 Squadron*

St. George, Stamford. In a moving ceremony the congregation listened as
the Squadron Commander said:

"Reverend Sir, I ask you to receive the Squadron Standard for No. 100
Squadron for safe lodging in the House of God until such time as it shall
pass to dust like those whose courage and devotion are enshrined in its
history."

Replying, the Rector said:

"We receive this Standard into the safe keeping of God's House, here to
hang for all time as a reminder to those who pass by of Man's duty to God,
to his Sovereign and to his country."

Squadron activity was again restricted by ice and snow at the beginning
of 1986 although detachments were sent to Akrotiri and Kinloss and the
Squadron also participated in a maritime exercise based at the French Naval
Air Station at Landisvisiau. In June the Squadron made its last flight check
of Belize radar and the Rushton detachment transferred to RAF Machrihanish
in the Mull of Kintyre whilst the Kinloss runway was being re-surfaced.
The Squadron also operated from Machrihanish during August and
September when it was deployed for another maritime exercise. The following
month it was based at Bergen|Flesland for a major exercise when it carried
out simulated attacks to test the U.K. Air Defence System.

Any romantic ideas about the Mull of Kintyre, inspired by the "Beatles",
do not appear to have been shared by the personnel of 100 Squadron on
detachment at Machrihanish. This war-time base is probably the most
isolated base in Britain with Nissen hut accommodation and few amenities:
Rushton detachments were to operate from here for over a year. During this
period 'Operations' at Wyton were puzzled by strange foot-notes to routine
signals which reported progress on the escape tunnel.

Surrounded by wire, the base resembled a prisoner-of-war camp so an
'escape committee' was formed which laid down a number of ground rules:
an escape tunnel would be constructed; all tools would be stolen; all earth
from the diggings must be hidden and the entrance and exit must be concealed.
The 'prisoners' worked with alacrity and, in a short time, concealed soil
caused ceilings to sag making it necessary to dispose of it elsewhere. The
outcome was that a lot of it found its way to Cambridgeshire by air! With
the tunnel completed a formal break-out took place and the entrance and
exit were concealed for the last time and the tunnel was forgotten. One day,
however, a tractor, ploughing outside the wire, fell into the excavation. On
the base there was a minor drama at first as it was thought that someone
was trying to break into the airfield. There was also an irate Scottish farmer.
Peace was restored when the Squadron borrowed a JCB to fill in the
workings!

Machrihanish, however, did have its consolations. Rushton detachments
from Kinloss usually flew to and from the Hebrides range at 15|18,000ft
but the location of Macrihanish made it possible to return at 2,000ft. Crews
lucky enough to have both targets shot off early in a sortie would return via

the 'scenic route': Tiree, Staffa, Coll, Sound of Jura with, perhaps, a practice approach at Islay|Port Ellen. Another highlight was a night at the Argyll Arms at Bellochantuy 'where many a happy evening was spent.' On one occasion the detachment's arrival was greeted with:"You frightened the life out of me when you flew over this afternoon. I thought you were going to hit the chimney pot!" Another remarked: "I saw you waving as you flew along the beach."The Commanding Officer, Wing Commander Reg McKendrick, was present at the time but reserved his comments until the next morning when he discreetly drew the detachment commander's attention to the order prohibiting low flying in the area!

Bad weather delayed the start of operations in 1987 although the Akrotiri and Machrihanish detachments were in full swing early in February. Two ex Royal Navy Canberra TT18s, equipped to carry two air-launched banner targets, were added to the Squadron's strength in March and, in May, the Squadron acquired a minor Electronic Counter Measures capability when its PR7s were modified for 'chaff' ('window') dropping. The Hebrides detachment returned to Kinloss in July when the runway re-opened and, later in the year, the Squadron took part in maritime exercises from Landisvisiau and Monte Real in Portugal and an ADEX flying from Leck in northern Germany.

1987 was the year of 100 Squadron's 70th birthday. On the weekend of the 4th|5th October 290 Association members and guests, including 50 Canadians and 7 Aussies, joined the Squadron itself at Wyton for the festivities. Every era of the Squadron's history was represented from ex-Lieutenant Roy Shillinglaw of the Fe 2b days to young Canberra crews of '87. Amongst other guests were former ex-100 crews who flew in for the party to give a thrilling display with their Phantoms, Lightnings and a Hawk. An AEW Shackleton from Lossiemouth joined in and, of course, 'City of Lincoln' stayed awhile before taking off for a nostalgic display. Following the Wyton reunion the Canadian contingent were guests at a reception given by the Mayor and Borough Council of Cleethorpes. There was another nostalgic visit to the old airfield at Waltham followed by a service at the Squadron Memorial.

The Squadron's hard work in such a wide range of tasks was formally recognised in October when it was the inaugural recipient of the 'Sky-fame Trophy' which is presented annually to the 18 Group unit which had been most effective in its role during the previous year.

1988 saw some variation in the Squadron's exercise bases when Keflavik in Iceland and Nordholz in Germany were added to the list. Another exercise took the Squadron to Bergen where it carried out simulated low-level attacks on shipping well north of the Arctic Circle in the vicinity of Lofoten and Vestfjord. In May practice interceptions were flown over the Bristol Channel for the Royal Navy School of Fighter Control and, in August, a Canberra was sent to the Bilbao Air Show for static display. This caused considerable interest as it was the first Canberra to visit Spain. The year ended with the loss of TT18 WK127 which left the runway at Wyton on landing and the undercarriage was retracted to avoid hitting the control tower. Fortunately, the crew escaped without injury although the aircraft was a write-off.

More variety came in 1989 when, in addition to its usual tasking in Cyprus and the Hebrides, a detachment went to Kinloss where crews carried out trials into the use of the Canberra for Short Range Maritime Patrol (SRMP). This proved to be a very popular exercise as it gave crews the excuse to fly at 250 ft investigating every ship in sight! Meanwhile, on the weekend of 13th|14th April, Wyton hosted celebrations to mark the 40th Anniversary of the first flight of the Canberra.More than 1,500 current and ex-Canberra aircrew and engineering officers attended. Another SRMP exercise took place in September when the Squadron operated from Lista simulating low-level attacks on naval targets. In October the Squadron operated from Wittmundhafen in Germany in an exercise to test U.K. *Air Defences.*

The '90s began in much the same manner as previous years with the Hebrides detachment in February although the Akrotiri APCs did not begin until March. It was to be an eventful year.In April the Squadrom operated from Keflavik again and, on the 27th, two Canberras flew out to the Royal Netherlands Naval airfield at Valkenburg to take part in the 45th Anniversary celebrations of 'Operation Manna'. Saturday, the 28th, was taken up with sight-seeing and a most impressive opening ceremony and reception. On the 29th, 45 years to the day after 100 Squadron Lancasters had dropped food supplies to the Dutch, the Canberras carried out their fly-past at Ypenburg, the site of 100 Squadron's first Manna drop by Lancasters. Timed to coincide with the exact dropping time of 14.30 hrs they were 15 seconds early though it is unlikely the error was noticed by the crowds of spectators who lined the runway on the two fly-pasts. The event was a great success, charged with poignant memories for both the Dutch spectators and ex-Manna participants who had returned to Holland for the occasion.

Overseas training flights to Spain were introduced and Canberras made two visits to the Spanish military airfield at Madrid|Getafe. Exercise 'Hornet Sail' took place in May when Squadron aircrew sailed a 32 ft. yacht from the Joint Services Training Centre, Gosport, to Brest and returned by Canberra with the crews who flew the aircraft outbound returning by sea.

Tragedy hit the Squadron on 27th June when E15 WH972 crashed in bad weather on the approach to Kinloss. Skipper, Flight Lieutenant Cameron Locke and Navigator, Flying Officer Gordon Jackson ejected but Cameron was killed whilst 'Jacko' had severe spinal injuries. Just three days earlier they had attended the annual reunion and 'Jacko' had read the Lesson at the Memorial Service. As reported in the newsletter at the time Association members, as in days gone by, shared the Squadron's grief. 'Jacko' went on to make a good recovery and is now flying again.

By August the war in the Gulf was looming and the Squadron's Akrotiri detachment was withdrawn. In its place the Squadron flew a large number of sorties transporting priority freight between the U.K. and Cyprus for onward transportation to the Gulf. Again, working behind the scenes, the Squadron played an important part in the conflict and felt a sense of pride that twenty or so former members had acquitted themselves so well flying Tornados and Buccaneers. Squadron groundcrew, as ever, played their part in the Gulf which led to a reduction in routine flying from Wyton. At the same time the Rushton detachments were stepped up to prepare Air Defence Units for deployment in the Gulf. This pattern continued into 1991 and it wasn't until June that the APC detachment returned to Cyprus.

Thursday, 16th March 1991, was a black day for Wyton and the Squadron: Group Captain Reg McKendrick, the Station Commander and former Commanding Officer of 100 Squadron, Flight Lieutenant Stephen Wilkinson, also ex-100 and Flight Lieutenant David Adam, Navigator from 231 OCU, were killed when T4 WJ877 crashed on take-off and exploded on the A141 March – Huntingdon Road. R.A.F. Wyton was stunned by the loss. Group Captain McKendrick had been a most popular C.O. – as one former Squadron member put it: ". . . the old boss was a smashing man who had time for both the Chiefs and the Indians." He was also a good friend to the Association which will always be indebted to him for his guidance in its formative years. Stephen Wilkinson and Dave Adam had flown in the Canberra Flight in the Battle of Britain 50th Anniversary fly-past over Buckingham Palace and were very popular on the Station.

By June it was confirmed that the faithful old Canberras would be withdrawn and that the Squadron would re-equip with Hawks. No doubt it was with a feeling of loss that crews flew the last exercises of the year from Montijo, near Lisbon, and from Leck and Stavanger. By September only 10 Canberras remained and the first three Hawks had arrived. In October, 1991, two Canberra TT18s with air-launched banners took part in live firing exercises in Egypt turning round at Birigat.

A happy departure from the normal routine took place on the 24th October when Wing Commander Keith Douglas, Squadron Commander, Air Vice-Marshal Herrington, CB, Association President, and Flight Lieutenant Adrian Dawe flew out to the Isle of Man to present Roy Shillinglaw, the Association's oldest member, with a framed Canberra print signed by all the members at the reunion dinner during the summer. Roy, then 92 years of age, had felt unable to attend the last reunion and the print was given as a token of esteem to our oldest member. "The visit was a great success; he was thrilled to see us and insisted we stay for a splendid lobster lunch during which he delighted us with his famous anecdotes of his time on 100 Squadron."(Wing Commander Keith Douglas.)

The year ended with the final Hebrides detachment in November and the last 100 Squadron Canberra sortie was flown on the 18th December.

Between January 1972 and December 1991 100 Squadron operated a total of 48 Canberras in a remarkable number of roles. This is in addition to the earlier Canberra period, 1954 – 1959, and must constitute something of a record in aviation history. For the benefit of the hundreds of men who flew and serviced the Canberra in the last twenty years Squadron Leader Tuthill has researched the "fate" of each one and these are detailed in Appendix Five. It is believed that some of the airframes were bought by a Japanese car manufacturer who will recycle the high quality aluminium for engine parts.

100 Squadron started 1992 under the command of Wing Commander John Pitts and was equipped with 12 Hawks. The Squadron was given two weeks respite from tasking while it completed conversion to the new aircraft. To the layman, conversion from one type of aircraft to another may not mean very much and the author is grateful to Flight Lieutenant F. Coulton for bringing to light some of the work and problems involved.

Many of the ex-Canberra pilots attended a short refresher course at Valley whilst navigators received their training at Squadron level. Some new crews joined the Squadron from Tactical Weapons Units and front line squadrons. Their specific tasks were to familiarise air traffic control and the Ops Wing at Wyton with Hawk type operations and to establish a new set of Standard Operating Procedures for 100 Squadron. Many Canberra groundcrew were converted to the Hawk but, as the number of aircraft on the Squadron increased, more Hawk-qualified groundcrew were posted in. As with their predecessors in earlier days the groundcrew have been complimented on the high serviceability rate achieved. Unlike their predecessors they were fortunate in being able to erect a most impressive bar – "The Boneyard" – in their new quarters!

Inevitably there were changes in personnel: Squadron Leader Benn was posted from Harriers at Wittering to become the first Hawk Flight Commander replacing Squadron Leader Wilkin who became a Staff Officer at H.Q. 18 Group. There were two or three transfers to the Canberras of 360 Squadron whilst others went to fly Jaguars or navigate the Tornado GR1 and a group of young navigators joined the Squadron for their first tour.

Due to the change in aircraft type the Squadron lost three of its previous roles: Rushton target towing, radar calibration and Pluto 5 calibration sorties – the last two because of the Hawk's shorter range. On the other hand, the much faster and more manoeuvrable Hawk led to roles being expanded and the addition of new ones as with its support of 56 Squadron. 100 Squadron crews are now trained in low level evasion techniques in order to support the advanced radar phase of the 56 Squadron conversion course. Joint Maritime Exercises have been maintained as a Squadron role with the addition of Forward Air Controlling (FAC) with the Army. The Hawk's versatility has been advantageous in flying more numerous and useful attack formations against ships and targets on the ground. The Squadron continues its role with APCs in Cyprus and fighter control training in the U.K. and it also has an important role in introducing young crews to fast jets before moving on to the front line.

It is to the credit of the Commanding Officer, aircrews and groundcrews that a banner detachment flew to Cyprus with the new aircraft in January 1992, so shortly after the change-over, the transit including an additional stop in Athens. Otherwise, UK tasking resumed as before. However, the Hebrides Rushton detachment and flight checking roles were lost but were balanced by a new requirement for co-operation with Forward Air Controllers and a marked increase in low level fighter affiliation exploiting the Hawk's low-level performance.

In July '92 the Squadron and 100 Squadron Association celebrated "The Big One" – 100 Squadron's 75th Birthday. Over 300 attended the festivities with reunions within a reunion as former Vildebeest flyers and Japanese P.O.W.s got together; Lancaster crews met up with their Canadian buddies; there was a sprinkling of Aussies from the Singapore days and, even, Tom Scully, a wartime flyer with 100 Squadron RAAF. World War 1 was represented by proxy by Norman McCreath whose late brother, Angus, flew Fe 2Bs on the Western Front. A day's extension to the main reunion was held at Waltham where 70 or 80 assembled at "The Jug and Bottle" for a nostalgic tour of the airfield followed by a Mayoral reception at Cleethorpes Town Hall.

Another Hawk was added to the Squadron strength in August and the build up of aircraft continued throughout the rest of 1992 and 1993. Number 100 Squadron was back in business and a new era had begun.

Following established practice two Squadron Hawks flew in salute over the Memorial at Holton le Clay on Remembrance Sunday, still well attended by wartime flyers and the people of Holton le Clay who remember them so well.

January 1993 gave a good indication of the busy year to come. The flexibility of both the Hawk and its personnel was ably demonstrated with a very short notice detachment to Gibraltar. Coupled with this, rumours of a squadron move began to gain more substance.

Throughout the Spring the Squadron continued with its busy schedule detaching to Norway, Scotland and Cyprus to take part in both national and international exercises. In late April the squadron move was confirmed and the new home declared as RAF Finningley near Doncaster, South Yorkshire. The move was planned to take part in late Summer 93.

The Squadron Navigation Trophy was greeted in May with heavy showers, nevertheless crews valiantly battled through to produce a worth winning pair – Flt. Lt. Cook and Fg. Off. Casabayo!! The summer months also saw the Squadron going to France and Cyprus as well as beginning earnestly to pack up the buildings at Wyton prior to the move to Finningley.

August was a month for farewells, with dinners and photocalls being held to bid goodbye to Wyton and its people. On the 31st August the Squadron detached to what seemed like the cour corners of the country after a 12 aircraft flypast, later to reunite at Finningley on 21st September 93 to begin official operations. Despite the turmoil of moving, the Squadron mounted detachments to Italy and Denmark and the longest Hawk Flight on Squadron record was logged – 2hrs 55mins. The rest of the year passed with more exercises in Scotland and Norway as well as the ubiquitous APC's at Akrotiri. Meanwhile, the squadron personnel and families became progressively more familiar with life in Yorkshire.

1994 has now dawned and with it the prospect of another busy year for the Squadron with several major exercises already planned and the expectation of a substantial changeover in aircrew personnel. Let us hope this year proves as interesting and profitable for the 'Ton' as the 76 which have gone before.

As 100 Squadron greets yet another new year, little more remains to be said unless one tries to count the hundreds of fighter pilots, air defence units, warships of the Royal Navy and every NATO fleet who owe their own efficiency to the men who fly the skull and cross-bones. The end of the 'Cold War', with the break-up of the Soviet Union and Warsaw pact, brought a feeling of euphoria to East and West alike only to be superseded by uncertainty as new trouble spots flared up. The Royal Air Force leads Europe in support of the United Nations' increasing peacekeeping role in these trouble spots. Number 100 Squadron has operated in almost every conceivable role in the RAF: attack and defence; transport and training; innovation and development; reconnaissance and radar navigation. With such a tradition 100 Squadron can take its place with the best into the 21st century and beyond.

# Message from Wing Commander John Pitts

## Officer Commanding 100 Squadron – February 1994

100 Squadron has quite recently settled into its new base at RAF Finningley and has also just completed a second very successful year of operating the Hawk aircraft. The versatility and economy of the Hawk in the Squadron's role has far exceeded expectations and has attracted universal and extremely favourable comments from our users. Additionally, the Squadron was justifiably proud when, on 16th October 93, it was awarded the 18 Group Skyframe trophy for operational performance and efficiency over the previous 12 months.

Admittedly, the modern, agile target facility the Squadron provides does not and cannot have anything like the glamour and danger of an active front line role and, although the crews are inevitably unable to boast the same brave, heroic and often outrageously perilous exploits as their wartime predecessors, the current tasks are nonetheless essential in promoting the effectiveness of the defensive systems of all 3 Services. Simultaneously, the Squadron's role provides an excellent and evolving medium in which crews can gain invaluable experience of a front line style of operations while performing their jobs as penetrating target formations.

Indeed, the value of the Squadron has been such that aircraft and crew numbers have been steadily increased during the 2 years of Hawk operations and the more recent supplement of engineering personnel to carry out second line servicing at the new base now makes the Squadron one of the busiest and largest in the Royal Air Force; it is also one of the very few fully autonomous units in existence in today's Service.

Even before the demise of the Canberra, the Squadron faced the threat of disbandment and contractorisation under the Government's Options for Change initiative. However, the Hawk, which was only seen as an interim solution until April 1995, has enabled exploitation and development of the Squadron's role to such an extent that contractorisation of the style of flying the Squadron now performs is, to say the least, proving more difficult to contractorise than originally envisaged; additionally, the advantages of the flexibility, effectiveness and the inherent mutual training benefits of a 'uniformed' operation have of late assumed a higher and very favourable profile together with considerable sympathy in the corridors of power, so much that there can be some cautious optimism with regard to the Squadron's future.

In penning the closing remarks to Arthur White's sterling account of our Squadron's exploits over some 75 years of virtually uninterrupted operations, I find that, although the hardware and style of operations on the Squadron have evolved both substantially and dramatically over the years, the professionalism, spirit and pride on the Squadron is manifestly entirely unchanged. Apart from highlighting that today we have both men and women in the cockpit and amongst our support personnel and also pointing out 'observers' are known as navigators, I can justly and most aptly recognise the efforts of all current Squadron personnel by reiterating verbatim the words of Major C G Burge; as Squadron Commander, he wrote his conclusion to the Annals of 100 Squadron exactly 75 years ago:

"My task as CO was considerably lightened by the energetic and wholehearted support which I, at all times, received from one and all serving under me. Pilots and Observers, always full of determination and keenness, unselfish and cheerful at all times, won for themselves and the Squadron the greatest admiration. Like gentlemen and sportsmen they played the game throughout. No less can be written concerning the Ground Personnel. Their task was no light one and their devotion to duty greatly contributed to the success of the pilots and observers. Although their work was less romantic their task entailed great hardships and hard work . . . they too "kept it going". Lastly I cannot speak too highly of the "Esprit de Corps" which so strongly existed . . ."

I have been as proud as any of the long list of Commanding Officers to be at the helm of Number 100 Squadron and sincerely hope that many others will be able to follow. Meanwhile, I and all the proud men and women on the Squadron will continue to do our utmost to preserve the true spirit, the tradition and the lifeblood of one of the oldest and most distinguished Squadrons in the Royal Air Force. "Lets keep it going"

February 1994                          Wing Commander John Pitts

# POSTSCRIPT

As this story unfolded and I read or heard so many first hand accounts of those involved I became more and more impressed with the spirit, resolution and humour of the men who have made 100 Squadron. I tried to imagine the feelings of the Fe 2B flyers in their flimsy machines as they crossed the German lines in the dark. What went through the minds of those Vildebeest men as they flew,in vain, knowing full well the odds against them, into murderous anti-aircraft fire to halt a relentless foe? How did those Lancaster crews repeatedly "press on" through flak and hell-fire and land their, often, burning and battered 'planes in England again and then, on "stand down", sing "The 100 Squadron Boys" in the Mess?

The same indomitable spirit persisted through the post-war years of comparative peace. In the "Cold War" period the tension was always present and 100 Squadron was there amongst the best never knowing if the next 'QRA' would be the real thing. In its training and trials roles 100 Squadron learnt how to "toss bombs over the shoulder" – some of the bombs were 25lb practice bombs; some were 1,000 pounders – but they *could have been* NUCLEAR! 100 Squadron made sure it "could do it" if called upon but, more importantly, it made sure the front line squadrons could do it as well. "Without 100 Squadron we wouldn't be able to do our job."

In his conclusion to "The Annals of 100 Squadron" Major Burge recalls Lord Trenchard's words to him at a time when it was thought the Squadron would be disbanded:

"It's traditions which count and which make people keep straight and, although the Squadron has been disbanded, those who belonged to 100 Squadron should remember in the future *what a Squadron they belonged to!*"

Although this is a story of men it seems fitting to bring it to a close by reproducing one lady's view of 75 years of Squadron history.

## *100 SQUADRON LADIES GUEST NIGHT – FEBRUARY 1992*

No pictures alas, these words must suffice,
Herewith the Squadron seventy and five.
New trophies, old stories, new faces,
The tapestry weaves and comes to life.

Behind, our Standard keeps guard.
From Ypres, Malaya and on to Berlin.
Silk, palest blue, tasselled and flowered,
Brave ghosts of many Dinings – In.

With flowers and candles, blue and gold,
One Hundred Squadron here unfold.
In pools of light young eyes are bright,
But in corners shaded memories are unfaded.

First, our ancient aviator ninety four,
Wyton too far for Roy Shillinglaw.
Those early eyes that saw, in the dark,
His old 'lattice – tail' as old as the Ark.

Royal Flying Corps tales and magical names,
Trenchard, Von Richtofen and France,
Bombs, bombing and night games.
Boys became men in a trance.

Ten years in Malaya and then despair.
Advancing Nippon takes most of the flock,
Dark Singapore days and heavy the air,
Sarang Tebuan Jangan Dijolok!

Tattered remnants head south, still keen,
Spares, torpedoes and silver outward bound.
Deep in Selat Sunda does silver gleam?
Sumatra, Java and P.O.W. compound.

Phoenix under Southern Cross did rise,
Salute Royal Australian Air Force 100!
Memories of jungle green, now in ties,
Ghosts live on …unhindered.

Back in old England with Lancs.
Night after night we paid dear.
There were parties and girls, even Yanks!
So many good-byes, year after year.

Tonight, flashes of sequins on shoulders

Was that how it once looked below?
Memories still sharp though much older,
Was it noisy tonight on the Ruhr?

Places and names come faster now,
As peace brings brush fires abroad.
Malaya, Egypt, Christmas Island, Mau Mau,
The Lincolns our answer did once afford,

But on, to Canberras and trials anew.
To Stamford's chequer board we owe
Those bold cummerbunds, gold and blue.
Then the pace, for a while, will slow.

The war is now at its coldest.
Victor moths your wings unfold,
Blue Steel your deadly chrysalis,
Q.R.A., detachments, dispersals untold.

Our silver once again records history,
Winged lady here on this table
Tells of excellence and past glory.
Bomber Command Squadron most able.

Again Standard will rest. But not long
Before we are off once again,
Now testing our own defence song.
So rich the R.A.F.s grain.

And now, young Hawks, it's your turn.
The stars you yearn are in reach.
Remember to laugh as you learn,
You too, will be called on to teach.

So which young woman here tonight
Will sit in my place in her turn?
Will she scribble the scene and ponder the sight
And will her own memories burn?

                          Mrs. C. Herrington.
                          February, 1992.


100 Squadron is still flying. There can be no better way to end this story
than by reiterating those other words of Lord Trenchard seventy five years
ago:

                    *"KEEP IT GOING!"*

A. W., November 1992.

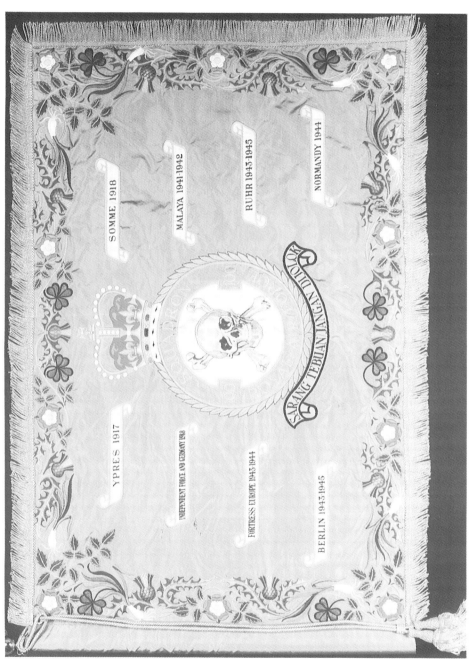

The New Squadron Standard
Presented by MRAF Sir Michael Beetham GCB, CBE, DFC, AFC
14th December 1984

# APPENDIX ONE

## POETRY AND MUSIC

"Oh! East is East and West is West,
But 'out there' the twain do meet,
And 'Erbert Smiff' greets Vere de Vere
On the same old Mess Room seat.
Here there is neither East nor West
Money nor breed nor birth,
For you've all got to grin, when your luck's
      not in,
And you've all got to prove your worth."

(From "The Annals of 100 Squadron,)


*"100 SQUADRON LAMENT.*

For months in England, on the spree,
With the Squadrons on H.D.
Count Zeppelin's crimes were an awful length,
But we struck six airships off his strength.

     And we brought them down in flames
     And we brought them down in flames,
     And we brought them down in flames
     And they haven't been there since.

Then some "brass hat" at Adastral House
Tried his best to start a grouse,
To form "One Hundred" for overseas,
He picked his men from the best H.D.s

     And they sent us out to France,
     And they sent us out to France,
     And they sent us out to France
     To show them how to bomb.

We landed on the Western Front,
From Isel le Hameau was our first stunt,
And we soon ken from Jerry's moans,
That he didn't like the Aeros with the skull and
cross bones.

> For they blew up all his railways,
> For they blew up all his railways,
> For they blew up all his railways
> And amunition dumps.

Our pilots got well known round there
So they moved us up to a place called Aire,
And we bombed his 'dromes till the Hun wished he
Could run across the Major they called Christie.

We "wrote off" his best 'drome,
We "wrote off" his best 'drome,
We "wrote off" his best 'drome
And also the Menin Road.

Then Jerry, just to show his spite,
Bombed London with his 'planes at night.
The people said, You silly clowns,
Why not go and bomb his towns?

> So they pushed us off to Ochey,
> So they pushed us off to Ochey,
> So they pushed us off to Ochey
> To get square with the Hun.

Well, Jerry must have thought the same,
And he tried his best to stop the game.
We all remember that fine night
That brought the Squadron their first fright.

> For he tried to wipe out Ochey,
> For he tried to wipe out Ochey,
> For he tried to wipe out Ochey
> But the Cafe stands there yet.

The "wind up" there no man could stick,
And everyone paraded sick,
Then someone said t'would be "the goods"
To move up further in the woods.

And everyone was happy,
And everyone was happy,
And everyone was happy,
For there was rest, sweet rest.

When we got rid of our F.E.s
We got to work with the twin H.P.s,
And Jerry said, by what we hear,
That the only one he had to fear,

Was good old "100 Squadron,"
Was good old "100 Squadron,"
Was good old "100 Squadron,"
We hope to meet again.

(Corporal J.R. Bird. "The Annals of 100 Squadron.")


*"THE VILDEBEEST."*

The Vildebeest, a quaint old bird,
Of rather gaunt appearance,
Between its tummy and the ground
Has heaps of buckshee clearance.

It sports a lump upon its back,
Has legs so long like Tamils,
A flight lined out, across the 'drome,
Looks like a string of camels.

Found in Malaya and Iraq,
It flies in hefty circles,
Its motive power is stuck in front
And loudly it capurtles.

Unlike the usual type of bird,
It lays its eggs whilst flying.
They vary both in size and weight,
And cleave the air a-sighing.

The Vildebeest's patriotic charms,
Are painted on its chassis,
Red, white and blue, a tasteful hue,
So dignified and classy.

(From Seletar Station Magazine.)

*THE HUNDRED SQUADRON BOYS.*
(*Air McNamara's Band.*)
(Note: Names and verses varied with arrival of new Squadron and Flight
Commanders and Section Leaders.)

1.      We are 100 Squadron – we're the boys who know the score,
        If anyone denies it we will spread them on the floor,
        At bombing and beer and billiards and all the Cleethorpes
                Hops,
        We've got the gen – we're the leading men – we certainly
                are the tops.

CHORUS
        While the bombs go bang and the flak bursts clang and the
                searchlights blaze away,
        We weave all over the starlit sky and wish we'd gone by day.
        Oh! Hamilton, Hamilton save us now,
        We can't abide the noise,
        A credit to Butch Harris are the 100 Squadron boys.

2.      Oh we love to nip in smartly to a little buzz bomb site
        And smartly nip off home again and get to bed at night.
        We're saving our night vision up for other earthly joys
        And now we're safely in the Mess meet the 100 Squadron boys.

3.      I'm Wing Commander Hamilton and I am Number One
        And I very strongly deprecate the things that are not done.
        If you ask my crew if I have any faults they will tell you
                in accents sweet,
        "You can see the ants as we stooge over France at altitude
                zero feet."

4.      My name's Dave Robb and they gave me the job of settling "A"
                Flight's hash,
        Three ops a year and gallons of beer and look at the extra
                cash,
        Believe it or not, this ribbon I've got, diagonal white and
                red,
        Was won for drinking fifteen pints in fifteen seconds dead.

5.      My name is Scott and I'm rather hot at dishing out the bull.
        I don't believe in wrapping my Flight in yards of cotton
                wool.
        Oh, Flannel's the stuff if you flannel enough but you can't
                flannel me,

So that'll be five bob in the box and couple of hours P.T.

6.    My name is Traff and I joined the RAF – well pretty near the
            start,
      My trade is navigation but I'm a bit of a wolf at heart,
      I've a popsy here and a popsy there and I don't care if
            they're wed
      So long as their husbands don't come home and find me still
            in bed.

7.    I get my beers from the bombardiers – my name is Zaggerman,
      So raise your hat to a desert rat the Lawrence of El San,
      I lost my curls to the harem girls who thought me lots of
            fun
      For I was never known to overshoot or make a dummy run.

8.    I'm Flight Lieutenant Thompson once the terror of Tobruk,
      My desert dicing days would fill a pretty weighty book,
      But since I got to Grimsby they've demoted me By Heck!
      And now I'm one of the lesser Sheiks of Barnolby-le-Beck.

9.    My name's O'Donovan Iland and I'm Number One A.G.
      And 190s and 109s are all the same to me.
      I'll man the mid-upper with any old Skipper so long as he's
            learned to fly,
      You can only live once – it's a matter of months – and it
            doesn't take long to die.

10.   My name's Vin Knight, I'm the leading light of the airborne
            plumbers guild,
      And every night my dreams of glamorous coutesans are filled.
      There's a girl named Lou – she'd appeal to you – if you
            haven't been introduced
      She's big and blonde and terribly fond of me and my plus 12
            Boost.

(Anon. Waltham: 1943 – 1945.)

*BEHIND THOSE SWINGING DOORS*

'Twas Saturday night and the Ops Room was chill
Though the "King's Head was merry and gay
And Groupie and Wingco and Bradford did wait
For the Form B that was on its way.
"What's keeping those aircrew?" the Wingco exclaimed,
"They ought to be up here," he said,
And little they knew, that every darned crew
Was safely inside the "King's Head".

CHORUS

Oh the doors swing in.....the doors swing out,
The aircrew pass in but they seldom pass out.
The Squadron I fear has gone right on the beer
Behind those swinging doors....behind those swinging
          doors.

"I've tannoyed and tannoyed." the S.I.O moaned,
"But no-one has answered my call,
The ops meals are spoiled and the cooks are all oiled
In the Flight's there is no-one at all!"
Dear Squadron, Dear Squadron come back to us now,
There's briefing at quarter to three,
The Wingco is groaning with tears in his eyes
Oh bring back my Squadron to me.'

CHORUS.
Oh the doors swing in . . . the doors swing out,
The aircrew pass in but they seldom pass out
"You can stuff all your ops whilst there's plenty of
          hops
Behind those swinging doors . . . Behind those swinging
          doors."


At last Groupie guessed at the horrible truth
And down to the village they went,
They drove with a roar right up to the door
And called on the boys to repent.
"Dear Squadron," they wailed, "In your duty you've
          failed,
You'd better start mending your ways
In time to save Groupie from losing a ring,

It's always the C.O. who pays!"

CHORUS.

Oh the doors swing in, the doors swing out,
The aircrew all heard them but never came out.
They said, "It's our right to drink Saturday night
Behind those swinging doors . . . Behind those swinging
        doors."

Each Saturday night at the "King's Head" Saloon
The Squadron blows in with its pay
And they spend it on beers till its up to their ears
And never go home till it's day!
"Dear Squadron," Butch Harris wrote after a while,
"I've heard of your Saturday night.
If you press on regardless the other six days
You can take it from me . . . It's alright!"

CHORUS.
Oh the doors swing in, the doors swing out,
The aircrew pass in but they seldom pass out
And Butch is there too, just imbibing a few
Behind those swinging doors . . . Behind those swinging
        doors!
(Anon. Waltham. 1943 – 1945.)


The following did not originate on the Squadron but it seems appropriate to
include them here.

*THREE CHEERS FOR THE MAN ON THE GROUND*
(*E. Sykes. 1942*)

Wherever you walk you will hear people talk
Of the men who go up in the air;
Of the dare-devil way they go into the fray
Facing death without turning a hair.

They'll raise a big cheer and buy lots of beer
For a pilot who's home on leave;
But they don't give a jigger for a flight mech or
      rigger
With nothing but props on his sleeve.

They just say, "Nice Day," and then turn away
Without a mention of praise;
And the poor bloody erk, who does all the work,
Just orders his own beer and pays.

They've never been told of hours in the cold
That he spends sealing Germany's fate;
How he works on a kite, till all hours of night
And then turns up next day at eight.

He gets no rake off for working till 'take off'
Or helping the aircrew prepare;
But whenever there's trouble it's "Quick! At the
        double!"
The men on the ground must be there.

Each flying crew could tell it to you;
They know what this man is worth;
They know he is part of the R.A.F.s heart
Even though he stays close to the earth.

He doesn't want glory, but please tell his story;
Spread a little of his fame around.
He's one of the few, so give him his due:
"Three cheers for the man on the ground!"


*ODE TO A DARK LADY*
A beautiful, comely maid was she,
Her lovely form a joy to see,
She came as swiftly as the night,
As graceful as a bird in flight,
Into the green years of our life.
Not sweetheart true nor loving wife,
But dark, mysterious, proud, unknown ,
To cherish, love, but never own.
Respectfully we learned to pay
Our tributes to her day by day,
And as our lives with hers entwined,
Our joys, our fears, our inner mind,
Became a mutual living thing
To take upon our journeying.

She opened wide her arms to share
With us the perils of the air.

Her steadfast spirit, loyal, true,
Was with us always as we flew.
She never faltered, even though
She might be wounded, weak and slow.
We raise our glasses, drink a toast,
Remembering a very host
Of things that time cannot transcend,
A gallant mistress, servant, friend,
We loved her to the very end,
My Lady Lancaster.

Audrey Grealy. 1982.
(Published in "Poems With Wings" 1983. Published in the Wickenby Register News Letter October. 1982.)

# APPENDIX TWO

*BOMBER COMMAND "A BALANCE SHEET"*

Since 1945 controversy has raged over the Bomber Offensive on Germany and many attempts have been made to decry the achievements of the crews of Bomber Command. The success of particular raids has been called into question by such statements as, "It only disrupted German war production for a few days." This implies that the whole effort had not been worthwhile. As one writer put it:" If such statements are true one wonders what the outcome of the war would have been had the attacks never taken place!"

The following 'balance sheet' has been compiled from Group Captain Saward's "Bomber Harris" with additional statistics from "The Bomber Command War Diaries." (NOTE: Much of Group Captain Saward's information is based on personal consultations with Herr Albert Speer, Hitler's Minister of Production.)

*THE ACHIEVEMENTS*

For 3½ years Bomber Command was the only means of striking directly at Germany.

60% of German cities detroyed by 955,044 tons of bombs.

47,307 mines (approx 33,000 tons) were laid in enemy waters, ports and shipping lanes.

The Allied bombing offensive caused a progressive reduction in German military output so that losses exceeded replacement rates. This was compounded by the fact that German artillery (88mm anti-tank guns and ammunition) had to be withdrawn from the Eastern Front along with 900,000 men to defend German cities against Bomber Command's attacks. Hence, Bomber Command proved to be Stalin's 'Second Front'. (Albert Speer.)

German aircraft production was reduced and emphasis switched to fighter production to combat Allied bombers. This saved Britain from further German air raids by German bombers earmarked for this purpose. (Albert Speer.)

It also deprived the Luftwaffe of the potential to impede the Allied invasion of Normandy when even moderate air attacks could have severely disrupted if not halted the landings.

Allied aircrew reduced the Continental transport system to chaos.

Between April, 1944 and January, 1945 German oil production was reduced by 75%. [Note. Bomber Command night attacks were more effective than American daylight attacks because of the heavier weight of bombs, mixed with incendiaries, used by the R.A.F. (Albert Speer.)]

In its tactical role Bomber Command provided invaluable support for all the Allied armies, including American, thus preventing another 'Somme'. ["Your chaps made it easy for us." (Field Marshal Montgomery to Air Marshal Harris.)]

*"BATTLE OF THE SHIPS"*

Number of enemy vessels sunk at sea by bombing:       26
    "    "    "        "        destroyed in port:   300
    "    "    "        "    sunk by air laid mines:  1102

              Total, including 39 "U" boats:   1428
                       Tonnage: 1,083325 tons.

This represents 31.2% of ALL enemy shipping lost in the Atlantic and North West European waters.

In addition Bomber Command and the United States Air Forces destroyed 111 "U" boats in production at inland factories. Bomber Command's 'share' is estimated to have been at least 50%.

Finally there was the intangible effect on the morale of the British people. After the 'blitzes' of 1940 and 1941 men, women and children could listen to the laboured drone of hundreds of "ours" climbing on course for Germany. Many, living near a bomber airfield, would count the 'planes taking off – and count them again on their return. The following day they would learn, with grim satisfaction, the details of the night's raid.(Ed.)

*THE COST TO BOMBER COMMAND*

| | |
|---|---:|
| Aircrew killed in action or died while P.O.W.: | 47,268 |
| Aircrew killed in flying or ground accidents: | 8,195 |
| Aircrew killed in ground battle action: | 37 |
| Total killed: | 55,500 |
| Prisoners of War: | 9,838 |
| Wounded in aircraft: | 4,200 |
| Wounded in flying or ground accidents in U.K.: | 4,203 |
| Total Aircrew Casualties: | 73,741 |
| Total R.A.F. Ground Staff killed in World War 2: | 1,470  men |
| | 91  WAAF. |

*AIRCREW CASUALTIES BY NATIONALITY*

|                |        |       |
|----------------|--------|-------|
| R.A.F.         | 38,462 | 69.2% |
| R.C.A.F.       | 9,919  | 17.8% |
| R.A.A.F.       | 4,050  | 7.3%  |
| R.N.Z.A.F.     | 1,679  | 3.0%  |
| P.A.F.         | 929    | 1.7%  |
| Other Allied   | 473    | 0.9%  |
| S.A.A.F.       | 34)    |       |
| Other Dominion | 27)    | 0.1%  |

*TOTAL AIRCRAFT SORTIES AND CASUALTIES*

Sorties: 389,809   Lost: 8953   Operational Crashes: 1,368

Total Aircraft Lost: 10,321.
All casualty statistics from "Bomber Command War Diaries" –
Martin Middlebrook and Chris Everitt. (Viking).

# APPENDIX THREE

## Prisoners Of War
## The First World War

There are a few accounts of prisoners taken on the Western Front in "The Annals of 100 Squadron". In general it seems that all were treated within the terms of the Geneva Convention. There is only one account of actual brutality although other cases are hinted at. There are references to the pleasure of 100 Squadron flyers meeting up with other comrades who had been taken prisoner and several wrote of German attempts to trick them into revealing information under interrogation. The general complaint, apart from the resentment at being taken prisoner, was the very poor quality of food. It should be remembered, however, that by 1918 most of Germany was suffering from the effects of the Allied blockade. The following accounts are condensed from "The Annals of 100 Squadron."

On their first operation Lieutenants Swart and Fielding Clark made a forced landing behind enemy lines. (See main text.) Swart went in search of a French telephone post leaving his Observer with the aircraft. He was accosted by a German patrol but bluffed his way clear by asking them if they had seen his automobile! He hurried back and tried to restart his aircraft but failed so he and Fielding Clark destroyed their maps and as much of the aircraft as possible without setting fire to it.

There followed several days, dodging German patrols and gun emplacements, in an attempt to reach Switzerland. They had considered making a break towards the French lines but were deterred by heavy gun barrages from both French and German positions. After three days without food they came to a village where there was a number of German Army wagons lined up which they searched, in vain, for food. It was then they noticed a light shining from a hut, built on raised foundations, near a dam. Swart peered through a crack and "saw a Hun sitting at a table and, at his right hand side stood a jar of honey." To his observer he said, "I'm going to jump in and deal with that Bosche and, if there's anyone else, you look after him."

Swart dashed into the hut and attacked the German with a stick but the blow caught him on the shoulder. He then grabbed the German by the throat throwing him back onto a bed. At this point the Observer entered the hut but was struck in the chest by a second German, who had been lying in a corner bed, causing the Observer to lose his balance and fall through the doorway and drop nine feet onto the ground below. The second German promptly bolted the door and went to the aid of his comrade but Swart held on on whereupon his new adversary grabbed a Mauser and poked it into Swart's back. Realising that the game was up Swart surrendered but his original foe was now behaving like a madman punching and kicking his attacker until "one side of his face looked more like pudding."

Meanwhile the Observer had tried to get help from the German garrison in the village but was unable to cross the ditch. (He was still weak from an attack of fever.) Shouting, he returned to the hut just as Swart's 'victim' was preparing to shoot him. The cries caused the two Germans to pause and confer and, in the intervening seconds, Swart managed to explain that they were only looking for food. To some extent, the Germans were mollified.

The outcome was that Swart and Fielding Clark were taken for interrogation to St. Avold where a General told them they did not treat the German officers like gentlemen as they turned the questioning into a farce! The rest of the war was spent in prison camps at Metz, Karlsruhe, Landshut and Holzminden.

Air Mechanic W. Hawkins, flying as Observer with Lieutenant Fulton, wrote of his experiences after making a forced landing near Audenarde in Belgium. Warned by a group of Belgians that they were in enemy-held territory they decided to take off again although their aircraft was badly holed bu 'Archie' and machine gun bullets. A short time later they were forced down again and had just managed to destroy the machine when they were captured and taken to Coutrai where they were billetted with other British airmen and infantry.

The following day Hawkins, in a party of 80, was moved to Ghent and imprisoned in a dungeon containing "five filthy beds". In the evening they had their first meal of the day which consisted of a slice of black bread and 'ersatz' coffee and this was repeated at 5.0 a.m. the next morning. The party then boarded a train for Haltern and there was no more food until they arrived at the camp, "which looked filthy and black", the following day. In the 'decontamination house' hair was shaved to the scalp and they showered without soap. Hawkins described a number of Russians, who had been working in France, as human skeletons "with heavily swollen ankles – many of them dying there."

On transfer to another Group he met another 100 Squadron flyer, A.M. Robb. Meals consisted of coffee, "noon pig-wash", a kind of black fish, "some yellow matter we called 'sandstorm' horse beans and sauerkraut." Hawkins and a Corporal Davidson of the D.L.I. made abortive escape attempts in June and August, 1918, and for their pains they received 14 days in the cells. After this the two were separated but Hawkins struck up a friendship with a French officer who had been sent to the camp by mistake. In October they hid themselves in a parcel office just outside the wire. After six hours work on the wire-protected windows they broke out at 1.0 a.m.

and eventually reached Winterswyck in Holland. Hawkins arrived in Gravesend the day after the signing of the Armistice.

On the 30th September, 1917, Second Lieutenant Bushe and Observer Lieutenant Colbert bombed a Zeppelin shed at Ghentrode and completed their mission by shooting up aircraft on the ground. This last venture cost them their Fe 2B which was hit by an 'Archie' burst. The aircraft crashed in a ploughed field near Meulebeke and turned over. Shortly after setting fire to the 'plane they were captured and there followed a long, slow train journey to Karlsruhe via Liege and Cologne. At Cologne open hatred was shown to them by local citizens and they were refused food by the German Red Cross.

At the quarantine camp in Karlsruhe they existed on two bowls of soup, five English biscuits and a small piece of bread each day. After 14 days they were transferred to Clausthal – a rail journey of 30 hours and, again, with no arrangements for food. Lieutenant Colbert wrote of the brutal German Commandant who greeted them making it very clear that he was the boss.

Two escape tunnels were dug but one flooded and the other was discovered by the guards. Conditions deteriorated with the approach of winter: there was no fuel for the stoves, little food and snow up to five feet deep. The prisoners were glad to work if only to keep warm and they constructed an ice rink and toboggan runs to provide themselves with winter sports! Indoors, there were weekly concerts and sketches.

In the Spring a third tunnel was started but, following a warning from his brother, who had 'lost' 27 officers in another camp, the Commandant "appeared like a raving madman" and instituted another search to the dismay of the prisoners. In August Lieutenant Colbert met another 100 Squadron officer, Lieutenant Goddard, who had been transferred from Heidelburg.

With the signing of the Armistice food parcels were distributed without censorship and the prisoners finally departed for the Baltic port of Warnemunde on the 11th December.

Lieutenant Louis Taylor's Fe 2B was trapped by a balloon barrage in Luxemburg after bombing Trier. Taylor actually 'flew' the aircraft, balloon and net to crash-land in a field. He had put the nose down but, with the engine flat out, the ASI registered only 30 mph! His observer, Lieutenant Le Fevre, managed to extricate him from the aircraft but they were almost immediately captured.

Lieutenant Taylor's account is almost entirely confined to descriptions of repeated interrogations by "swaggering German officers and gaudily dressed officials". Both Taylor and Le Fevre refused to divulge any information beyond their rank, name and number. An amazing number of ruses were adopted by the Germans to trick them into talking but to no avail. The day after their capture they were taken back to the site of the crash where they inspected the wreckage. A German Squadron Officer adopted a friendly approach and commiserated on the loss of their 'plane leading to an attempt to compare its performance with German aircraft.

The German tried to goad them by speaking of the vast superiority of German machines. The Commandant threatened to withhold food unless Taylor answered his questions. Addressing the interpreter Taylor replied, "...he should know a Britisher well enough to know that kind of threat will not help."

They were moved to another camp where they were thrown into a dirty, concrete cell. Food was greasy, inedible black bread and 'acorn water'. Guards jeered calling out, "L'Allemagne ober England", "King George Kaput!" and "Schweinerei Englander." One guard, in a fury, ordered Taylor to stand up when he approached and threatened him with a revolver when he refused. Taylor angrily displayed his Lieutenant's 'stars' on his shoulders and shouted back at the guard whereupon "he suddenly stammered and slunk away like a whipped puppy."

Further interrogations took place at Conflans. One ploy was an attempt to get the prisoners drunk. Another was to put them in a cell with a 'captured French pilot' but neither Taylor nor Le Fevre were taken in. An offer was made to drop a letter over the lines "if he would tell them where". On another occasion the two were placed in a recreation room with pictures of aerodromes on the walls. One of these was entitled "Ochey – Squadron of 1A Handley Pages under the Command of Major – and Squadron 100 RFC Fe 2B. Lieutenants Taylor and Le Fevre paid no particular attention. The rest of the war was spent in the Karlsruhe prisoner of war camp.

## PRISONERS OF THE JAPANESE

The Squadron Archives contain personal diaries of the experiences of 100 Squadron airmen who survived the tragedy of Singapore only to spend the next 3[1/2] years in conditions of appalling brutality and degradation at the hands of the Japanese. The diaries, which are mentioned in the main text (Malaya), are: "100 Squadron versus Imperial Japan," by Flying Officer Basil Gotto; "Into the Sun," by Sergeant Claude Thompson (R.N.Z.A.F.) and "The Diary of a Japanese Prisoner of War," by Flying Officer Tom Lamb. In total these diaries far exceed the length of this book and are too great to reproduce here; indeed they merit publication in their own right. The author, however, believes that this history would be incomplete without further reference to them and there follows a brief synopsis of Tom Lamb's and Claude Thompson's experiences as prisoners.

Although widely separated during their captivity both had very similar experiences beginning with the actual materials they got hold of to record their experiences. In each case they obtained exercise books from a school where they were held shortly after their capture and both record hoarding small scraps of paper and reducing the size of their writing as time went on. Ingenious means were devised to hide their records from ever-searching and suspicious guards – Tom hid his in the hollow leg of a bamboo stool and managed to bring them home with him after the war. Claude's were hidden in the roof space of his prison to be retrieved 40 years later from the local police.

Tom's comrades, 'Al' Allanson and Buck Taylor, had survived the flight of the last two Vildebeests (q.v.) and were badly beaten up at their initial interrogation. They were eventually placed in a tiny concrete cell with a bucket for a latrine.

Nearby were a number of native prisoners who, on one occasion, made a violent commotion. The reason was to witness the punishment of another native for some offence and all the prisoners were led to a courtyard for the spectacle. The unfortunate native was tied to a whipping post and received twenty stokes with a rattan cane leaving 'his back a gory mess.'

On their journey to a new camp at Palembang the prisoners were billetted overnight at a seedy Chinese hotel. To their amazement they were served with ham and eggs for breakfast but they were further amazed to learn, from their guards, that they had to pay for it themselves! That was to be their last decent meal for over three years.

At Palembang 27 prisoners were crammed into a small room; their main meal was a bowl of plain boiled rice and an occasional watery soup and prisoners suffered the ordeals of interminable 'tenkos' – roll calls where they numbered off in Japanese and were clubbed for making errors or failing to bow to guards. Work consisted of clearing jungle for landing strips, loading or unloading ships and trains and, in Claude's case, laying railway track.

Conditions deteriorated with every move. In total Claude travelled 3,000 miles to camps throughout Sumatra, Java and Singapore. Up to 250 men were battened down in stinking holds whilst stretcher cases were laid over the covers. Tropical downpours soaked excreta into the holds already foul from the dysentery sufferers below. Within the camps food rations were calculated on three scales: one for outside work parties, one for camp workers and the lowest for the sick. The top scale was barely at subsistence level. Outside work parties could earn a small pittance with which they could augment their rations but, as time went on, the currency was of little value.

Both writers, 1,000 miles apart, tell of prisoners organising lectures in their spare time. Tom writes of lessons in English, Spanish, French and Dutch and in navigation . Claude refers to lectures in psychic science and accounts of life in Australia, America, Canada, New Zealand and England. Some prisoners had copies of classical literature which they circulated between themselves. But throughout their narratives is the constantly recurring tale of inhumanity, disease and starvation rations.

The nadir of Claude's experience came with a 28 day sea voyage to Sourabaya. For once the Japanese made some effort to return the prisoners to some vestige of health at "Bicycle Camp." The prisoners already there were aghast at the appearance of the newcomers – ragged, bent and emaciated by disease – and wondered if that was the shape of things to come for themselves. After a month's 'rehabilitation' they were formed into work parties laying railway track through the jungle with a quota of two kilometres per day. Back at the camp some prisoners had given up all semblance of hygiene – even refusing to wash or shower which was a luxury. The result was that many of them were badly infested with 'crabs' and conditions were becoming so bad that they were forcibly bathed by the other prisoners.

In the jungle, working up the line from camp to camp, rations were augmented by rats, grubs, locusts, iguana, snakes, crocodile, dogs, bracken and nuts from rubber trees. They were tormented by leeches, mosquitoes, scorpions and hornets and their skin was covered by masses of ulcers. Conditions were no better for Tom Lamb in Sumatra. Dogs and snakes were, again, on the menu. Outbreaks of Beri beri and dysentery decimated the prisoners to the extent that graves could not be dug quickly enough.

*It was to be a week after the war ended that they learned* peace had finally come. Their Japanese captors could not do enough for them sending food, chocolate, clothes into the camps. In their respective camps, so far apart, Tom and Claude wrote of the preparations – and the delays – to airlift them out. Both were amazed and impressed when one of the first Dakotas to land brought Lady Louis Mountbatten to see for herself the conditions under which they had lived. They themselves, embarrassed by their rags, squalor and illness were quickly reassured by Lady Louis who insisted on inspecting the camps and, even, the latrines.

Nearly 3,000 miles away, in Japan, Ted Geldard and Bill Rafter, 100 Squadron prisoners of war, were in Fukuora No. 2 Camp whilst Sid Lawrence of 36 Squadron was at a camp nearby. Sid had been on the Japanese Hell ship, 'Kuora Maru' which embarked 2,200 prisoners for Japan but only 200 survived the voyage. The group worked in the ship-yards near Nagasaki and are amongst the few Europeans to survive the Atomic bomb on the city. Ted recalls:"We didn't know what it was at the time, of course, but there was a massive explosion and we thought an ammunition plant had blown up. A couple of days later the Americans dropped leaflets telling us about the Atomic bombs on Hiroshima and Nagasaki and that the Japs had surrendered unconditionally. We were told to take over the installations – which we did."

### STALAG IV B

Although reference has been made in the main text to members of 100 Squadron who were Germam prisoners the only detailed accounts available, at the time of printing, come from Jim Noble and an article in "Intercom" by A.C.A. member H.G. McLean. Two of these articles have been condensed to show one facet of life in Stalag IV B and the ingenuity of 100 Squadron Navigator Sergeant Eric Gargini.

"Gargini, or 'Marconi', made the clandestine radios we had in Stalag IV B which greatly contributed to keeping our spirits high for, through his efforts, we had the facts every day from BBC London as to the progress of the war. Indeed, towards the end, these facts quite likely helped to depress the morale of our guards for it was no uncommon thing to see members of the Wehrmacht studying the map of Europe, which was regularly updated, drawn on our wash house wall. His radios were made from odd bits and pieces – practically anything could, seemingly, be utilised – as long as he could get just one valve and these were obtained through the collaboration of the French prisoners.

I well remember his lecture on the principles of television given to us one evening in December, 1943. One of his inventions sticks in my mind. He cut both ends off a small tin, secured a piece of wood, strut wise, across one end, and drove a nail through the centre of this. To the nail he attached one end of a twin electric cable and he secured the other to the rim of the tin. The end of the cable was connected to the lighting supply and the tin lowered into a bucket full of water. The current was switched on and in five or six minutes we had boiling water! I have tried this, myself, only to fuse the supply! In my book he was, indeed, a genius." (H.G. McClean.)

"Eric built the first receiver to produce the first British news service in Stalag IV B. Another hut inmate took down the broadcast and I was given a hand-written transcript which I took to the office of the 'British Man of Confidence' in the German Headquarters. I dictated the news to a Geordie, named Brodie, who typed it out under the noses of 'Jerry' who would not expect the British to do this so openly. I then took the type-written sheet to each RAF hut in turn where each barrack chief would read out the news. The news was conveyed by word of mouth to the British Army compound, the South Africans, French, Dutch and Poles.

The radio was kept in a compartment in the brick floor of the hut near Eric's bunk. I only discovered this when 'Pickaxe Charlie', a German feldwebel who always carried a pick-axe to tap the floor, came into the hut. I was sitting on Eric's bunk when he said, "Don't move your feet.' Jerry tried hard but failed to find the set. On one occasion it was thrown from hut to hut as the search went on.

I also attended lectures in radio and television given by other inmates who, in civilian life, had been employed as BBC techicians. What is not known about Eric, apart from being a first class navigator, is that he was always air-sick for a few minutes after take-off and it took a brave man to do his duty as efficiently as he did under these circumstances." (J. Noble) [Eric died in 1991 after a brilliant career in electronics. Ed.]

*And Another Story about IV B*
The survivors of Warrant Officer Preston's crew (see above and main text) who were shot down over Holland were transported by rail truck through Germany to Stalag IV B at Muhlbert which is south of Berlin and east of the Elbe in what was to become Russian occupied territory. Forty seven years later Jim Noble recalled some of the events in his two years of captivity.

The camp was divided into a number of compounds each with a large gate leading to the street. Each nationality and/or Service had its own compound and, officially, they were not allowed to mix. In the event, French, Poles, Dutch, Serbs, South Africans, British Army and RAF aircrew, with a few groundcrew captured in the Dodecanese, did manage to meet in the 'street' from time to time. Prisoners were housed in wooden huts, about 150 to each hut, with brick floors. They slept in two tier wooden bunks. There was a separate compound for Russian prisoners who, because Russia had not signed the Geneva Convention, were treated and fed very badly indeed. Later, a separate compound was provided for Italian prisoners when Italy changed sides in the war! The latrines were in the centre of the compound and consisted of long wooden seats constructed over two underground concrete tanks or cess pits. Also in the compound was another wooden hut referred to as the 'Education Hut'.

### THE GREAT COAL BRIQUETTE ROBBERY

As the war progressed fuel became scarce and airmen were despatched, under guard, to neighbouring woods to collect wood for the fires. The work was dirty and, in view of the poor rations, arduous. Washing facilities were basic with just cold water and no soap. Another, official, ration of fuel was coal briquettes which were stored in a building in the Army compound. The RAF decided to raid the compound and advised the Army of its intentions. Believing they might get the blame and be punished by the Germans the Army objected to the scheme but they were advised by the RAF that if they created any problems "there might be a few accidents."

By some means the RAF devised a number of large plywood boxes, with four carrying handles. Each member of the team had ten cigarettes with which to bribe guards if necessary and, just before curfew, they made their way into the street to mingle with prisoners from other compounds and thus made their way into the Army compound. Among the team of 'robbers' was a Pilot Officer Ings, who was quite short in size, and a tall New Zealander called Terry. Armed with a crowbar Ings stood on Terry's shoulders and forced the window of the store.

Once inside they forced the door from its hinges to allow the rest of the team to enter. With boxes full of briquettes the team returned to the hut and the door was replaced. Back in the huts other prisoners had removed part of the brick floor and excavated some of the earth beneath to make room for the briquettes. "The whole thing was planned like a bombing raid and there were no casualties!"

A duty roster was drawn up for each of the many raids until they decided their activities should cease when the Germans began to solve the puzzle of the disappearing briquettes.

### THE TUNNEL THAT FLOPPED

As it was nearer the perimeter fence it was decided to start the tunnel from the 'Education Hut'. Amongst the prisoners were some who knew something about tunnelling and a request was sent to all huts for timber to shore up the roof as digging progressed. The timber was found by prisoners 'donating' one in three of the wooden slats which made up their bunks. All went well and the tunnel reached beyond the fence to open farmland. Unfortunately a local farmer, working in his field, found his tractor plunging into the ground as the roof of the tunnel fell in.

Discovery of the tunnel caused a lot of panic amongst the guards and they deliberated on what to do about it. The outcome, "in typical, orderly German fashion", was to make the Russians pump the sewage from the latrine cess pit into large drums. This sewage, normally spread on the fields, was poured down the hole. "It would be a brave man," recalls Jim, "who would venture into that tunnel now and those who donated the slats from their bunks slept very badly until the end of the war!"

### CAMP CONCERTS

With the aid of costumes, make up, a gramophone and records supplied by the Red Cross the RAF occasionally put on a camp concert – the theme of the sketch, usually, being skits against themselves. The concerts seem to have been popular with the Germans if only to relieve their own boredom. On one occasion the theme was the British Colonial Empire with red-coated soldiers, armed with wooden guns, defending a fort. At regular intervals the gramophone played "Land of Hope and Glory" when the actors would stop in their tracks and salute. The Germans were confused at all this and never realised that the actors were taking the mickey out of them for a change.

On another occasion the crew of a B17 shot down near the camp didn't believe that the actors, dressed in 'drag', were British especially as Germans were sitting in the audience. They thought it was some kind of elaborate, German plot to make them talk. It was some time before they would accept that this was a British run show in a German camp.

### CHRISTMAS DINNER 1944

By this time, largely because of Allied air attacks on communications, Red Cross supplies were rationed to one parcel for 12 men. Christmas Dinner consisted of a piece of bully beef, some tinned German soup and a small piece of beef from a quarter of a cow shared between 1500 men. Dessert was a soggy biscuit with German jam made from turnips. Tea was mint tea "normally used for shaving" and the coffee was made from acorns. An airman knocked on the door to call in the guard, who was standing outside in the freezing cold, and invited him to join in the repast. The RAF type took the guard's rifle, laid it beside a bunk and they sat down for the meal. At the end of the meal he was given a British cigarette, his rifle was returned and he was then escorted outside to resume his sentry duty. "I believe only the RAF could have done such a thing!"

Sergeant Gargini (Standing – Left)
with crew at O. T. U.

*MISCELLANY*

Outside the camp was a flak battery where Italian soldiers were being trained. When Italy changed sides they were imprisoned. "One day they were outside as allies of the Germans – next day they were inside as allies of the British!"

The Camp Commandant was heard to say that the French walked around as though they owned the camp; the Dutch would like to own it; the Poles knew they didn't own it and the British couldn't give a damn who owned it.

One day a feldwebel noticed the shoulder flash of a Polish member of the RAF. "He went berserk and drew out his sidearm. A German speaking RAF officer warned him he would have the RAF to deal with if the Pole was harmed." He calmed down and the incident passed.

A group of Polish women resistance workers were brought to the camp after the Warsaw uprising. "It was strange to hear women's voices after two years." The RAF made collections to give the women soap and other comparative luxuries. Polish males came round the RAF compound trying to barter for what few extras there might be but they never gave them to the women.

The prisoners of Stalag IV B were released by the Russians in 1945. Their only possessions were the clothes they stood up in and a small haversack.

# APPENDIX FOUR

## *The Hundred Squadron Association*

A number of attempts have been made to form an association of former members of 100 Squadron beginning with informal get-togethers of World War 1 flyers in the early '20s and similar attempts after World War 2. In the early '80s two separate strands developed which, eventually, came together in 1984.

The first of these was the "Waltham Association." Two former members of the Squadron, Jimmy Flynn and Jon Procherea along with other wartime personnel – including Roland Hardy, Jim Holmes and 'Johnnie' Johnson – met to form an association of those who had served at R.A.F. Waltham (Grimsby). Membership was open to all who served at Waltham and included 100 Squadron, 142 Squadron and Station personnel. The idea was taken up by Ian Reid, a young telephone engineer who had always been fascinated by the exploits of the Waltham flyers, and he became Secretary/Treasurer of the new Association.

Reunions, attended by 40 or so members and guests, were held annually from 1982 until 1986 at the Royal Crest Hotel where members would assemble for a dinner party on a Saturday evening to be followed, on the Sunday, by a visit to the Village Hall at Holton le Clay for coffee followed by a service at the Squadron Memorial.

The second strand originated in Canada. In the summer of 1984 a group of Canadian ex-100 Squadron aircrew, led by Squadron Leader Dave Robb, DFC, AFC, RCAF (Retd,) and his former gunners, Monty Kerr and Bob Gibson, met at Trenton R.C.A.F. base to inaugurate a Canadian 100 Squadron Association. About 30 ex-Waltham flyers were present and, amongst other activities, they raised most of the funds required to commission a painting by Graham Wragg depicting three Waltham Lancasters leading a 'gaggle'. The painting now hangs in the Winnipeg Air Museum.

The strands came together on the 14th December, 1984 when the Squadron received its new Standard from Marshal of the R.A.F. Sir Michael Beetham GCB,CBE,DFC, AFC,FRAeS. The ceremony was attended by members of the Waltham Association and other former members of the Squadron including Dave Robb from Canada. In the course of the festivities the, then, Squadron Commander, Wing Commander Mike Purdie, Dave Robb and a few others got together to formulate plans for a 100 Squadron Association.

The outcome was the Inaugural Meeting and Reunion on the 19th|20th October, 1985 held at R.A.F. Wyton. A draft constitution was agreed with a Committee of: Chairman (who will always be the Squadron Commander), Secretary, Deputy Secretary, Treasurer, Newsletter Editor and six Area Members representing different regions of the country. There is also a Canadian Member and a Squadron Liaison Officer. Subsequently it was decided that the Association should have a President and Air Vice Marshal W.J. Herrington, CB, RAF (Retd.) who had commanded the Squadron during the "Victor" era was invited to take on the task.

The aims of the Association are:

(a)      To provide a bond and a link between present and former Squadron members by providing an Association membership list to all members.

(b)      To foster good comradeship among present and former members of the Squadron.

(c)      To encourage and promote social contact between present and former members of the Squadron.

There is provision for Honorary Membership for those with particularly close associations with the Squadron and one of the first to be recognised in this way was Ian Reid for his efforts with the Waltham Association. An amendment to the constitution gave members' widows the right to membership although they do not have voting rights.

The Committee meets two or three times a year and the Annual General Meeting is combined with the reunion. Contact between the Association's 200 members is maintained and encouraged by quarterly newsletters; there is an active Canadian 100 Squadron Association with which there is close liaison and exchange of newsletters; there is also a 100 Squadron R.A.A.F. Association with similar links.

The important difference between the Waltham Association and 100 Squadron Association is that the latter was conceived as an on-going organisation whereas the former was limited to the period 1941 to 1945 and, in fact, is now inactive. This is best illustrated by the fact that in 1992 100 Squadron Association's oldest member is Lieutenant Roy Shillinglaw who served in World War 1 and our youngest members currently serve on the Squadron. In fact, the Association is proud to record that every aspect of the Squadron's history is now represented in its membership.

Since the formation of the 100 Squadron Association Southern Area Member, Mr. E.J. Clark, has meticulously researched records from Flanders to Malaya, the Dutch East Indies and Waltham and, in 1990, produced the Squadron's first Roll of Honour recording the names of 672 Officers. Non-Commissioned Officers and Airmen who died on active service in two World Wars. The Roll of Honour is now displayed in an oak cabinet in the Station Chapel at R.A.F. Wyton.

*COMMANDING OFFICERS,AIRCRAFT AND BASES*
*COMMANDING OFFICERS*

| | |
|---|---|
| Major M.G. Christie, CMG,DSO,MC. | 21st March, 1917. |
| Major W,J, Tempest DSO, MC. | 11th December, 1917. |
| Major C.G. Burge OBE. | 16th June, 1918. |
| Squadron Leader | |
|    Hon. L.J.E. Twistleton-Wykeham-Fiennes | 1st February, 1920. |
| Squadron Leader J.V.Steel, OBE. | 30th November,1920. |
| Squadron Leader F. Sowrey. | 19th February,1921. |
| Squadron Leader N.M. Martin CBE. | 10th August, 1922. |
| Squadron Leader H.F.A. Gordon. | 10th September,1923. |
| Squadron Leader L.T.N. Gould | 10th October, 1925. |
| Squadron Leader W.B. Farrington. | 16th January, 1929. |
| Squadron Leader L.G. Le B. Croke. | 13th January, 1931. |
| Squadron Leader A.H. Paull. | 18th November, 1935. |
| Squadron Leader J.G. Walser. | 20th November, 1936. |
| Squadron Leader G.F. Simond. | 13th September,1937. |
| Wing Commander R.N. McKern. | 16th January, 1939. |
| Squadron Leader J.G. Kerby. | 5th September, 1941. |
| Squadron Leader A.W.D. Miller. | 11th December, 1941. |
| Wing Commander J.G.W. Swain. | 26th December, 1942. |
| Wing Commander R.V. McIntyre DFC. | 24th April, 1943. |
| Wing Commander D.W. Holford | 20th November, 1943. |
| Wing Commander J.F.Dilworth. | 17th December, 1943. |
| Wing Commander R.V.L. Pattison,DSO, DFC. | 3rd March, 1944. |
| Wing Commander A.F. Hamilton, DSO,DFC. | 20th September,1944. |
| Wing Commander T.B. Morton, DSO,DFC. | 7th March, 1945. |
| Wing Commander EBC Davies. | 1st July, 1945. |
| Wing Commander G.J. Bell. | 1st April, 1946. |
| Squadron Leader D.G. O'Brien. | 23rd May, 1948. |
| Squadron Leader R.A. Jell, DFC,AFC. | 17th July, 1950. |
| Squadron Leader R.I. Alexander, DFC. | 1st December, 1952. |
| Squadron Leader H.B. Hunt,DSO,DFC,AFC. | 21st April, 1954. |
| Squadron Leader C.P.H. Kunkler | 10th January, 1955. |
| Squadron Leader R.A. McPhie | 14th January, 1957. |
| Wing Commander M.M.J. Robinson | 1st May, 1962. |
| Wing Commander W.J. Herrington. | 30th September,1964. |
| Wing Commander H.M. Archer, AFC,AFRAeS | 4th January,1967. |
| Wing Commander B.M. Burley. | 1st February, 1972. |
| Wing Commander B. Harcourt-Smith. | 10th December, 1973. |
| Wing Commander J.D. Harvey | 5th January, 1976. |
| Wing CommanderP.N. Le Marquand | 31st December, 1976. |
| Wing Commander J.W. Blockey | December, 1978. |
| Wing Commander J.N. Landeryou MBIM | December, 1980. |

Wing Commander C.R. Adams. AFC.                    August, 1982.
Wing Commander M.J. Purdie.                        October, 1983.
Wing Commander R.J. McKendrick.                       June, 1986.
Wing Commander K.M. Douglas, MBIM.              December, 1988.
Wing Commander R. Metcalfe,MBIM.                      June. 1991.
Wing Commander J. Pitts.                          1st January, 1992.


BASES                                             AIRCRAFT TYPE

| | | |
|---|---|---|
| South Farnborough Hants. | 23rd Feb. 1917 | F.E.2b&d.B.E.2e. |
| St. Andre Aux Bois. | 21st Mar. 1917 | |
| Izel le Hameau. | 1st April 1917 | |
| Treizennes | 16th May, 1917 | |
| Ochey. | 5th Oct. 1917 | |
| Villeseneux. | 1st April 1918 | |
| Ochey. | 12th May 1918 | Handley Page 0-400 |
| Xaffevillers. | 10th Aug. 1918 | |
| Ligescourt. | 16th Nov. 1918 | |
| Det. St. Ingelvert. | March, 1919 | |
| Det. Quilen. | March, 1919 | |
| St. Inglevert. | June, 1919 | |
| Returned to England. | Sept. 1919 | |
| Baldonnel. Co. Dublin. | Sept. 1919 | Bristol F 2b |
| Spitalgate Lincs. | 4th Feb. 1922 | Avro 504 K. DH9A |
| Eastchurch, Kent. | May, 1924 | Vickers Vimy. |
| Spitalgate. | July, 1924 | Fairey Fawn. |
| Weston Zoyland. | 11th June 1926 | Hawker Horsley. |
| Spitalgate. | 30th Aug. 1926 | |
| Bicester. | 10th Jan. 1928 | |
| Weston Zoyland. | 14th April1928 | |
| Bicester. | 19th May. 1928 | |
| Donibristle. Fife. | 3rd, Nov. 1930 | |
| Gosport. | 3rd June 1932 | |
| Catfoss, Yorks. | 15th June 1932 | |
| Donibristle Fife. | 27th Aug. 1932 | |
| | Nov. 1932 | Vickers Vildebeest |
| Gosport. | 8th June. 1933 | Vickers Vildebeest |
| Donibristle | 30th June 1933 | |
| Seletar, Singapore. | 5th Jan. 1934 | |
| *Disbanded*. | February. 1942 | |
| Grimsby (Waltham) | 15th Dec. 1942 | Avro Lancaster. |
| Elsham Wolds. | 1st April 1945 | |
| Scampton. | 3rd Dec. 1945 | |
| Lindholme. | 8th May, 1946 | Avro Lincoln. |

| | | |
|---|---|---|
| Hemswell. | 28th Oct. 1946 | |
| Dets. at Chile, Malta, | | |
| Shallufa (Egypt). | | |
| Waddington. | 23rd March 1950 | |
| Det. at Tengah (Singapore). | | |
| Tengah. | 31st May. 1950 | |
| Waddington. | 22nd Dec. 1950 | |
| Shallufa. | 20th May, 1952 | |
| Waddington. | 18th Aug. 1952 | |
| Wittering. | 2nd Aug. 1953 | |
| Eastleigh, Kenya. | 7th Jan. 1954 | |
| Wittering. | 22nd March 1954 | E.E. Canberra B2,B6 |
| Dets. at Gaydon,Wyton, | | PR7 at Wyton. |
| Christmas Island. | | |
| *Disbanded.* | 1st Sept. 1959 | |
| Wittering. | 1st May, 1962 | H.P. Victor B2. |
| Disbanded. | 30th Sept.1968 | |
| West Raynham. | 1st Feb. 1972 | Canberra B2,PR7, |
| | | E15, TT 18. |
| Marham. | 5th Jan. 1976 | |
| Wyton. | 5th Jan. 1982 | |
| | Jan. 1992 | BAe Hawk T.1|T.1A |

# APPENDIX FIVE

## 100 Squadron Canberras 1972 – 1992

| WD | 948 | To Manston 3|77 for Fire Fighting School. |
|----|-----|------|
| WE | 113 | To 231 OCU 1|82 |
|    | 188 | To 231 OCU 1|76 |
| WH | 666 | To Zimbabwe AF as 2205 3|81 |
|    | 667 | Crashed Akrotiri 11|80 |
|    | 670 | Scrapped – 12|91 |
|    | 718 | For sale Action. |
|    | 724 | Scrapped 4|76 |
|    | 739 | To 19 MU 7|76 |
|    | 779 | To 231 OCU current. |
|    | 848 | To 231 OCU. |
|    | 849 | To 231 OCU. |
|    | 903 | To Marham 12|77 for fire practice. |
|    | 948 | Crashed Holt 8|77 |
|    | 957 | To St. Athan for storage 1|82. |
|    | 964 | To St. Athan for storage 2|82. |
|    | 672 | Crashed Kinloss 6|90. |
|    | 981 | For Sale Action. |
|    | 983 | Scrapped 12|91. |
| WJ | 567 | Sold locally. |
|    | 603 | To Wattisham 12|80 for BDR use. |
|    | 610 | Crashed West Raynham 6|72. |
|    | 614 | To B Ae 2/72 for conversion to TT18 for R.N. |
|    | 636 | Held for 'Life Sampling'. |
|    | 640 | To No. 2 School of TT 11|81 for ground instruction. |
|    | 678 | Overstressed during PIs: to Abingdon 11|85. |
|    | 680 | Sold. Awaiting details. |
|    | 682 | For spares recovery. |
|    | 715 | Scrapped 7|92. |
|    | 728 | To RAE Farnborough 2|76. |
|    | 753 | Crashed Marham 6|78. |
|    | 756 | To 231 OCU current. |
|    | 861 | To No. & Squadron. |

        877    To 231 OCU: Crashed Wyton 3|91.

        975    To Marshalls, Cambridge. Now in Bomber County Museum Cleethorpes.

WK   106    Scrapped Marham 3|76.

      116    Crashed Akrotiri 2|82.

      118    Sold to Air Museum in Staffordshire.

      123    To Manchiung, Germany. Wings now part of B" 99+34 (ex-WK 137)

      124    To Manston for rescue training.

      162    Crashed Alconbury 8|85.

      164    To Foulness 7|82.

WP   515    To St. Athan for storage 8|89.

      519    Held for 'Life Sampling'.

      538    Held for BDR use.

XA   536    To Abingdon 9|78 for BDR use.

*ACKNOWLEDGEMENTS*
The author wishes to express his appreciation to all the following for their assistance and co-operation in preparing this book.Air Vice Marshal W.J. Herrington, CB, RAF (Retd.) for initiating the work, for his valuable help with proof reading and editing and for his article on the 'Victor' era.Wing Commander A.J. Brookes whose Official History of 100 Squadron 1917 to 1977 forms the central core of this book.

*THE FIRST WORLD WAR*
The late Major C. Gordon Burge, OBE, for compiling "The Annals of 100 Squadron" which provides a most detailed account of 100 Squadron's early years from February 1917 to November, 1918.Roy Shillinglaw for his video recording of his experiences in the First World War.Mr.Norman R.J. McCreath for his taped recollections of Lieutenant Angus McCreath's experiences in the First World War.Notes from Professor A.J.P. Taylor's lectures on The First World War.

*THE INTER-WAR YEARS AND MALAYAN CAMPAIGN*
G. Bell, M. Britten, S. Dannam, E. Geldard, B. Gotto, E. Hallam, R. Hampson, L.Hughes, Wg. Cdr. J. Kessey, DFC,RAAF,(Retd.), T. Lamb, R.S. Mager, W. Rafter, E. Redshaw, P. Scully (RAAF),Mrs. Sedgeley, C.Thompson (RNZAF) David Vincent, A.A. Wiseman BEM.
Group Captain A.J. White, Australian High Commission, London.
R.A.A.F. Records, Canberra.Captain P.F.C.Elphick R.N.(Retd.) and Sydney Taverner (article on Malayan Traitor "Clipped Wings-The Collapse of British Air Defence, Malaya" by Philip Rivers.)

*WALTHAM*
Peter Burnett,F.W. Bury, F. Butler, E.J. Clark, Martin R. Cooke, J. Carson, G.J.A. Crowley-Smith, F. Dorman, K. Drury, A. Gamble, J.D. Game, R.G. Gibson, W. Greenslade, Roland Hardy, C.A. Johnson, C.M. Kerr, E. Mawer, J.S. Metcalfe, Ursula Moessner, J. Noble, F. Ockerby, Sqn.Ldr. D. Robb,DFC,AFC,RCAF (Retd.) S. Savage, G. Sidebotham, H.J. Taylor, Rev. M. Thompson, G. Vickery, J. Littlewood.

*1945 to 1992*
SquadronLeader G.M. Bailey,AFC, RAF (Retd.). Flight Lieutenant J.A. Barker, RAF (Retd.), Flight Lieutenant J.P. Barker RAF (Retd.) Squadron Leader E. Brewin, RAF (Retd.) Squadron Leader J. Clubb, RAF (Retd.), Flight Lieutenant.B. Collen DFM, RAF (Retd.) Flight Lieutenant F. Coulton Wing Commander R. Jell DFC,AFC, RAF (Retd.) Wing Commander J. Pitts, RAF.,Squadron Leader Derek Tuthill R.A.F. (Retd.)

*PUBLICATIONS*
"Leadership in Battle." Sir John Smyth VC. (David and Charles.)

"Royal Air Force Squadron Badges." Peter C. Smith. (Balfour.)"The German Air Force in the Great War." G.P. Neumann. (Portway)."History of the Second World War" with particular reference to Arthur Simpson (with co-operation of Major Tokuji Mortimato and Mutsuya Nagao) and Lieutenant Commander F.C. Van Oosten. (Purnell)
"Bomber Harris". Group Captain Dudley Saward, OBE. (Cassell)."The Bomber Command War Diaries". Middlebrook and Everitt. (Viking).
"Bombers Over Berlin". Alan Cooper. (William Kimber).
"The Avro Lancaster". Francis K. Mason. (Aston).
"Grimsby Evening Telegraph."
"RCAF at War. 1939 to 1945" Milberry and Halliday.
Imperial War Museum. Channel 4 Documentary: "Schoolboy Flyers and Wild Sow"(Pforzheim raid and accounts of German Night Fighter Pilots.)
"Bomber Squadrons of the RAF" – Philip Moys (McDonald).
"Christmas Cracker Island". Air Vice-Marshal Wilfred Oulton.

*ADDITIONAL POETRY*
Mrs. C. Herrington – "Ladies Guest Night."
Eric Sykes – "Three Cheers for the Man on the Ground."
Audrey Grealy – "Ode to a Dark Lady."

A final word of thanks to those members of 100 Squadron and the 100 Squadron Association, not mentioned above, who have telephoned, written or dropped the odd snippet of information which has been so important in "putting flesh on the bones" of this story.

*BIBLIOGRAPHY*
	"Leadership in Battle" by Sir John Smyth V. C. (David & Charles)
	"The German Air Force in the Great War". Neumann (Portway)
	"Royal Air Force Squadron Badges". Peter C. Smith (Balfour)
	"History of Second World War". (Purnell)
	"Bomber Harris" Gp. Capt. Dudley Saward OBE (Cassell)
	"Bomber Command War Diaries". Middlebrook & Everitt. (Viking)
	"Bombers Over Berlin". Alan Cooper (William Kimber)
	"The Avro Lancaster". Francis K. Mason. (Aston) DELETE
	"R. C. A. F. at War 1939 – 1945" and "Bomber Squadrons of the RAF"
	"Schoolboy Flyers and Wild Sow". Channel 4 Doc.
	"Christmas Cracker Island". A. V. M. Wilfred Oulton

# ADDENDA

The Editor is extremely grateful to Mr. A. N. Greaves who has sent the following extract from his late father's diary.

*EXTRACT FROM THE DIARY OF LT. W.H GREAVES. (OBSERVER WITH 100 SQUADRON ON THE WESTERN FRONT.)*

*1st October 1918*
I was detailed for a raid on B------ but after standing by until 0200 hrs. the "washout" came through.

*2nd October 1918*
Today I have beaten the record by not getting up until 1530. In order to wake myself up I went for a trip in the old bus. My word, it is a fine sight to fly over the old battle areas by day. Below, one can see ruined villages and fields full of shell holes. There are patches in the forest where trees have been torn up by shells and everywhere can be seen traces of the terrible struggle of the earlier war years. In the evening I was again detailed for a show on one of the hottest objectives but, once again, the weather was kind to us. So instead of bombing Germany we had a good rag in the Mess on account of one of the skippers going home on the following day.

*3rd October 1918*
After breakfast we went for a day test and, my word, had a narrow squeak in taking off, clearing the trees by the skin of our teeth. About 1730 I was detailed for a show so visited the operation room and studied orders and course. Dinner was a rush affair and a race to my quarters to get into my flying gear. This consists of my ordinary uniform (in case of a landing in Hunland) 3 pairs of stockings, jersey, muffler wound round neck and head, flying helmet, sidcot suit, fur boots and gloves. In my pockets I carry cigarettes, a couple of white handkerchiefs in case of getting pipped, torch and maps.
When the pilot, Lt. Gower, the front observer, Lt. Ross and myself reach the aerodrome the air mechanics were running the bus up so we did not have long to wait before we could taxi out. Everywhere on the 'drome was a scene of activity and signals, mysterious to the outsider, were flashing everywhere. At last our turn to take off came so the engines are opened full

and the roar of same is tremendous. We race along the ground and, having nearly I ton of bombs on board, the machine had to strain every 'nerve' to get off the ground. We are soon clear of the 'drome and slowly we get our height, 2000 feet, and commence on our course. Everything below is pitch black but by our compasses and "lighthouses" we reach the lines. All along the battle-front can be seen the never ending flash of guns with the occasional star shells lighting up the scene below. I give another hasty check on my guns and find them O.K. We are now over Hunland and, evidently, the 'bosch' can hear us as the searchlights are being frantically flashed over the sky but they cannot find us yet.

At last we are picked up by one and immediately dozens of others are on to us. I have a busy time firing down at them with my machine gun which seems to put the wind up them as some lights go out and others dodge away from us. All around us are bright flashes of bursting 'archies' varied by other forms of Hun hate such as 'flaming onions'. We carry on hardly altering course except to go round a barrage. We finally reach our target and I feel the good old H.P. (Handley Page) give a leap as the bombs are dropped. We can see the explosions below and it gives me great delight, knowing as I do, the rotten work the Huns used to do on innocent people and towns in dear old England. How different is our work from theirs. We bomb important military circles and they, the first thing they find. Having got rid of our 'pills' we start back and, my word, we did have to go through some 'Hate'! It was like a Crystal Palace firework display but a little more dangerous. Seeing the puffs of bursting shells all round it is difficult to realise that it is possible not to be hit. We get a warm time until we cross the lines at 7000ft and then we are left in peace and soon see the beckoning lights of our 'drome. We land and climb stiffly out of the bus after being in the air for 4I hours.

None of us are able to hear anything on account of the gunfiring and engine noise but, by shouting like mad, we are able to carry on a conversation and compare notes. The A.M.s push the faithful old bus into the hangar and tie it down to sleep whilst we are met by the C.O. who resembles a dear old father to us. He is delighted at having us back safely and pleased with our work and takes us off to the Mess for coffee and something to eat. Whilst indulging ourselves, we give our verbal reports to the R.O. and answer the various questions of others. I then go to bed and sleep like a top, forgetting about Hunhate, wars and flying and dream pleasantly of glorious feeds of Lyons' cream cakes and ragtime bands.

*4th October 1918*
Today I did not get up until 1100, had lunch after which I played footer in a match against 97 Squadron-result a draw 1–1.

*5th October 1918*
I drove into Nancy, a ride through ruined villages. In Nancy I did some shopping and greatly amused my companions by going into a shop and buying some girls' garters. They were of pale mauve and blue silk and very good for the eye-sight. In the evening I was on another 4½ hour show to Mezieres, again with with Lts. Gower and Ross. We dropped 1 550lb and 8 112lb bombs and I fired 300 rounds.

*6th/9th October 1918*
Nothing special to report except the occasional visit from Fritz without any damage being done.

*10th October 1918*
I was awakened by 'Archie' fire at 0600 but it was so darn cold that I would not get up and watch how the Huns operated. General Trenchard called and saw us in the afternoon and congratulated us on our good work.

*11th/20th October 1918*

Due mainly to dud weather we have had a quiet spell with plenty of visits to the cinema, concerts and games of footer.

*21st October 1918*
Another night show to Mezieres, this time with Lts.Proctor and Sherman. We dropped 16 112lb. bombs and had a petrol line severed by 'Archie' . I managed to crawl out on the wing and held it in place until we landed.

*23rd October 1918*
Nothing happened during the day but in the evening we did a show to Metz dropping 16 112lb. bombs. The pilot was Lt. Taylor who did a fine job getting us home with a dud engine. Lt. Lewis was the other crew member and we flew for 3.35 hours at 5000ft.

*24th October 1918*
Had a visit from an American war correspondent who stayed for lunch.

*28th October 1918*
Prince Albert (later King George VI) visited the Squadron during the day.

*29th October 1918*
A bad day with three crashes and four killed. Our own engine went dud but Lt. Proctor landed us safely.

*30th October 1918*
Operations washed out due to weather and then petrol leak.

*31st October/4th November 1918*
Rumours of an armistice abound resulting in many parties but nothing definite and operations continue.

*5th November 1918*
Another night raid to Gillingen. Lt. Taylor was the pilot and Lt. Shillinglaw* the other crew member. We flew at 6000ft. and carried 14 131lb. bombs.

*6th November 1918*
Trip cancelled owing to oil leak.

*7th November 1918*
Did various day tests and practices with Lt. Evans as pilot.

*10th/11th November 1918***
   We took off at 1700 for a night bombing raid on Hellingen aerodrome and bombed at 1930 after flying over the target for 30 minutes at 6500ft. We carried one 550lb and eight 112lb bombs but the 550 pounder would not release. A heavy mist came up and we could not see the landing flares. After circling for 30 minutes we crash landed, writing off the kite but fortunately the bomb did not explode and we only received minor injuries. Lt. Crocker was the pilot and Lt. Best the other observer.

*11th November 1918*
   Peace declared.

   \*    See main text
   \*\*   Officially the last operation of the war. See main text.

Lieutenant Greaves died at the age of 84 in 1982 (Ed.).

## "WINGS FOR VICTORY"

A chance remark in the R.A.F.A. Club, Cleethorpes, following the Remembrance Day Service at Holton le Clay in 1993 led to a search for news of a Lancaster purchased by the people of Grimsby as part of their war effort. The following acount adapted from 100 Squadron Association's Newsletter No. 24.

From Ian Reid we learned that two Lancasters were 'presented' to the Squadron on 2nd October 1943, when Squadron Leader Bell received two log books – "the compilaton of which was to consist of the operational records of two of the Squadron's Lancasters". The story is complicated by the fact that FOUR Lancasters arrived at Waltham at approximately the same time: JB 602, JB 603, JB 604 and JB 605. Of these it seems certain that JB 604 was one of them as Ted Mayfield DFM recalls a Grimsby Council official coming out to Waltham at the time "with a certificate of some sort to be signed by the crew."

One of the Squadron's first Lancasters, which took part in the Squadron's first raid with Bomber Command, St. Nazaire, was ED 583 which is referred to in the main text. John Prochera flew as air-gunner in this aircraft and described the "Wings for Victory" symbol painted on its nose. ED 583 was to take Lawrence Stow and his crew through most of their tour. On 4th October 1943 it exploded over North Toresby on a training flight killing Capatin Morgan, a tour-expired American on the Squadron, and his crew.

The story of JB 604 is told by Ted Mayfield DFM, who was Flight Engineer in Flight Lieutenant K. A. Major's crew:

"Lancaster JB 604 'S' was allocated to our crew on delivery to 100 Squadron, brand new, on 3rd November 1943. Its original letter was 'J' but this was changed to 'S' between the 4th and 15th December 1943.

A few seconds after a midnight take off for Berlin on 23rd December 1943, JB 604 shuddered violently and icy draughts of air blew around the inside of the aircraft. The Mid-upper gunner looked through the inspection panel into the bomb bay and discovered that the 4000lb bomb had fallen from its mountings and dropped onto the bomb doors, forcing them partly open. At that time we were flying at 300ft over the centre of Grimsby. The residents were lucky that the bomb doors held otherwise there would have been considerable damage to the town and many casualties. It would also have blown our aircraft out of the sky."

The 'cookie' was jettisoned over the North Sea from 3500ft. and. after flying around for an hour to lighten the fuel load, the crew landed safely at Waltham. Ken Major and crew completed their tour in JB 604 on 20th February 1944.

Both Ted Mayfield and Lawrence Stow speak highly of Flight Lieutenant

Ken Major who is described as 'a super bloke and a very good friend'. He went on to become Flight Commander at 1668 C. U. and then trained as master bomber on Mosquitoes for 'Tiger Force'. He was killed whilst flying an experimental SR A1 on Battle of Britain Day 1949. Four nights later JB 604 with Flying Officer V. L. B. Jones and four members of his crew were lost on a raid to Schweinfurt when they crashed on the mill at Marly, near Dijon. They were: Flying Officer Jones, Flight Sergeant Grinrod (Bomb Aimer), Flight Sergeant Sullivan (Wireless Op.), Sergeant Turner (Mid-upper Gunner) and Seargeant Messinger (Rear Gunner). Flight Sergeant Ken Head (Flight Engineer) and Flying Officer Basil Garlick (Navigator) survived as POW's. The Squadron Commander, Wing Commander Dilworth and his crew were lost on the same raid. Today only Ken survives.

On 24th February 1994, Ken and his wife and relatives of the lost crew members attended a military ceremony at Marly hosted by the Mayor and citizens at a 50th Anniversary ceremony to 'honour the memory of five English airmen buried in the town'. Two crews represented 100 Squadron but the fly past was cancelled because of bad weather.